*Global Markets Transformed*

D0705968

# Global Markets Transformed
## 1870–1945

Steven C. Topik and Allen Wells

*The Belknap Press of Harvard University Press*
CAMBRIDGE, MASSACHUSETTS
LONDON, ENGLAND

To my father, Kurt Topik, who aroused in me a love of history
and a curiosity about faraway peoples and places.

—Steven Topik

~

To my children, Anna, Dion, Emily, and David,
and to my first grandchild, Alexander Robinson Wade.

—Allen Wells

Originally published as Chapter 4, "Commodity Chains in a Global Economy," in
*A World Connecting: 1870–1945*, ed. Emily S. Rosenberg (Cambridge, MA: Belknap
Press of Harvard University Press, 2012), a joint publication of Harvard University
Press and C. H. Beck Verlag.
German language edition © 2012 by C. H. Beck Verlag.

Maps by Isabelle Lewis
Book design by Dean Bornstein

*Library of Congress Cataloging-in-Publication Data*
Topik, Steven.
    Global markets transformed : 1870–1945 / Steven C. Topik and Allen Wells.
        pages   cm
    Includes bibliographical references and index.
    ISBN 978-0-674-28134-9 (alk. paper)
    1. Commercial products. 2. International trade. I. Wells, Allen, 1951–
II. Title.
    HF1040.7.T66   2014
    382.09'041—dc23          2013031036

# Contents

# Introduction

The seven decades after 1870 have been labeled the "Second Industrial Revolution," the "Era of High Imperialism," the "Great Acceleration," and the "Great Transformation."[1] By any measure the global economy underwent a remarkable transformation. Thanks to unprecedented gains in industrial and agricultural productivity, an exponential increase in commerce, investment, and immigration, and sweeping improvements to transportation, communication, and distribution, the world's population doubled, trade more than quadrupled, and output multiplied fivefold. New monetary and property standards, nascent multinational corporations, and international conventions and organizations facilitated such fundamental changes. Many people, however, experienced the grim side of these developments: It was also an era of colonialism, racism, and an unprecedented concentration of wealth. A succession of deadly wars and the degradation of landscapes ensured that these improvements in productivity came at a high cost.

It was a time when the principles of liberal economic thought were first systematically applied to parts of the international economy and when "globalization" first became clearly manifest.[2] But globalization did not mean that everyone was brought into lockstep with Europe and North America. Although the logic of capitalist investment and trade imposed themselves in ever more parts of the world, heterogeneity and diversity also became more striking. There were many ways to respond to similar market pressures. While international trade, prices, and technologies affected most everyone, people often felt the impacts differently, in ways that may have had greater cultural or political resonance than economic.

We will illustrate the evolving dimensions, contradictions, and functions of the world market during this period by focusing on the material and conceptual sinews of trade and the commodities that tied together continents and fueled commerce. We do not reify the economy. In fact, the world market was "a rather abstract, theoretical fiction" with great variations and cyclical swings.[3] But our studies of the international trade of wheat, rice, hard fibers, rubber, sugar, coffee, tea, cacao, and other commodities will show that it is a useful concept in appreciating the movement of enormous amounts of goods and capital, as well as millions of people. Market forces operated through humans in varied, unpredictable, and even contradictory ways, reflecting local customs and past lessons as much as contemporaneous opportunities.

We begin with how historians have conceived of our period, and then turn to an overview of the world economy and its characteristics between 1870 and 1945. After painting with a broad brush the contours of the Great Divergence—the growing gulf between the haves and those who had little—we examine the apparent contradictions that emerged between liberalism and state capitalism or socialism, laissez-faire individualism and organized capitalism, free trade and colonialism, and the irony of creative destruction and its environmental implications. After a brief visit to the cotton-driven First Industrial Revolution we discuss the Second Industrial Revolution and its defining characteristics. Then we explore the sinews of the world economy in greater detail: the legal frameworks, monetary standards, shipping, canals, rails, and telegraphs, and the changing sources of energy that fostered ever-larger markets. That is followed by discussions of industrial linkages to copper and industrial metals, oil, and rubber that were made possible by key advances in transportation and communication.

After this extended overview of economic framework, we turn to the heart of our story, the various commodity chains that carried the bulk of cross-border commerce: staples such as grains, especially wheat and rice, and the hard fibers needed to package them; and stimulants like sugar, coffee, tea, chocolate, and tobacco. These agricultural products were not just marginal luxuries. By 1913 food made up more than a quarter of world exports, and grains and stimulants were truly global in their reach.[4] Other commodities will be addressed for comparative purposes.

Although historians generally distinguish the period 1870–1914, an era of relatively free trade and export-led growth, from the following three decades, which wrestled with world wars, depressions, and growing state intervention in economic matters, we examine the entire seventy-five years because so many of the dynamics, aspirations, and assumptions were linked. Although overall world trade expanded until 1914, stagnated in the 1920s, and shrank dramatically during the 1930s, disputes between liberalism and protectionism, industrialism and agrarianism, and public and private interests marked all seven decades.

## Historical Disagreements

Was it the best of times or the worst of times? Scholars have characterized this three-quarters of a century in strikingly different ways. For Whig historians, defenders of empire, or champions of free trade, it was a time of progressive diffusion that spread the benefits of civilization and brought God and the written word to benighted peoples. This is the Henry Stanley, Teddy Roosevelt, and Jules Verne eighty-days-around-the-world version of modernity, which had Europeans and neo-Europeans, such as those in North America, Australia, and Argentina, "discovering" and improving all with which they came into contact. To apologists, this was a time of expanding freedoms—of trade, worship, and scientific research.

Contemporaries who rued the consequences of what was often cast as social Darwinism saw the titanic struggle between fit and unfit races, winners and losers, in much darker hues. Here one thinks of Joseph Conrad ruing in *Heart of Darkness* that "the conquest of the earth, which mostly means the taking it away from those who have a different complexion or slightly flatter noses than ourselves, is not a pretty thing when you look into it too much." The light-skinned, in European and North American minds, brought progress and development, all too often orchestrated by the terrible killing power of the automatic guns that permitted the great issues of the day to be decided, as Prussia's prime minister Otto von Bismarck predicted in 1862, "by blood and iron."

Some commentators and scholars have stressed technological innovations and the growth of markets (though not necessarily unfettered markets). Sometimes these improvements were seen as the teleological triumph of reason and science. According to this view, technical progress imposed itself on ever more people in ever more distant parts of the world. But the machine was not neutral. It was seen as a "civilizer" that proved the superiority of Western Europeans.[5] Proponents contended that reason, race, technology, and prosperity were inextricably tied together.

Yet reason and "racial science" also gave rise to an unreasonable "Age of Extremes" that discarded liberalism for a "triumph of the will," and substituted totalitarianism for laissez-faire. In the United States, racism became widespread and politically volatile in the wake of the abolition of slavery and the end of Reconstruction.[6] In the theories of US eugenicists German Nazis found reinforcement for their racial ideology and practices, leading to the cruel and bloody Holocaust that spread through Central and Eastern Europe.

Gazing from a Eurocentric perspective, the historian Eric Hobsbawm characterized the time as the "Age of Empire," while the Marxist theorist Rudolf Hilferding labeled it the period of "Finance Capital."[7] To leftist militants like Nikolai Bukharin and Vladimir Lenin, it was the era of "monopoly capitalism." Rather than a world open to progress shaped through a freer diffusion of trade, capital, and technology, this historical conjuncture, such critics fulminated, was rent by imperial possessions, monopolies, and cartels.

Perhaps surprisingly, outside of Europe the most dynamic regions generally were not part of formal empires. Indeed, recent research has underlined the importance of Asian entrepreneurship and inter-Asian trade in the East Asian industrial model that emerged in our period. Trade *within* Asia grew faster than in any other region in the world. Even those that were colonial subjects, like Australia, Canada, and South Africa, effectively won their independence in this period. India would not be far behind, achieving its freedom in 1947. So if formal empire made its mark on our seventy-five years, it also wrote its final chapters. Moreover, if the economic theories of John Gallagher and Ronald Robinson are to be accepted, "free-trade imperialism" motivated empire builders. This hotly contested perspective would inspire a rash of studies on neocolonialism, dependency theory, and world systems that complicates our understandings of methods of formal and informal colonial rule.[8]

Our approach acknowledges the central role that Western European and North American capitalists, laborers, and technology played in the metamorphosis of world trade and finance and agrees that entrepreneurs on both sides of the North Atlantic were fundamental to the era's profound transformations. As historian Jürgen Osterhammel recently observed: "The history of the nineteenth century was massively made in and by Europeans. . . . Never before had Europe generated a similar excess of innovation and initiative, while at the same time unleashing overpowering force and arrogance." But we agree with him that European exceptionalism has been exaggerated.[9] Not all changes originated from or were dictated by European and North American capitalists. The world beyond Western Europe and North America was hardly an undifferentiated "Third World" that continued to meander along in time-honored ways. Despite widespread representations of the non-Europeanized world as "Oriental" in this period, in fact radically differentiated economic transformations occurred in many parts of the globe between 1870 and 1945.

As Say's Law had pronounced a century before, products created their own demand. Or, in the words of Brazilian diplomat J. F. de Barros Pimentel, "A century ago, the public pressured to have the commodities. In modern times, we observe the pressure of goods over the public. It is the inverse system: provisions [dominate] over populations. The globe's inhabitants do not search for goods as much as products seek consumers."[10] So what was produced in overseas agrarian areas not only responded to the appetites of affluent industrializing areas but shaped their tastes and notions of "decent" standards of living. The imported became centerpieces of national identity and class definition, from tea and wheat in the United Kingdom to coffee and sugar in the United States and Germany.[11] Thorstein Veblen may have ridiculed "conspicuous consumption," but goods that were previously undreamed of suddenly became status symbols or markers of modernity for the fortunate. Over time these goods filtered down to the general public and became mass necessities.

The vastly intensified labor of the working class also funded diversions of the leisure class that spread across borders: sumptuous retreats sprung up in Marienbad, Bohemia, and Battle Creek, Michigan; sin cities emerged in Casablanca, Havana, Shanghai, and Rio de Janeiro, and overseas tours led by the British Thomas Cook Company and travel guides written by the German Baedeker company catalyzed a global tourist industry. Leisure became commodified into manufactured things that could be exported: cheap publications like dime store novels and newspapers, player pianos and music rolls, records, Victrolas and other phonographs, and, of course, moving pictures. Tropical products, like chocolate, coffee, bananas, and tea, also fed these newfound leisure pursuits.

## Why Study Commodities?

Tracing the evolution of a number of commodity chains during this era illuminates how agricultural, pastoral, and mineral-producing areas of the world—many in Latin America, Asia, Oceania, and Africa—were linked commercially to Western European and North American financiers, industrialists, and consumers. Commodity chains reveal connections among people who were distant and unfamiliar to each other; they linked inhabitants of different continents with markedly diverse lifestyles and cultures, who sometimes worked under contrasting modes of production. Rather than concentrate exclusively on diffusion or homogenization brought about by the industrial center imposing itself on an agrarian periphery, as many economic histories of this period have done, we study commodity circuits to demonstrate the inherent variety and interplay of world commerce and the contributions of the areas outside of Europe and North America.

Defining a "commodity" is no easy task, given the thorny nature of scholarship on this subject. The Ricardian or Marxian definition posits a commodity as a good produced for exchange to create profit, rather than one strictly made for use by its maker. The value of the commodity was determined by consumers rather than by its producer. We prefer this broad definition to the more restricted one recently in vogue with economists and businessmen who think of commodities only as raw materials or, more specifically, bulk undifferentiated and unbranded goods. To us, commodities were the result of dynamic and contingent processes of commodification, what some sociologists call "value chains," which sometimes included producers, processors, transporters, exporters, wholesalers, and retailers. Anthropologists, however, remind us to take into account cultural differences in how commodities have been perceived and utilized over time. They were not always market-bound tradable things. Things moved in and out of a commodity state, appreciated as much for their practical uses, their lore, and their symbolic value as for their roles in exchange and accumulation. They also had gendered meanings determined by households and subcultures as much as by individuals.[12] Because this was such a transitional moment in the global economy's expansion, in one locale goods could sometimes be produced solely for exchange, whereas in another the same product carried locally generated cultural and symbolic significance. World history enables us to understand how malleable commodities and their social roles were, just as we hope to show how the movement of these goods reveals the contours of world history.

To be sure, commodities often acquired new meanings and uses as they traversed oceans and were turned into imaginative new products. But it was also true that in the original producing areas the significance and even the essence of these "goods" (we use the term recognizing its embedded and sometimes inaccurate value judgment, given that sometimes these goods were bad for producers or consumers) were altered as they were bent to the needs of foreign and domestic consumers. Examining the transformation of primary goods into finished products illuminates the workings of the world economy, because it requires consideration of a host of legal, technological, political, and social institutions that facilitated and accompanied such changes. Therefore, we first consider the conventions necessary for trade to flow and blossom, *before* entering into a detailed discussion of the commodity chains.

We pay particular attention to commodities that transcended national borders, even though the vast majority of economic activity in the world before 1945 was still dedicated to home and local production. It is impossible to consider the bewildering array of goods that circulated globally during this era, so we will concentrate on a few key products that were representative of the diversity of agricultural, mining, intermediary, and industrial processes.

We have chosen these products not because they were new to the world economy in 1870. Most, in fact, were not; some had already traveled internationally for centuries. Rather, they were selected because they were some of the most valuable globally traded products of the time. They not only fulfilled new social, cultural, and economic roles and elicited remarkable technological and institutional innovations, but they confounded some of the basic assumptions that contemporaries held about world trade. They allow us to follow goods from where they were grown, mined, or raised, to their processing and transformation for the market as they were packaged, branded, advertised, and placed in stores and stalls, to their final consumption in distant lands in remarkably different forms with usually quite different social meanings. Following these commodity circuits provides a heuristic device for understanding the complexities of global integration during this crucial era.

CHAPTER ONE

# Transformations

Given the sweeping changes that occurred, it is not surprising that winners and losers littered the new economic playing field. British, US, German, and French trade, capital, technology, and spheres of influence spread across the globe while eminent older empires such as the Ottoman, Chinese, Austro-Hungarian, Spanish, and Portuguese declined and fragmented. Western Europe, North America, Russia, Japan, and some parts of Latin America fared relatively well. Africa, the Middle East, and most of Asia (significantly, areas most afflicted by colonialism) fared less well. Clearly, transformations were far from uniform.

Even on the more prosperous continents, economies did not grow steadily and predictably. Intensified capitalist relations led to more frequent and destabilizing booms and busts, deflations and inflations. It was only in this period that economists began to theorize that economic cycles were inherent to capitalism. The economic concept of "cycles of accumulation," in which dramatic downturns ultimately and painfully cleared the way for later growth spurts, would come later. More unsettling to investors and producers alike, the economies most closely involved in international trade and finance found themselves most affected by global ups and downs. The seventy-five years after 1870 were marked by the first worldwide depression in the early 1870s, a downturn that lasted into the 1890s, followed by a European *belle époque* from the late 1890s until 1913 (save for the 1907 panic), unsettled conditions in the wake of World War I, and then what was, at least until recently, the most devastating and longest-lasting international commercial and financial crisis the world had ever experienced, the Great Depression. And just as the global economy was digging itself out, the pernicious effects of World War II would cripple huge swaths of the globe.[1]

Not only were sharp contrasts evident in different parts of the world, but their temporal character ensured that the benefits of "progress" were far from obvious for contemporaries. Preceding generations had bequeathed cultures of violence, unfree labor, cumbersome concepts of property and wealth, and monopolized markets to the denizens of this new age. Indeed, critics like Lenin, Bukharin, Rosa Luxemburg, and Hilferding asserted that such "market imperfections" (to borrow a concept from liberal economics) were not just anachronisms or anomalies, but fundamental to the expansion of imperialism and industrial capitalism. Closer integration to the world market did not necessarily mean shared values, social structures, or prosperity. The pressures of the international economy may have melded together local peoples and markets, but they also wrought fissures and fragmentation in areas newly affected by world commerce. In some regions, market integration offered greater productivity, choice, and convenience to many. Elsewhere, market expansion resembled military campaigns imposed at the end of a bayonet at frightening cost.

If this era was the high tide of private property, privatization of land, and less-restrictive trade, it also witnessed the birth of the "organized capitalism" of trusts, cartels, and conglomerates, as well as socialist and fascist command economies. Hobsbawm has noted: "Still, it does not much matter what we call it ('corporation capitalism,' 'organized capitalism,' etc.), so long as it is agreed—and it must be—that combination advanced at the expense of market competition, business corporations at the expense of private firms, big business and large enterprise at the expense of smaller; and that this concentration implied a tendency towards oligopoly."[2] Even in South and East Asia, where family firms and partnerships continued to be the predominant form of business organization, there was a tendency toward concentration, just as there was in Latin America with its large plantations and relative handfuls of enormous mines, banks, and factories.

Certainly, new technologies rewarded economies of scale and scope while permitting centralized supervision and international coordination of an unprecedented order.[3] But the impetus to control these markets mocked ideologues who preached the virtues of individualism and competition. This gave rise to political movements, such as the Populists in the United States and anarchism and socialism elsewhere, that denounced large banks and corporations and sought more cooperative or communal endeavors. Their actions reflected what economic theorist Karl Polanyi called the reformist "double movement" or what Marx referred to as revolutionary "contradictions," as states, groups, and individuals sometimes moved to mitigate or overturn the consequences of intensified market relations.

And for all of these new forms of organization and responses to rapid change, we should remember that many of the world's inhabitants were still peasants living in rural villages, often with communal forms of landownership. For them the rush of events in the center of the world economy could be a distant rumble, though often they came to feel its aftershocks.

Striking contrasts frequently were evident within the same country, as skyscrapers in modernized city centers were juxtaposed with sod or wattle-and-daub huts in the countryside. The differences in power, wealth, lifestyle, health, and labor systems often became so great that the rural and the urban were treated as separate realms and the populations as almost racially distinct. Over time some of the contrasts diminished in the more affluent areas as primary cities colonized their hinterlands, and in the process transmitted technological advances and social institutions, while absorbing ever more migrants from the countryside.

Difference imposed itself not only in lifestyle, but also more intimately in the quality and length of life itself. Unlike the post–World

War II period, the areas of fastest population growth prior to 1945, such as the United Kingdom, Western Europe, and North America, were also the areas of rapid economic growth. In the United States, life expectancy began to grow quickly after 1870, jumping from forty-five years at birth for white males to sixty-five years in 1939–1941, a remarkable advance given that the total population was ballooning. Despite crushing wars, Scandinavia and other countries from Northern and Central Europe like Germany and the Netherlands reached life expectancies of sixty years by 1945. European offshoots, like Australia and New Zealand, experienced some of the most dramatic gains in longevity, attaining an average of sixty-seven years by the end of World War II. Latin Americans, with the exception of Argentines and Uruguayans, did not enjoy such demographic improvement. Most of them could expect to live only into their forties. In Africa and Asia (outside of Japan), where most of the world's people lived, population grew more slowly *and* the average person often could not expect to live past the age of thirty or forty.[4] So global life spans grew at historically unprecedented rates in some locales but so too did the gap in life expectancy between those in the richer countries and those in the poorer. Even within the same country, differences in longevity grew, as advances in sanitation and public health initially were concentrated in the cities. The medical discoveries of this period offered to the affluent included commodified and branded miracle drugs, such as aspirin, penicillin, and quinine, and increasingly modern practices from professionalized physicians and nurses. The poor continued to rely on folk remedies and shamans or simply suffered and died.

## Constructive Destruction?

Distress and economic progress were not simply sad coincidences; they were often causally linked as they accompanied the carving up of Asia, Africa, and the Middle East by European powers. As Hilaire Belloc wrote in a sardonic ode to the colonial *mentalité,* the Europeans won out abroad—particularly in Africa—not so much because of the brilliance of their civilizations or the strength of their faith, but because: "Whatever happens, we have got / the Maxim gun, and they have not." Although the full poem was in fact a searing indictment of colonialism, it did correctly point to Europeans' military advantage, if not their perceived moral superiority.

Over time, however, the diffusion of weapons by arms dealers and states undercut the early edge of the armed. Outlaws also took advantage: Chicago's policemen feared that "Tommy guns," first designed for trench warfare during World War I, might fall into the hands of Al Capone's mobsters. The Plains Indians and later the Apache in the US Southwest used rifles not just for hunting but also for raiding and self-defense. Revolutionists as well as militaries used dynamite to explosive effect.

Weapons industries reflected the contradictions of science and industrialization. Modern weaponry integrated precision engineering, standardization, assembly-line manufacturing, and automatic technology with durable and light materials to create potent engines of slaughter. When economist Joseph Schumpeter extolled capitalism's "creative destruction," he saw it as a virtue that removed barriers to rapid progress.[5] Perhaps he did not take into account that some of the largest corporations to arise from the Industrial Revolution, companies like Colt, DuPont, Siemens, IG Farben, and Krupp, profited handsomely from building devastating weapons of destruction. By the end of World War II, guns were capable of hitting targets miles away, guided missiles could fly over the English Channel, and airplanes were dropping powerful bombs, culminating in the atomic bombs dropped on Hiroshima and Nagasaki. Tragically, morality did not keep step with scientific "progress."[6]

When applied to livestock, the killing technology of Chicago's stockyards lowered the price of meat, making it available to the working class in the most affluent cities. At the same time, the "disassembly lines" of Chicago's Armour and Swift meat-processing plants were scientifically efficient means of terminating millions of animals' lives and transforming their skinned, cut-up carcasses into dozens of new commodities, from meat to shoes and buttons. These multinational corporations, which spread their operations to Latin America and beyond in the 1920s, used everything but the squeal in their merciless creative destruction that was the precursor to the industrial assembly line.[7]

A particularly striking example of the contradictions of technology was Alfred Nobel's inspired invention of dynamite. Mixing nitroglycerine and silica, he arrived at an explosive that not only was much more powerful than gunpowder, but, when joined to his invention of the blasting cap, was safe and controlled. The result was a godsend to miners, tunnelers, and builders more generally because it made their professions much safer. Dynamite went global not only because the more stable explosive could travel safely but also because Nobel's firm built dynamite factories in many countries. Although his invention was useful in the building and construction trades, he was denounced as a merchant of death. But as a pacifist, Alfred was earnestly distressed about the destructive genie he had let out of the bottle. Nobel willed a sizable part of his $9 million fortune to reward constructive scientific and other intellectual advances with a major prize. Perhaps the most ironic part of his penance was the creation of the Nobel Peace Prize, funded by explosives earnings.[8] Construction and destruction, peace and war danced to unpredictable rhythms in volatile couplings.

## The Great Divergence

This era magnified what historian Kenneth Pomeranz has called "the Great Divergence." Taking exception to the conventional wisdom, at least in the West, that Europe had enjoyed wealth and technology superior to the rest of the world since the Middle Ages, Pomeranz contends that the West's margin over Asia materialized only after 1750 and then more for economic and geographic reasons than for cultural or racial ones. Thereafter, wealth, technology, and military power became concentrated among a few countries and in a few corporations in one corner of the world to a degree that had never before been experienced.[9] By 1880 the developed world's per capita income was about double that in the "Third World." It was to be over three times as high by 1914 and reached a five-fold difference by 1950, despite the devastation Western Europe experienced during World War II.[10]

Indeed, the wars brought about a divergence even within the developed economies, because such burgeoning economies as the United States, Canada, Australia, New Zealand, and Argentina were spared the ravages of war. The United States' per capita gross domestic product (GDP) jumped from a fourfold advantage over the average of "the periphery" in 1870 to almost ninefold in 1950, while Western Europe's lead grew more slowly from 3.5-fold to 4.7.[11] The democratically impoverishing Great Depression and World War II would lessen the divergence somewhat, but nonetheless in 1945 it was still far greater than it had been in 1870. Even these shocking numbers mute the reality of the gaping divide. The world's richest entrepreneurs and robber barons controlled more wealth than many small countries.

Sharp differences did not just stand out between countries on distant continents. Even within the same country immense inequalities were apparent, though not as great as those between richer and poorer countries. This Gilded Age saw plutocrats in enormous estates lighting cigars with five-dollar bills while millions of hungry proletarians huddled in teeming, filthy slums.[12] Tropical plantations may have provided delights such as coffee, sugar, and bananas, for the first time available to the new urban class of consumers in Western Europe and North America, but planters' ostentatious mansions were ringed by peasant huts or barracks and hungry, barefoot children, all too often hidden from the view of a well-armed *patrón*. Meanwhile, many people, particularly in Africa and Asia, continued to till their land and tend to their livestock as they had for as long as anyone could remember.

Contemporaries attributed this chasm to differences of race, religion, or climate, or to a clash of civilizations. The global divide was viewed as a confrontation of civilization versus barbarism not only by self-satisfied European and North American plutocrats but by many elites in the periphery. By the end of the period, explanatory concepts such as "underdevelopment" and "imperialism" began to replace the older cultural, religious, or racialist distinctions. Despite the urge to spread Western ways and homogenize the world during these years, *difference,* often growing differences, marked the gap between the daily lives of the globe's impoverished populace and those who benefited from the era's changes.[13]

## Environment as Resource and Victim

Although our book concentrates on human involvement in the world economy, we would be remiss if we overlooked the collective impact of humans' explosive new productivity and trade on the natural environment. Economic growth and medical advances helped the world's population expand at the fastest rate in history to that point, doubling from 1.2 billion people to 2.5 billion in seventy-five years, and, as noted, in many areas life expectancy increased. Coupled with peoples' expanding ability to produce—total world output grew 500 percent by some estimates—and a growing appetite to consume, as well as the capability to access remote areas because of improved infrastructure, "nature" was losing its domain. While virgin prairies and grasslands were put to the plow, yielding bountiful returns, human intrusions also brought on disasters. Irrigation may have turned some deserts into fertile fields, but overfarming and grazing transformed once-prosperous lands into dust bowls.

Movement by actors in the world economy into formerly uninhabited areas had contradictory consequences. As Europeans and North Americans encountered parts of the globe formerly unknown to them in the Amazon, the American West, central Africa, and Siberia, plant and animal extinctions became commonplace. Development for some species often spelled tragedy for others.

Conservationists like John Muir in the United States began to see the threat of human sprawl and fought to maintain "pristine" nature. But they were unusual. In most places a "primitive accumulation" occurred in which the flora and fauna were treated as resources for human use and profit. "Darkest Africa," for example, became a natural bounty rather than a wilderness. Its great herds of elephants were slaughtered for their tusks just as the millions of buffaloes of the North American prairies were sent to near extinction. Brazil's vast coastal forest, the Mata Atlântica, was felled. And on the oceans, humans overran many islands. There, as well as on the continents, exotic species were introduced with occasional disastrous consequences for indigenous creatures and plants.[14]

Human audacity was not new, of course. For millennia some people thought their gods had bequeathed them ownership of the beasts and plants. Civilization and suzerainty had by definition long been equated to the domination of nature.[15] What changed was not ideas but rather how technocrats and scientists began developing techniques for massive frontal assaults on nature. Environmental degradation went hand in hand with commodification. Human societies with markets increasingly became market societies dominated by the urge to sell and buy in ever more parts of the world. Land, forests, and wildlife increasingly were perceived either as private property or as barriers to progress. This capitalization of nature in turn demanded new legal institutions, titles, financial instruments, and exchanges.

## Cotton and the First Industrial Revolution

By 1870 the First Industrial Revolution had already caused cheap cotton textiles to replace precious metals, spices, silks, sugar, and tobacco as the principal engine of long-distance trade, though international commerce in all these commodities, with the exception of spices, grew rapidly throughout our period. The steam-powered loom, fed by Welsh and British coal, and Eli Whitney's cotton gin had revolutionized textile and clothing manufacturing. Where cotton had provided a mere 4 percent of clothing in the United Kingdom and the United States in 1793, a century later it had reached 75 percent. That this industrial powerhouse was fed by slave labor in North American cotton fields appeared to augur its demise once Abraham Lincoln abolished slavery. After all, on the brink of the American Civil War, the United States provided two-thirds of the world's total supply and fully 80 percent of the cotton manufactured in Britain.[16]

But cotton growers in the United States and elsewhere came to realize that they did not need slaves. King Cotton would continue to drive the economy of the southern United States after the Emancipation Proclamation, thanks to debt peonage, but now producers in Egypt and India, who took advantage of peasants, sharecroppers, and debt peons, could offer competition, thanks to even lower labor costs. By the last decades of the nineteenth century cotton was no longer the engine of world trade, because many areas, from Brazil and Mexico to South Africa, Uganda, and China, now grew their own. For the period 1860–1887, cotton ranked ninth in the value of seaborne trade, valued at less than one-fifth of grains or sugar and less than one-fourth of coffee. US exports of cotton regained antebellum levels by 1880 and doubled by 1895, but stagnated thereafter. The swelling US domestic market for textiles compensated somewhat for declining foreign demand, but domestic cotton production grew slowly and inconsistently, as it did worldwide. It would soon encounter stiff competition from other natural and synthetic fibers.[17]

As textile manufacture matured, investors from the first industrialized countries as well as native entrepreneurs in Latin America, Southern and Eastern Europe, and Asia, especially Japan and India, imported machinery and set up their own factories. They then appealed to their governments for tariff protection, further reducing the international circulation of textiles though increasing sales of machinery from the core to the periphery. This was the first stage of what became more generally known after 1930 as import substitution industrialization (ISI). Cotton was an early victim of what economist Raymond Vernon termed the "product cycle": the life trajectory of a new technology that initially provided great monopoly rents to "first movers" who first mastered more-efficient techniques and expanded markets.[18] While continuing to profit, first movers of cotton manufacturing lost their international advantage and their dynamism as the technology diffused. We will see this pattern repeated over and over again in areas as disparate as steel smelting and the telegraph and commodities from grains to rubber. New products demanding different raw materials from far-flung parts of the globe would take the baton in a global relay race to lead the continued expansion of the world economy.

## Free Trade

The battle over tariffs on international trade was of enormous import for the course of world commerce. In 1870 Britain clearly enjoyed a privileged position in the world market thanks to its industrial head start in cotton textiles and other products, domination of global shipping, prosperous and sophisticated financial system, and access to imperial markets. There was little wonder, then, that British statesmen and politicians were quick to invoke classical economists like Adam

Smith and David Ricardo on the advantages of free trade and the invisible hand of the market. Although one could attribute the concept of laissez-faire to earlier French Physiocrats, economic liberalism by our period spoke with a British accent. Her Majesty's imperial officials, as well as British investors, wage-earning workers, and consumers, all came to see advantages in lower duties on trade.[19] England's economic missionaries set out to convince statesmen and borrowers across the globe of the necessity of the gold standard, low tariff duties, limited government, and the primacy of the private sector—all of which would benefit British manufacturers, merchants, and bankers as well as their empire.

Political leaders and capitalists in other countries could be excused for not being as enamored of free trade. The unequal distribution of global capital led many governments to be suspicious of its benefits. Even in regions that enjoyed the most success in this age of export-led growth, such as the Americas, or later industrial giants such as Germany, Russia, and Japan, there was heated debate about the wisdom of open markets and privatization. Protectionism continued to vie with free trade, as defensive-minded political elites developed sophisticated economic discourses in favor of greater autarky.[20] Some statesmen sought to extend the idea of a tariff barrier to entire regions under the aegis of commercial unions. Each major economic power flirted with such unions: the French created their own union with other "Latin" countries, the United States' policy of Pan-Americanism tried to coordinate trade in its imagined "backyard," Britian would build its own imperial preferences in the 1920s and 1930s, the Germans followed suit in Central Europe, while the Japanese imposed their economic will on their regional neighbors.

Elsewhere there were efforts to protect narrower markets. In Latin America, protectionist lobbies exercised great weight in Brazil, Peru, and Mexico at the end of the nineteenth century.[21] Moreover, regional strongmen or *caudillos,* who still exercised considerable sway as late as the 1870s and 1880s, were key actors in the struggle to marshal resources. *Caudillos* acted like warlords in China or chieftains in Africa, who themselves were fervent advocates of local autonomy, even if sometimes that was seen as a step toward eventual greater regional unity. So it is no surprise that warfare and political upheavals hindered economic development and investment. As a result, the export performance of most of Latin America remained shaky until the last decades of the nineteenth century and most of Africa and Asia fared even worse.[22]

Although some of Latin America's national leaders were among the most fervent disciples of the Manchester School's free-trade policies, conditions in that hemisphere necessitated responses different from those in England. In the "New World" the economies demanded significant state interventions, not only in transportation, banking, and public utilities, but also in the key export sectors, such as coffee and rubber. Nonetheless, liberalism continued to be an ideological and rhetorical desideratum of state policy even if it was obeyed more in the breach than in practice. They spoke liberalism; they acted interventionism.

The desirability of free trade also proved controversial in the United States. The defeat of the Confederacy in 1865, after the United States' bloodiest conflict, failed to put to rest divisive debates over the tariff, which continued to be a contentious matter for the nation's two major political parties. The Democrats were especially wary of big government, and Populists and then Progressive Republicans demanded greater state intervention in the economy. These parties remained suspicious of foreign investment even as it flooded into the country. Anti-British sentiment became so inflamed that the United States and Britain only narrowly escaped war in the early 1890s.[23]

For the most part, Canadians did not share such anti-British feelings (with the notable exception of the Québécois), but they pursued a middle ground, seeking freer trade by reducing their colonial ties while still remaining a part of the Commonwealth. Freer trade, however, meant turning away from London. The majority of their trade shifted from the United Kingdom south to the United States in these years. In 1870 Canada imported over half of its consumption goods from the United Kingdom and only a third from the United States; by 1911 just a quarter of its imports came from the British and 61 percent came from its southern neighbor.

Canada's experience contrasted rather sharply with those of other British colonies, such as Australia, New Zealand, and South Africa, which received over half their imports from Britain. Around half of Canadian exports, on the other hand, continued to go to Britain. They surpassed Australia but were considerably lower than New Zealand, and South Africa, which sent over three-quarters of their exports to the United Kingdom.[24] India, South Africa, and Rhodesia had success in the international market, but all three were under the aegis of British colonialism and paid a price in terms of severe internal inequalities.

The situation was different in most of Asia and Africa, which had not been subjected as thoroughly to British or Iberian influence. There, tribal and village authorities meant fragmented sovereignties; the great majority of the population consisted of subsistence peasants and herders who probably did not find foreign trade appealing. In such locales, European powers frequently attempted to foster monetary markets by statute or through force of arms. Even Japan, which was the most successful Asian economy at industrializing and expanding trade, abandoned its efforts at integration into the world economy to seek a self-contained imperial trading unit, the Greater East Asia Co-prosperity Sphere, once the Great Depression made its government wary of free markets.

It would require the near collapse of international trade and capital flows during the First World War and then the Great Depression of the 1930s to force major changes in commercial and financial thinking. Only then did theory catch up with the piecemeal policies of politicians engaged in crisis management. The severe dislocations of trade and financial flows generated new ways of understanding the global economy and of appreciating new roles for states.[25] Initially the advent of state planning was largely unplanned and unsought. This occurred in both agricultural and industrial export economies. After the First World War the leading powers, with the exception of the USSR, attempted to return to classical liberal economics by reinstating the gold standard and lowering barriers to trade and international investment. However, the Soviet Union and parts of Eastern Europe that increasingly fell into its orbit after the war turned to state planning for ideological reasons as well as for survival. During the 1930s the self-regulating market ceased to regulate itself even in Western Europe as commodity prices and trade dropped precipitously. In the face of deflation, unsettled financial markets, and political unrest, even European and North American governments turned to protecting home industries and widened the scope of public investment and regulation.

Exporting countries attempted to follow suit. Domestic markets in most of Latin America, for instance, already had expanded and diversified considerably under export-led growth. Consequently, ISI became increasingly attractive as a means of lessening reliance on imports. Politicized and radicalized urban workers, and, in a few countries such as Mexico, peasants and workers in the export sectors, demanded greater state attentiveness and a social safety net.[26] Similar statist efforts occurred in India and in Japan's sphere of influence, which included its colonies of Korea and Formosa as well as its growing influence over Southeast Asia and China. The Keynesian Revolution, even if it was not yet called that, began to challenge free-market liberalism in theory and practice.

## The Second Industrial Revolution

The late nineteenth and early twentieth centuries were at once a natural extension of the First Industrial Revolution and a fundamental break with the past. A bevy of changes occurred in everything from the materials utilized, the sources of energy, the organization of production and business, the application of science, the nature of the most dynamic sectors, and even the nations now commanding the heights of this new wave of industrialization. Whereas the English had gained their head start in the eighteenth century through the application of coal to develop steam power, after 1870 they gradually ceded leadership to the United States and Germany. Although coal, steam, and iron continued to be important, now oil, electricity, and steel took precedence. Chemists became as important as engineers as they created aniline dyes, dynamite, and nitrates for fertilizers and munitions. Scientifically based, capital-intensive technology led not only to newer, more efficient, and larger-scale production methods, but to new materials such as rubber, steel, and cement, and new industries, such as weapons, electronics, the telegraph, the typewriter, the bicycle, and the automobile. Many of these new materials and products rewarded economies of scale. Assembly lines with continuous-flow production and standardized interchangeable parts eventually led in some places to the "American System" and Frederick Taylor's concept of "scientific management" predicated on greater efficiencies (what critics viewed as greater labor exploitation) through enhanced work norms and time-and-motion controls.

Other mass-produced products, particularly foods and medicines, were now packaged, branded, and advertised to facilitate their conquest of global markets. By the post–World War II era, consumers in the West craved goods that were not even dreamed of in 1870; farmers and peasants for the first time could imagine buying factory-made clothes or store-bought foodstuffs that heretofore had characterized city life. The advent of department stores (and the consumer credit they extended) in the late nineteenth century in Western Europe and the United States, like Le Bon Marché, Harrods, Selfridges, Macy's, Marshall Field's, and Wanamaker's, and catalog stores, such as Montgomery Ward and Sears, Roebuck & Co., began to widen the market for ready-made mass clothing.[27]

Even though the growth of the world economy was no longer driven primarily by cotton, the British continued to be a driving force behind its expansion. By revolutionizing production and transportation technologies and expanding credit mechanisms, the United Kingdom and Ireland were responsible in the latter half of the 1870s for almost 40 percent of the world's manufactured exports. To export finished products, they had to import raw materials for their factories as well as food and drink for their growing urban populations, because their climate and the limited fertility of their land could not sustain them. That is why almost two-thirds of world trade in the forty years before 1913 was in primary products. The United Kingdom and Ireland accounted for just under a third (and northwestern Europe another 40 percent) of all imports of primary products. The world economy was driven by the relatively small islands of the United Kingdom and a cramped northwestern Europe, which were monetized and dependent on the outside world. Competition in the factories of Manchester, London, and Sheffield and on the European continent dropped export prices of manufactured goods, creating accelerated demand abroad. At the same time the gnawing British appetite for food and raw-material imports at least initially raised prices in agricultural exporting countries while London cemented its position as the world's banking and finance center.[28]

The pound sterling, which became the official unit of the British gold standard in 1821, replaced the Spanish, Mexican, and Peruvian peso in most countries by the 1870s, to eventually become the currency standard for world trade. This greatly reduced transaction costs and facilitated lending. As London became the world's commercial *and* financial center, the United Kingdom could sustain for a while the lead it had taken in the First Industrial Revolution (see Table 1.1, p. 34).

Britain's need for raw materials and food for its booming factories and population meant huge trade deficits. It financed this imbalance from its "invisible" earnings achieved through interest on commercial and public loans, profits on foreign direct investments, shipping and insurance charges, and currency exchange transactions. Historian Niall Ferguson does not exaggerate Britain's preeminent role as the motor of world trade when he writes: "Yet the fact remains that no organization in history has done more to promote the free movement of goods, capital and labour than the British Empire in the nineteenth and early twentieth centuries."[29]

## States, Markets, and Monopolies

Despite the dreams and aspirations of the most radical champions of liberalism and the free market, turn-of-the-century economies were not unregulated. Expensive and far-reaching new technologies demanded public oversight of the private sector. States played an important role in subsidizing, regulating, and in some cases constructing costly infrastructure to lubricate the wheels of commerce. This was also true in some of the export economies in Latin America, Asia, Oceania, and, to a lesser extent, Africa that were more recently integrated into the world market.[30] Elsewhere, traditional modalities of trade remained largely uninterrupted, and, not surprisingly, states' presence in the economy was barely noticed.

The roles of merchants, officials, and information itself evolved in response to the evolution of the market. Even as late as 1870 most specialized knowledge of the market was local, sporadic, and heterogeneous, controlled mostly by specific actors at different points in a commodity chain—growers, traders, transporters, processors, dealers, wholesalers, retailers, and peddlers. Closely held information on trade and personal relations of trust aided the continued importance of ethnic and familial trading diasporas, such as the Cantonese,

Tamil, Gujarati, Sindhi, Persian, Hadhrami, Armenian, Syro-Lebanese, Moroccan Jewish, Basque, Scottish, and Ashkenazi Jewish networks.[31]

Over time, information became more widely disseminated, systematic, and standardized, first by merchants and shippers, then by trade gazettes, newspapers, wire services, and commodity and stock exchanges. The telegraph that began linking distant contiguous areas and the undersea cable that tied together continents sparked the need for commercial, legal, and scientific conventions. European languages—French for diplomacy, German for science, and English for business—supplemented by the forces of colonialism and imperialism, became widely used among anonymous elites across the globe. Even areas that did not experience colonialism directly, like Japan, introduced modern conventions, but with their own twists. But the urge to "modernize" (another word and concept that became fashionable in this period) did not always connote the desire to homogenize. Outside forces were often perceived as pernicious and malignant. Reaction to them frequently inhibited diffusion rather than encouraging it.

There is ample debate among economic historians about whether this era of globalization primarily meant the growth of the free market, secure property rights, liberalism, the gold standard, and free trade, or whether it was characterized more by imperial and domestic government intervention and the emergence of monopolies. In fact, both were in evidence. Consolidation and monopoly were particularly noticeable in modern transportation sectors like railroads and steamships, in communication marvels like the telegraph, and in heavy industries dependent upon government contracts, such as armaments. It was also found where new energy forms and systems were utilized, such as oil and electricity, and with certain new raw materials that governments deemed to be of strategic value, like rubber. Standard Oil controlled over 90 percent of the oil refined in the United States in 1880, US Steel at the turn of the century produced almost two-thirds of the industry's steel, while the Rhine-Westphalian Coal Syndicate controlled the same share of coal in Germany.[32]

Concentration also emerged in intermediary capital goods sectors, such as machinery that was sold to manufacturers rather than to consumers, who remained blissfully unaware of the components that went into these goods. Among the pioneering machinery firms, notes business historian Alfred Chandler, "rarely did more than a handful of competitors succeed in obtaining a significant share of the national and international markets. These industries quickly became and remained oligopolistic or monopolistic."[33]

Much more evident to the general public in North America and Western Europe was that "bigness" was an indelible characteristic of such industries as perishable food and drugs, because processors found ways to profit from economies of scale and scope. Linking vertically between agricultural production (which they only occasionally did themselves), purchasing, processing, packaging, and distribution, some enormous, highly capitalized corporations that we are still familiar with today, such as the United Fruit Company, British Tobacco, Coca-Cola, Wrigley, and Quaker Oats, created international commodity chains within their firms to sell recently created products for mass markets.[34]

Huge corporations dominated not just because of technological imperatives or market demands. Financiers, who previously had profited from loans to governments and other financial instruments, emerged as key brokers who were best placed to take advantage of the more felicitous business climate. With the passage of joint-stock-company and limited-liability laws, financiers created large commercial banks that pooled the small investments of rentiers and the middle class to promote new innovative undertakings and expansions, all the while assembling trusts to restrain competition.

These enormous companies often had stockholders and even directors and managers from a number of countries, so increasingly they carried multiple passports. Although Lenin thought that nationalism and consolidation characterized the highest stage of capitalism and that they would lead the dominant imperialist nations to war among themselves, in fact multinational companies often preferred to cooperate with their international business associates rather than with their national compatriots. J. P. Morgan underwrote huge US combinations through his father's London-based company; the Rothschilds had banks headquartered in five countries; the American-based General Electric (GE) and the German firm Siemens undertook mutual projects; and French and British banks jointly underwrote loans. The governments of the countries in which these firms operated now were faced with divided loyalties. The new international scope created challenges for multinational corporations like Standard Oil in Austria, which found itself "caught between the international markets in which they operated and the national governments whose support they sometimes needed to protect their extended operations."[35]

Transnationalism was furthered by multinational corporations, bilateral and multilateral treaties between and among states, and international familial diasporas. This was also the beginning of what today are known as nongovernmental organizations (NGOs). Internationalists, sometimes working for "one world," banded together for causes as disparate as the conservation of nature, poverty relief, and health care.[36]

It should be noted that multinational combinations reigned among illicit organizations as well, hiding from government watchdogs rather than utilizing them. This was the era of the rise of immigrant street gangs, of some Chinese *tongs* that veered into illicit enterprises, and then later the internationalization of the Italian Mafia, which became an economic force with which to reckon.[37]

New technologies and capital accumulation also created what economic historian Alexander Gerschenkron termed "the relative advantages of backwardness." Formerly "backward" economies such as Russia,

Germany, and Japan did not need, he argued, to follow in lockstep Britain's blueprint for industrialization. Government oversight and foreign-financed and imported technology would help them leapfrog forward. Sometimes being very backward proved advantageous because, as economic historian David Landes has observed, "the greater the gap, the greater the gain for those who leap it."[38] Backward countries could grow faster than the early leaders because they could avoid their mistakes and take advantage of successful technologies as well as more plentiful international capital available for investment. Argentina, Australia, and Canada found their minimal colonial heritages and the dearth of inhabitants salutary once the world economy stimulated the demand, the means, and the investments to farm their fertile fields and transport their produce.

Advanced forms of capitalism were sometimes embedded in rural and poor settings where they were slow to spread and share their benefits. For instance, Mexico's export-led economy during Porfirio Díaz's dictatorship (1876–1911), which featured raw materials and staple goods, was characterized by crony capitalism, either by multinational companies and banks composed entirely of external capitalists or syndicates of politically connected foreign and domestic investors.[39] Argentina, Brazil, Chile, and Canada witnessed the presence of well-capitalized European or North American firms in transport and urban utilities, mining, banking, and the grain and beef industries. The domestic industrialization of Meiji Japan was aided by the weakening of the samurai oligarchy through land reform, but now concentration took another form, as *zaibatsu* or large financial cliques were created that worked closely with the state. But in this instance capital and management were domestic, though with foreign advice.[40]

Economic change also brought with it new social tensions that occasionally erupted in violence and radical political upheaval. The state–capitalist alliance in Mexico, for example, provoked the first social revolution of the twentieth century, and rapid industrialization in

Russia (and the disastrous consequences of the First World War) helped bring the Bolsheviks to power. Statist development in Japan spawned Asia's first imperialist power during the Age of Empire.[41] In China, European capital and technology were largely concentrated in neocolonial treaty ports under the authority of European powers. They contributed to unrest that overthrew the empire in 1911. Anti-European nationalism (and opposition to the occupying Japanese) would later stimulate the rise of the Communists and their ultimate triumph at the end of our period.

## Foreign Investment

The world had never seen as much foreign investment as was put in circulation between 1870 and 1929. This vast expansion of surplus wealth, monetary instruments, stocks, bonds, and loans encouraged more individual and corporate investment abroad. Although states supervised and regulated investments, it was the private sector, not states, that was responsible for the increase. Even when states borrowed to balance their budgets, pay debts, or invest in infrastructure, the lenders were usually a handful of international bankers. The banks making the loans were almost all Western European until the 1920s, when some US banks began placing loans abroad. Much of the capital raised in London, for example, was continental European, with smaller amounts coming from the Western Hemisphere, as well as India or Australia.[42] In addition, we do not know how much was invested by members of ethnic diasporas who never registered officially or how much went into partnerships rather than corporations. We do know that the stock offers often were as reflective of dreams or schemes as of concrete wealth. Nonetheless, they give us a general idea of the prodigious increase in international financial flows. Foreign investment surged from over £6 billion in 1870 to £23 billion in 1900 and £43 billion in 1914 (see Tables 1.1 and 1.2).

TABLE I.I

**Distribution of foreign investment, 1914, by investing regions (in pounds sterling)**

|  | Amount invested | % of total |
|---|---|---|
| Britain | 4,100,000,000 | 43 |
| France | 1,900,000,000 | 20 |
| Germany | 1,200,000,000 | 13 |
| Belgium, Netherlands, and Switzerland | 1,100,000,000 | 12 |
| United States | 700,000,000 | 7 |
| Other | 500,000,000 | 5 |
| *Total* | 9,500,000,000 | 100 |

Source: A. G. Kenwood and A. L. Lougheed, *The Growth of the International Economy, 1820–2000*, 4th ed. (London: Routledge, 1999), 27.

TABLE I.2

**Distribution of foreign investment, 1914, by recipient regions (in pounds sterling)**

|  | Amount invested | % of total |
|---|---|---|
| Europe | 2,500,000,000 | 27 |
| North America | 2,300,000,000 | 24 |
| Latin America | 1,800,000,000 | 19 |
| Asia | 1,500,000,000 | 16 |
| Africa | 830,000,000 | 9 |
| Oceania | 500,000,000 | 5 |
| *Total* | 9,420,000,000 | 100 |

Source: A. G. Kenwood and A. L. Lougheed, *The Growth of the International Economy, 1820–2000*, 4th ed. (London: Routledge, 1999), 27.

We should note that although much of this capital was invested in infrastructure and helped subsidize the public sector, some of it merely kept corrupt despots in power, enriching their families and cronies, or it enabled members of the political class or wealthy elites and corporations to buy up local assets and lands. And although foreign investment brought with it bridges, roads, and even schools, it also ensured the longevity of colonial or neocolonial regimes that sustained inequality as much as gunboats and troops ever did.

Over time the British found that their financial prowess had its limits and that London could not extend its reach into every corner of the world. Unwilling to protect its home market, the British gradually fell behind in the new chemical, electronic, and oil-based technologies, areas dominated by United States and German trusts and cartels. By 1913 the British share of global manufactured exports had fallen from 37.8 percent, where it stood thirty-five years earlier, to 25.3 percent; two decades later it was down to 19.5 percent. The British concentrated their trade ever more within their empire: from one-quarter of trade in 1871–1875, it rose to 41 percent in the depression years of 1934–1939.[43] Even within the empire, the United Kingdom ran trade deficits overall, showing positive balances only with South Africa. So Britain ceased being the workshop of the world, becoming instead its banker, investor, and shipper.

The same gradual retrenchment was evident in portfolio investments. The four decades after 1870 were a golden period for European overseas investments. Between that year and 1914, fully 40 percent of the world's foreign investment was British.[44] Surprisingly, in view of the conventional wisdom that this was the Age of Empire, European investors did not prefer to invest in their own colonies. Instead they focused on government bonds, railroads, ports, and urban improvements in independent regions like the United States and Latin America. Only after the First World War did Britain concentrate its investments in its colonies.

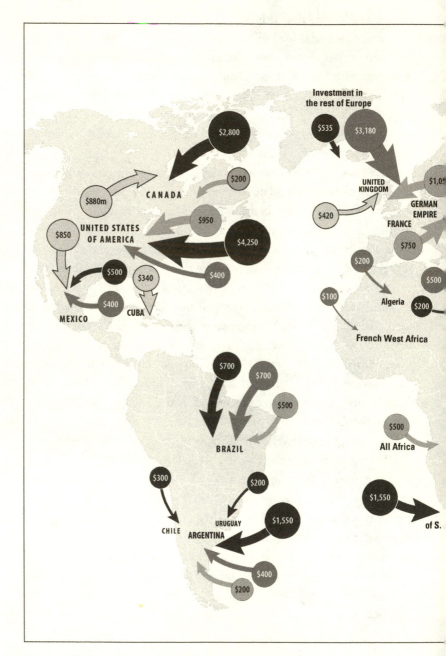

Patterns of foreign investment, 1914.

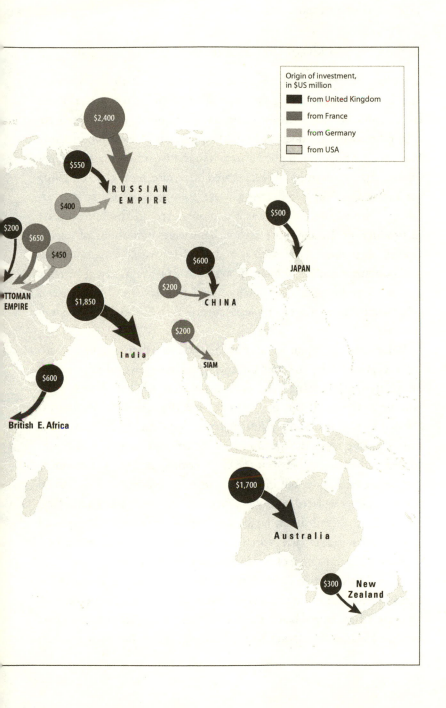

Origin of investment,
in $US million

- from United Kingdom
- from France
- from Germany
- from USA

$2,400

$550

$400

RUSSIAN
EMPIRE

$500

$200

$650

$450

$600

$200

CHINA

JAPAN

TTOMAN
EMPIRE

$1,850

$200

India

SIAM

$600

British E. Africa

$1,700

Australia

$300 New
Zealand

## Comparing Worldwide Production

Some parts of the world remained rather marginal to international markets. Notwithstanding the imperialist scramble for Africa in the last decades of the nineteenth century, that continent remained peripheral to world production (roughly 4 percent of total production). However, its population grew faster than the world's average, and per capita output outstripped its accelerated birth rate, more than doubling per capita GDP. This reflected a move from subsistence to market-oriented production as much as it demonstrated an absolute increase in production. In aggregate terms there were some hubs of export growth on the periphery, such as South Africa with its diamond and gold bonanzas. But in the main, growth was won at the cost of extreme inequality and exploitation as white settler enclaves and homegrown collaborator elites enjoyed privileged positions in Europe's sub-Saharan colonies.

Relative to the expansion in Europe and the Americas, Asia—with the exception of Japan—lost ground. Its share of world population, production, and international commerce declined. The fall was most notable in China. It was bad enough that the venerable empire was divided by warlords and foreign enclaves, and wracked by revolutions from the Taiping to the overthrow of the emperor in 1911; it also contended with civil war between the Guomindang and the Communists and Japanese invasion. But in addition its main exports, such as tea and silk, were either replaced by production elsewhere—tea in India and Ceylon (Sri Lanka), and silk in Japan and Italy—or, as with silk, replaced by synthetics, particularly North American and European rayon.[45]

We should add a note of caution about these findings, however. Calculating Asia's relative decline in the world economy underlines the danger in assuming that exports were an accurate measure of economic progress. China lagged behind in absolute and per capita exports in part because its large population had created significant domestic markets and dense settlement. It lacked marginal unpopulated areas appropriate to production of goods for Europe and North America—the main importers in this era.

Nonetheless, in a few products there were impressive export advancements worth noting. Indian cotton and textiles, tea, rice, and jute were world leaders, as were Indonesian (mainly Javanese) rubber, sugar, and tea and Malaysian rubber and tin. And opium was certainly one of the world's most valuable exports (in monetary terms). These crops and extractive undertakings were mostly successful in formerly marginal areas, like India's Assam district for tea, the Irrawaddy Delta for rice, Burma for jute, and Malaysia and Sumatra for rubber.

Moreover, it is plausible that the inward orientation of most Chinese, Japanese, and Indian production and the institutions and the skills they learned from this were ultimately to the good. Considered a detriment in the age of exports, they may have ultimately prepared these countries for dramatic explosions of exports that occurred in the last quarter of the twentieth century.[46]

The proof that prior development was often a disadvantage in export production is the fact that the areas that recorded the greatest aggregate gains were the sparsely populated Americas and some areas in the Pacific. Known as "new" or "vacant" areas, "neo-Europes," "settler colonies," or "Western offshoots," the United States, Canada, Australia, and New Zealand grew from a negligible share in 1820 to 10 percent of world output in 1870, then more than doubled their percentage of output by 1913, and reached almost a third of world production by 1950.[47] Per capita GDP jumped more than fourfold, reaching an estimated $9,288 (in 1990 US dollars), by far the highest level in history to that point and more than twice the level of Western Europe in 1950. We must bear in mind that in addition to enjoying favorable natural resource endowments, small native populations (important as the denominator in calculating per capita income and production), access to vast quantities of immigrants and capital, and in several notable cases the advantage of adopting the latest world technology under the umbrella of British free trade, neo-European lands benefited immeasurably because they avoided the world wars. Although hundreds of thousands of their soldiers died in those gruesome struggles, they benefited indirectly from the economic devastation experienced by their main competitors and trade partners. In particular the United States, which transformed itself from a debtor nation to a creditor, would, more than any other country, benefit from the Great War's deleterious impact on Europe.

Similarly, Latin America avoided the world wars and prospered from its export boom, more than tripling its share of output. Certainly Argentina and Uruguay's unparalleled success contributed greatly to that outcome. But many other nations throughout the region, such as Brazil, Chile, Colombia, Cuba, Mexico, Central America, and Venezuela, enjoyed more limited export booms. Latin America's per capita GDP grew 3.5-fold, reaching one of the world's highest totals by 1950. If Latin America "fell behind," as one influential volume has argued, it fell behind only the most prosperous economies of the world.[48] Some parts of Latin America, with their burgeoning markets and emerging native bourgeoisies, compared quite favorably with areas of Europe. Indeed, Argentina and Uruguay were among world leaders in both per capita income and trade after the turn of the century, while Cuba's economy, thanks to sugar and a welcoming market in the United States, also flourished. Chilean exports (first nitrates and then copper), Peruvian guano and nitrates, Bolivian tin, Mexican industrial metals and oil, and Brazilian coffee and rubber were all world leaders (see Tables 1.3 and 1.4).

We should caution that aggregate world economic data are "ballpark guesstimates" and are ideologically biased. Wealth is presumed to be measured by monetary market transactions. Gross National Product really measures Gross National Monetized Transactions. Self-sufficient production of goods and services, from peasant farming and

TABLE 1.3

## World GDP per capita, regional averages (in 1990 international dollars)

|  | 1820 | 1870 | 1913 | 1950 |
|---|---|---|---|---|
| Western Europe | 1,232 | 1,974 | 3,473 | 4,594 |
| Eastern Europe | 636 | 871 | 1,527 | 2,120 |
| USSR | 689 | 943 | 1,488 | 2,834 |
| Western offshoots (USA+) | 1,201 | 2,431 | 5,257 | 9,288 |
| Latin America | 659 | 698 | 1,511 | 2,554 |
| Japan | 669 | 737 | 1,387 | 1,926 |
| Asia (except Japan) | 575 | 543 | 640 | 635 |
| Africa | 418 | 444 | 585 | 852 |
| World | 667 | 867 | 1,510 | 2,114 |

*Sources:* Gene Shackman, Ya-Lin Liu, and Xun Wang, "Context of Change in the Twenty-First Century," http://gsociology.icaap.org/report/longterm.html; and Angus Maddison, *The World Economy* (Paris: Development Centre of the Organization for Economic Co-operation and Development, 2006), table B-21.

animal husbandry to domestic activities and barter, were not counted unless sold for money in a market where data was collected. So wealth and productivity became synonymous with commodification of goods and labor. Calculating them accurately relied on sufficiently strong, interested, and wide-reaching states that collected data. In supposedly "underdeveloped" areas, which for most of our period entailed the majority of the Earth's human population, data on economic activity was infrequently compiled, tabulated, monetized, or credited.

Another problem with data is the implicit assumption that increasing production or market activity was synonymous with improving welfare. As any reader of Charles Dickens's novels of the Industrial Revolution, such as *Hard Times,* Victor Hugo's *Les Misérables,* or the works of historian E. P. Thompson knows, rapid economic growth was usually attended by the appropriation of the labor and land of significant portions of the working classes. Their absolute welfare declined, at least in the short run, and this was true not only in cities. The "vacant"

TABLE 1.4

Economic output and population, by area (in 1990 international dollars)

| | 1820 | | 1870 | | 1913 | | 1950 | |
|---|---|---|---|---|---|---|---|---|
| | % of world economic output | % of world population | % of world economic output | % of world population | % of world economic output | % of world population | % of world economic output | % of world population |
| Western Europe | 23.57 | 12.80 | 33.61 | 14.80 | 33.52 | 14.60 | 26.26 | 12.10 |
| Eastern Europe | 3.33 | 3.50 | 4.13 | 4.10 | 4.49 | 4.40 | 3.47 | 3.50 |
| USSR | 5.43 | 5.30 | 7.59 | 7.00 | 8.59 | 8.70 | 9.56 | 7.10 |
| Western offshoots (USA+) | 1.94 | 1.10 | 10.18 | 3.60 | 21.65 | 6.20 | 30.65 | 7.00 |
| Latin America | 2.01 | 2.00 | 2.53 | 3.10 | 4.49 | 4.50 | 7.94 | 6.60 |
| Japan | 2.99 | 3.00 | 2.30 | 2.70 | 2.65 | 2.90 | 3.02 | 3.30 |
| Asia (except Japan) | 56.25 | 65.30 | 36.02 | 57.50 | 21.91 | 51.70 | 15.45 | 51.40 |
| Africa | 2.99 | 7.10 | 3.65 | 7.10 | 2.69 | 7.00 | 3.64 | 9.00 |

*Sources:* Gene Shackman, Ya-Lin Liu, and Xun Wang, "Context of Change in the Twenty-First Century," http://gsociology.icaap.org/report/longterm.html; and Angus Maddison, *The World Economy* (Paris: Development Centre of the Organization for Economic Co-operation and Development, 2006), table B-21.

or "newly settled" areas also experienced land appropriations through military campaigns that forcibly moved the indigenous populations off their lands in the last decades of the nineteenth century, such as Argentina's Conquest of the Desert, Chile's war against the Mapuche, and the United States' campaigns in the Midwest and West. More privately run attacks were carried out in the Australian Outback, New Zealand, and Mexico's northern deserts. Gross national product (GNP) in these areas grew even while entire ethnicities were exterminated or corralled onto reservations.

CHAPTER TWO

# The Sinews of Trade

Greed, desire, labor, capital, and sophisticated technology were not enough to catapult the world economy on a path to sustained development. As economic historians Douglass North and Lance Davis have shown, the creation and timing of economic institutions and infrastructure played a significant role and fostered path dependency, making some outcomes much more likely than others. Global expansion also often demanded large systemic investments and international agreements. In this chapter we discuss key underpinnings of the international economy, including currency standards; improvements to infrastructure, such as shipping, canals, railroads, autos, and airplanes, and the oil and rubber that they required; and vastly expanded communications networks, especially the telegraph, transoceanic cables, and radios, and the electric, copper, and aluminum industries that both resulted from them and facilitated their rapid expansion.

## Currency

The standardization of currencies was especially critical to the growth of commercial markets. The British pound sterling was the premier currency in the world economy, but in 1870 it was far from hegemonic. A bimetal silver/gold standard still reigned throughout much of Europe with the creation in 1865 of the Latin Monetary Union by France, Belgium, Italy, and Switzerland. The union was French emperor Napoleon III's brainchild, designed to counter London's monetary clout. It later added Spain, Greece, Romania, Austria-Hungary, Bulgaria,

Venezuela, and Serbia and Montenegro. The United States was officially bimetal as a result of the Sherman Silver Purchase Act of 1890. Latin American countries were mostly on the silver standard, thanks to the widespread circulation of Mexico's peso, as were most Asian currencies. Of course, the silver–gold divide refers to international and governmental transactions, because most of the world's inhabitants still lived largely outside a money economy, engaging mainly in subsistence or barter economies, where often natural goods such as bricks of tea, cocoa beans, salt, cowry shells, cattle, or cloth served as markers of value.

Nonetheless, monetization grew rapidly as governments minted the gold and silver bonanzas discovered in California (1848), Australia (1852), South Africa's Transvaal (1886), the Yukon in Canada (1898), Russia from the Urals to Siberia and the Amur region, and silver in Nevada and Colorado in the United States (1850s–1870s). Silver finds dwarfed gold discoveries, so silver's relative price dropped, which persuaded many bimetal countries such as France and its counterparts in the Latin Monetary Union and the United States to eventually make the move to the gold standard. The United States attempted to tie its new colonies to the dollar by sending out financial missions (and gunboats) to Latin America as well as to China to craft a "dollar diplomacy" that enhanced Wall Street's global financial position. Some countries such as Brazil had inconvertible currencies whose value was based on faith in the government but not backed by precious metals (except for brief, partial experiments). Merchant notes and bills of lading served as unofficial currency; by the twentieth century bank checks backed by private bank deposits began to circulate. China also enjoyed a rapid growth of paper currency that facilitated the spread of the money economy, domestic regional trade, and lower transaction costs. When the Great Depression disrupted the world economy, some aspiring empires, such as Japan, Germany, and the Soviet Union, responded to the crisis by creating trade currencies for bilateral exchanges.[1]

For all of these challenges to the pound sterling, the gold standard (whereby national currencies were convertible to gold) came to dominate in world trade and finance and played a significant role in their unparalleled expansion up to 1914. Issuing governments therefore had to store ample gold to back their currency. That was a boon to international trade, because foreign commerce would be the means of procuring gold for the vast majority of the world's countries that did not mine sufficient gold for their own needs. Balance of payments deficits would have to be addressed by adjusting prices or by reducing imports to avoid a gold drain and resulting currency depreciation. Governments could issue only as much currency as they had gold, so their actions were greatly circumscribed by international trade and finance. The private sector engaged in international exchanges, which supplied gold via trade surpluses. Private companies' political power was therefore strengthened. Because of the gold standard currency, exchanges were more certain and cheaper, facilitating commerce and international lending. This was known as the "self-regulating market."[2] Underpinning the gold standard was the desire to defend the value of money and therefore the assets of creditors and the wealthy by preventing inflation.

The drawback to the standard was that it was pro-cyclical. When the economy was thriving, money was abundant. But when there was an international downturn, governments could not issue more currency to prime the pump of economic activity. Prolonged slumps resulted. The world economy rode out the 1870s depression and the 1907 scare on the gold standard, but the First World War caused many countries to abandon it as world trade ground to a halt. Germany was the most crippled by war reparations and a historically unprecedented inflation.[3] Some forty countries returned to gold during the 1920s, but the 1929 financial crisis and the ensuing depression of international trade caused the British to abandon the standard in 1931. Others soon followed. Efforts to return to the gold standard after 1945 were halfhearted. The world would never return to the hegemony of the gold standard of the pre-1914 years, yet the world economy would boom as never before. Apparently gold was not essential to prosperous international trade after all.

## Shipping

If the standardization of currencies was of paramount importance, so, too, was the slew of infrastructural improvements that made their staccato-like appearance during these seven decades. The steamship was long considered one of the key markers of the transportation revolution. It *was* important, but its impact was not felt until the last third of the nineteenth century, yet freight rates had been declining since 1815.[4] Long-distance trade was already expanding rapidly before the conversion to steam, because of a combination of political, scientific, technical, and commercial improvements—such as the reduction of piracy; the elimination of navigation laws that had impeded multilateral shipping; the improvement of navigational instruments and nautical maps and an enhanced knowledge of winds and currents; the ability to build larger, more seaworthy transoceanic sailing ships; and the reduction of idle time in port. In the East, improved ports and their connections to their hinterlands were constructed in Alexandria, Mumbai (Bombay), Cape Town, and Calcutta (Kolkata), while new harbors were built at Aden, Port Said, and Singapore—to mention only the largest. In the Americas, a modernized Vera Cruz in Mexico, Belém, Manaus, Rio de Janeiro, and Santos in Brazil, Buenos Aires in Argentina, as well as Havana, Cuba, joined newly improved ports in New York, New Orleans, and San Francisco in the United States.

For Britain's manufactured products to flood first neighboring countries and then more distant ones and stimulate imports in return, the cost of transport had to fall and the capacity to carry large loads quickly and predictably had to grow. British sailing ships had dominated the seas before the First Industrial Revolution, so most of the nineteenth-century sea trade continued to be powered by wind on ships owned and manned by the British. As late as 1880, three times as much large-scale waterborne freight traveled by sail as by steam. With small loads, sailing ships had a much greater advantage. However, beginning in the 1880s steam came to drive ever-larger freighters built increasingly of steel rather than wood. Technical advances in steamships, such as the screw propeller, the iron and then (after 1880) the steel hull, the surface condenser, and the compound engine, made steamships lighter and more durable. These improvements enhanced carrying capacity and required less than a fifth as much coal, freeing up additional space for cargo. Steamers could now travel substantially greater distances without needing to refuel. The leading imperial powers, such as Britain, Germany, and the United States, which also held some of the world's largest coal reserves, established coaling stations on remote islands to provision the steamer trade.[5]

World trade and shipping in large vessels (over a hundred tons) grew at similar rates between 1881 and 1913. Both would stagnate in the 1930s and, of course, fall during the wars. Ship construction became increasingly mechanized and inexpensive, so that shipyards continued to serve as some of the largest manufactories of their time, just as some steamers were among the most capital-intensive machines of the era. By the end of our period, tanker ships were developed to transport oil, thereby clinching the transition from coal-fed steam power to oil-fueled steam power and finally petroleum-driven internal combustion engines.[6]

In addition to becoming bigger, faster, and safer, ships were transformed to serve and stimulate the growth of major new industries. The refrigeration of ships in the last quarter of the nineteenth century, for instance, permitted the rapid growth of the chilled and frozen meat industries. By the turn of the century, bananas also were benefiting from refrigerated ships to eventually become the leading internationally traded fruit, and would integrate formerly marginal areas of Central America and the Caribbean into the world market.[7]

Technological inventions and institutional innovations meant that in the period 1871–1914, when global trade underwent such spectacular growth, freight rates for commodities declined the fastest on the busiest oceanic routes because of fierce competition.[8] Before this revolution in shipbuilding technology, with freight rates declining, the rising cost of constructing a ship would have dissuaded investors from risking more capital in yet more expensive ships. Now shipping companies were forced to spend on more efficient ships and facilities, recouping the additional expense with the greater carrying capacity of the new ships and paying for it with lower-priced loans from international bankers.

Competition alone was not a sufficient motor of change. Some shipping companies received government subsidies to carry the mail, deliver colonial officials, or maintain merchant marine fleets as a backup in times of war. Also, many shipping companies were early conglomerates that also engaged in insurance, banking, and commerce on their own accounts, so what was a commercial loss for the shipping company could be a savings for a company's trading arm. In some cases, such as the Grace Line and later the United Fruit Company's Great White Fleet, the line's main purpose was to carry the company's cargo. Such multipurpose agricultural companies also built ports and increased the number of plantations they owned to develop new commodities like bananas and pineapples.[9]

This swelling of ship size and economies of scale that accompanied it meant ships were the most expensive capital goods of the era. But they would not have been economically feasible unless markets for goods and port facilities were large and efficient enough to unload and sell the goods. During the era of the spice trade, the simultaneous arrival of two ships could drive down the price of a precious commodity by glutting the tiny specialty market. But now a revolution in port facilities and land transport, often publicly financed or underwritten, as well as advances in warehousing and marketing, accompanied the dramatic explosion of shipping capacity. Multiple large shipments could be landed at the same time and still be profitable. Transport efficiency was coupled with remarkable changes in wholesale and retail marketing and distribution to satisfy swelling consumer cravings for overseas goods. Standards and prices for goods coming from myriad origins were increasingly negotiated at commodity exchanges that arose in key ports. All of these marketing innovations sped up turnaround time for shippers. This justified increased investments in ever-larger ships. Now mercantile corporations could maximize their use of the larger carrying capacity rather than suffer their ships' idling in ports, slowly being emptied or awaiting new return cargo.[10]

To take advantage of ever more commodious ships, the nature of the freight carried also changed. Early on, luxuries such as precious metals, spices, skins, and cloth that fetched high prices abroad drove long-distance trade. Now bulk commodities, goods that had a high volume-to-value ratio, such as coal, meat, and grains and tropical goods like chocolate, coffee, and bananas, became profitable to ship across oceans. The greater certainty of travel time under steam meant that goods that spoiled easily could now successfully traverse the seas, reaching large moneyed populations.

Still, the interrelationship between marketing economies and institutions (the cost of getting goods to the retail customer), freight economies, and the emergence of new long-distance cargo advantaged a relatively small part of the globe. Western European factories required ever more raw materials like cotton and lumber and fuel such as coal and later oil. Their populations could afford (and required as they left their farms) basic foodstuffs like wheat and more luxurious treats like sugar, coffee, and tea.

Those goods were exported mostly from a relatively small number of sparsely settled areas. Outside of densely populated Western Europe, the most dynamic economic regions were frontiers that were land rich and people poor. In these areas the cost and reliability of shipping became all the more important. Their few inhabitants meant land was relatively cheap in monetary terms (although often purchased with the blood of the indigenous peoples pushed off their tribal lands and of native animals) and labor was dear. Enjoying the greater productivity of fertile, well-watered lands, agricultural crops could be grown relatively inexpensively and shipped to Europe economically. However, the Europe-bound ships with their holds filled with coffee, cotton, or wheat had to return to the "vacant" agricultural lands where demand from the sparse and often poorly paid population was insufficient to fill them. They either filled up with ballast with little economic value or offered cheap fares to northern and southern Europeans who were being crowded off their lands at home. The passengers in turn worked the fields opening in the neo-Europes and provided a market for export of goods and capital from Western Europe. Thus, the freight revolution played a large role in the great transoceanic movement of peoples, most notably the movement of millions of Europeans to the United States, Canada, Argentina, Australia, Brazil, and New Zealand. As our discussion of grain, sugar, coffee, and tea commodity chains will show, sometimes the ships bound for the Far East and the circum-Caribbean contained Chinese coolies or Indian contract workers who benefited less from the change in latitude than immigrants bound to more temperate climes.

Lower transport costs that had enticed immigrants to less-populated areas also carried relatively cheap imports that competed successfully with local manufacturing and handicrafts. This undercut peasant agriculture and handicrafts in more established, crowded countries such as India and Eastern Europe, "freeing" population for emigration. So in its early phase during the nineteenth century, the Industrial Revolutions in Western Europe and the eastern United States contributed to the deindustrialization or the rerouting of goods to other parts of the world and the international movement of people.[11]

During their golden age the British had a near monopoly on building freighters because of their head start in shipyards, the steel and coal industries, and capital markets. In 1888 the British merchant marine had secured almost half the world's carrying power (the United States added another quarter of the total but it was mostly dedicated to domestic freight).[12] As late as 1918 the British steamer fleet was still 12 percent larger than the merchant fleets of all other European countries combined.[13]

The United States was slow to make its mark in international shipping after midcentury because between its Civil War and the early twentieth century its ships retreated from the Atlantic trade. Instead it concentrated on coastal and internal waterways such as the Great Lakes and the Mississippi, while its transoceanic cargo traveled on Western European ships—even if the goods were exported from tropical ports to the United States. Even for its trade in the Pacific, where the US Navy had opened ports in Japan and Korea, little public incentive was given to shipping. In 1882 total US federal subsidies were only one-quarter the size of those of an empire not known for its maritime prowess, Austria-Hungary. Where US ships had carried most of their country's cargo before the Civil War, they fell to about 40 percent in 1870 and down to about 20 percent by 1900, where it remained until the 1930s. Then the Great Depression and especially World War II permitted North American ships to gain dominance. By 1945 they plied the seas with almost two-thirds of the world's tonnage, an amount that had grown tenfold since 1870.[14]

Imperial as well as commercial motives drove the shipping revolution, because ships were the paramount means of projecting national power and influence overseas. The merchant marine served as an adjunct to navies and was essential to the building of Western European, North American, and Japanese empires. US admiral Alfred Thayer

Mahan had pushed for a "New Navy" already in the 1880s, underlining his view in his influential 1892 tome, tellingly entitled *The Influence of Sea Power upon History*. In 1911 First Lord of the Admiralty Winston Churchill championed the conversion of the British navy from coal to oil on similarly grandiose grounds: "The whole race and Empire, the whole treasure accumulated during the many centuries of sacrifice and achievement, would perish and be swept utterly away if our naval supremacy were to be impaired." Domination of the seas was critical, in his mind, to empire: "Mastery itself was the prize of the venture."[15] In the decades before World War I, as Germany also embraced the idea that strong navies signaled national power, German-British rivalry produced accelerated naval building in both countries.

States did not have a monopoly on the militarization of shipping. Private global arms dealers rose to prominence during these years. Merchant and financier Charles Flint was a member of the covert international fraternity of ship and weapons traders. As a private citizen he brokered deals to provide ships and modern weapons with, among others, an Ottoman sultan, the Japanese emperor, and republican presidents of Peru, Chile, Venezuela, and Brazil.[16]

Only some of the largest countries outside of Europe—Brazil, Argentina, and Chile—could afford to build, subsidize, and nationalize domestic merchant marines. In the cases of Brazil and Chile, they also ran large state-owned shipping companies (Lloyd Brasileiro and Compañia Sud-America de Vapores, respectively) that carried some freight internationally.[17] Domestic shipbuilding gained from their demand because they placed orders for ships and repairs with national as well as foreign shipyards. But the British merchant fleet clearly overshadowed their efforts.

The major exception to this model of European domination, as in so many other areas, was Japan, which moved quickly to address its deficiencies. During the prior two centuries of Tokugawa rule, ports had been all but closed off from foreign ships. Japan's geography, with its numerous islands and inland sea, and its precocious political capital (Edo, today known as Tokyo, already had a million inhabitants by 1800), had conspired against the creation of a modern merchant marine. But consternation over the British defeat of the ostensibly mighty Chinese fleet in the Opium Wars during the 1840s and 1850s, as well as the unanticipated appearance of Commodore Matthew Perry's American warships in Japanese waters in 1853, persuaded leaders that they had to modernize their maritime industries.

Close ties between strategic government concerns and the construction of a formidable merchant marine first became apparent in the Japanese attempt to conquer Formosa (today Taiwan) in 1874. The Japanese government purchased thirteen modern steamships to carry soldiers and gave them to a private company, Yūbin Kisen Mitsubishi Kaisha, contracted to carry out the invasion. The company initially had a monopoly on international trade as it opened service to Shanghai. After a merger in 1885 created Nippon Yūsen Kabushiki Kaisha (NYK), it became an entirely private company with routes to Korea, Asiatic Russia, India, and China. Over seventy local Japanese shipping concerns were merged in 1887 thanks to government subventions creating Ōsaka Shōsen Kaisha (OSK), which initially operated mainly in Japan and then branched out to Korea.

The connection between the maritime industry and war was further demonstrated in the Sino-Japanese War of 1894–1895 when the Japanese imperial government purchased fourteen ships and added them to the NYK fleet. At first these fleets relied to a considerable extent on imported ships, steamers from England and sailing ships from the United States. Gradually the government passed legislation that encouraged the growth of the domestic shipbuilding industry, insisting on the construction of larger vessels and inducing their shipping lines to purchase them. The naval buildup had military as well as economic purposes. It brought a Japanese victory against Russia in 1905 that surprised Western observers. After the war, capital and experienced shipbuilders shifted to the private sector. By 1910 half of the new merchant ships were built in Japan, giving rise to some of the world's largest and most sophisticated shipyards.[18]

Elsewhere in the Indian Ocean as well as in the Red and South China Seas, domestic non-Euro-American shipping was relegated to smaller sailing ships such as Chinese junks, Arab dhows, and Japanese *wasen*. Hence, in this most densely populated area of the world, coastal shipping—which could have excluded foreign merchant marines and stimulated domestic industry and commerce—was uncertain and expensive.

Besides Japan and Great Britain, all other major island complexes (Indonesia, Australia, Philippines, Madagascar, Cuba, and the rest of the Caribbean), for whom a domestic merchant marine would have stimulated commerce and development, were colonies. Their colonial masters were not interested in cultivating potential shipping rivals. The other major non-European export economies, such as Argentina and Brazil, focused on trade with Europe rather than developing domestic markets that could be served by national freighters.

Domination of high-volume freight by a dozen countries not only provided the world leaders a competitive advantage in terms of profits and lower costs, but also allowed them to develop insurance companies, large warehouses, and intelligence about freight and long-distance business conditions. Indeed, before the oceanic telegraphs, mail ships were the principal source of international news. The early steamship lines received large subsidies precisely so they would deliver the mail. Faster ships also meant greater international intimacy. Where mail and freight took six weeks to travel from England to Calcutta in 1840, by World War I the time had been cut to less than twelve days. Australia also was brought closer. From 125 days required to reach it from England at the beginning of the nineteenth century, the trip fell to a month a century later. The Dutch, who had required a year to reach their colony in Indonesia in the seventeenth century and still over a hundred days in 1850, could reach it in a month by 1900.[19] So shipping advances not only increased trade, they bound colonial systems more closely together.

Shipping advances also brought the Americas closer to Europe in travel time. Where sailing packets had required twenty-one days to reach Europe from the United States in the mid-nineteenth century, steamships could make the crossing in nine to ten days, which was reduced further to five or six days by the 1880s.[20]

## Canals

The unprecedented drop in the duration of ship voyages occurred because of changes on land as well as on the seas. Canals initially had been built to connect domestic markets, such as the Grand Canal in China and the Yangzi and Pearl River Deltas, canals in northern Italy and the Netherlands, and the dense riverine and canal systems in England, France, and Germany. In the United States, the Erie Canal connected New York City with the Great Lakes and eventually, through the Chicago River, down the Mississippi River. Because they issued out to oceanic ports, the interior waterways often made vast areas accessible to international trade.[21] However, generally they were narrow, so they inhibited economies of scale. They consequently lost trade to the railroad and motorized road vehicles. Sometimes, as with the Chinese Grand Canal, state budgetary decisions deprived the canals of maintenance funds.[22]

Most spectacular was the engineering feat that had been first accomplished in the days of Egypt's pharaohs, the Suez Canal. Designed by former French consul to Egypt Ferdinand de Lesseps and financed largely by French capital, this 119-mile-long passage finally connected the Red Sea to the Mediterranean (though bypassing the Nile) in 1869. Intended to assert French commercial and political control over Africa, the Middle East, and the Indian Ocean, the canal succeeded in stimulating international commerce beyond de Lesseps's wildest dreams. But it did not enhance French imperial aspirations, nor did it reorient the world economy from the North Atlantic back to the Mediterranean as was hoped. After the canal's opening in the 1880s, British ships accounted for 80 percent of the tonnage that passed through it. Their domination of Suez traffic declined over time, but as late as 1940 they still controlled over half the total passing through the canal.[23] Equally disappointing to the French imperialists was the British occupation of Egypt in 1882–1936. British control of the canal would be relinquished only in 1956.

Although ships needed two and a half days to pass through the canal and it could not accommodate the largest steamers, this was compensated by the great savings in time on the overall voyage—a 41 percent time reduction between London and Mumbai and a 26 percent drop between London and Hong Kong. (Australia benefited little from the canal because the circum-African route was not a great detour to the land down under.)

The other great canal of our period was built in Panama. The dream of avoiding the difficult and dangerous rounding of Cape Horn had inspired mariners dating back to 1521, when Ferdinand Magellan found his way through the straits named after him and located the long route from the Atlantic to the Pacific. But this dream became both possible and a pressing matter only when gold was discovered in California in 1848. Adventurers with gold fever would not wait for the slow wagon trains or the only somewhat faster rounding of the Horn. Routes across Central America became popular. With the United States now bicoastal, a canal became an important tool of national defense and fundamental in the building of a North American national market.

The same magnet that had attracted Magellan—the fabled China market—and the desire of French expansionists such as Napoleon III to establish a continental American colony (Mexicans defeated his effort to place Maximilian I on their throne in 1867) attracted the first serious effort at canal building. To the chagrin of North Americans, it was the French, not the Yankees, who initiated the project. Their success at Suez induced international investors to found a Panama canal company and bankroll it with the impressive sum of more than US$400 million. Unfortunately, de Lesseps attempted to apply the lessons learned in Suez, which proved ill-suited to the Americas. Although the Isthmus of Panama was less than half the distance of the Suez project (50 miles compared to 119 miles), the Panama Canal would have to be cut through dense jungle with torrential rains and a peak that rose to 360 feet above sea level rather than through flat desert sand as in Suez. That first company went bankrupt seven years after building was initiated, and its successor also failed. In 1902 the French company sold its canal works and its concession from the Colombian government to the US government. The Colombian Senate, wary of the United States' designs on Latin America made evident in the 1898 Spanish-American War, refused to permit the United States to take over the canal works. Proving Colombian concerns warranted, US naval forces then supported a rebellion that declared Panama independent. A French representative of the French canal company not only signed a treaty in the name of Panama and sold the nascent canal works but also ceded a fifty-five-square-mile canal zone over which the United States would exercise sovereignty for seventy-six years.[24]

As at Suez, this massive feat of engineering that greased the path of globalization began as a nationalist effort at empire building. The canal itself was built between 1904 and 1914 at an enormous cost in human lives and funds. The most expensive construction project in United States history up to that point, it cost around US$400 million. Less often mentioned is that the building of the canal cost twenty-five thousand to thirty-five thousand lives. The workers were mainly people of African descent from nearby Panama, Colombia, Jamaica, and Barbados. The North American enclave that developed in the Canal Zone had much in common with British settler colonies in Africa.

Historian Julie Greene notes that the Canal Zone was characterized by "large-scale mobilization and segregation of labor, special rewards and recognition of citizenship rights for certain (skilled, white) workers and a suppression of political dissent and forms of collective organizing deemed radical."[25] The canal's completion, hailed as a key step in the United States' move past continentalism to globalism, was celebrated in San Francisco at its Panama-Pacific International Exposition in 1915. But there was no remembering the workers or Panama at the festivities. The linkage between commerce and empire could not have been clearer. As the editors of *World's Work* proclaimed, the canal represented "the evolution of a new America. Our splendid isolation is gone ... we have become a colonial power with possessions in both oceans. And now we open under our own control one of the great trade routes of the world."[26]

Great hopes for developing Panama and the tropics in general were held out by US expansionists. Although earlier efforts at settling defeated southern Confederates in Brazil and Mexico after the Civil War had largely failed, medical advances such as the discovery of the effects of quinine, derived from the bark of the cinchona tree, and the isolation of the mosquito as the carrier of malaria and yellow fever made the tropics more hospitable to white European and North American colonial administrators and investors. The medical advances were tested and applied at the canals in Suez and Panama, attempted at dependencies such as Freetown, Liberia, and successfully implemented in Cuba during the US occupation after the conclusion of the Spanish-American War. Nonetheless, relatively few North American investors or colonists settled in the tropics. The most ambitious attempt, Fordlandia in the Amazon, was a complete failure.[27]

In both shipping and canal building, Great Power *realpolitik* and imperial pretensions wrestled with the forces of the marketplace. On the one hand, the greater capacity, speed, efficiency, and certainty of shipping stimulated trade, information, and competition. On the other hand, shipping lines experienced the same efforts at reducing competition that we will see in many other highly capitalized strategic areas of the world economy. For freight companies, the solution was shipping conventions (or collusion, as their critics scoffed) that coordinated the freight business through quotas and rate fixing. The conventions resulted from a transformation in the nature of ship ownership.

Where traditionally ships had been owned by groups of merchants, either as individuals or as a group such as the East India Company, the greater capital demands of steamships required well-endowed corporations, often benefiting from the protection of joint-stock legislation. Indeed, the British Parliament first created the protection of limited liability in 1855 with railroads, shipping companies, and banks in mind.[28] With this legislation corporations gained juridical identity separate from that of their stockholders. The investor was liable only for the amount of his investment, not for other company debts. Many pietistic Protestants found this shirking of responsibility reprehensible. Others, like Baptist John D. Rockefeller, considered it a welcome opportunity to get rich using other people's money. Despite an outcry, the legislation passed and the idea spread elsewhere as European and North and South American countries soon followed suit because this mechanism vastly facilitated the pooling of large amounts of capital, protected enormous long-term investments, and aided anonymous stock transactions.

The relatively small number and great investments of huge freight companies, as well as falling freight prices because of global competition inspired by the Suez Canal, convinced some companies to create international conventions or cartels. These agreements made the high fixed costs of maintaining existing fleets affordable and allowed participants to keep up with technological advances in this rapidly changing industry. Steam companies that belonged to the same cartel agreed to maintain rates rather than compete on price. They also agreed to honor deferred rebates to customers who used only ships within the conference, an early-day loyalty or frequent flyer card. The first convention began in the European Calcutta route in 1875. A China convention began in 1879 and a West Africa–London agreement in 1894. Various conventions also operated in South America among European steamers. British courts ruled the conventions legal in part because they did not successfully monopolize the traffic. Unscheduled "tramp" freighters that opportunistically steamed to wherever sufficient cargo or passengers awaited them were able to ignore the conventions and charge lower fares. In 1900 tramps constituted a third of world seabound cargo capacity, so they put a sizable dent in the conventions' ability to control pricing.[29]

## Railroads

Just as steam drove the First Industrial Revolution in production and transformed navigation, it also powered railroads. Railroads did not begin as a means of exporting or importing goods. Instead, they began their practical applications in Britain in the 1820s to assist the burgeoning coal industry. A fortunate confluence of mechanical power and fuel to transport the coal via the railroad to more distant factories ensured England's primacy in rails and industry. Although the railroad revolution is usually associated with the First Industrial Revolution, it in fact spurred the second one as well. In Europe alone as many miles of track were laid in 1880–1913 as had been put down in the heroic pioneer railway age of 1850–1880. Outside of Europe, tracks were laid down at an even faster pace. World rail mileage multiplied fourfold between 1870 and 1910 and grew again by half to 1930, despite the destruction caused by the Great War. However, the Great Depression, World War II, and the advent of the automobile and truck would all but stop the railroad age. Worldwide track fell by 1945, mainly because of its decline in the United States (see Table 2.1).

TABLE 2.1

World railroad mileage, by continent, 1840–1945 (in thousands of miles)

| | 1840 | | 1870 | | 1901 | | 1910 | | 1930 | | 1945 | |
|---|---|---|---|---|---|---|---|---|---|---|---|---|
| | Miles | % | Miles | % | Miles | % | Miles | % | Miles | % | Miles | % |
| Europe[a] | 2.6 | 47.0 | 65.4 | 50.1 | 181.8 | 35.6 | 212.1 | 33.1 | 236.9 | 25.0 | 252.9 | 26.9 |
| (UK) | 2.4 | 43.6 | 21.5 | 16.4 | 30.4 | 5.9 | 32.2 | 5.0 | 32.6 | 3.4 | 32.0 | 3.4 |
| North America[b] | 2.8 | 51.0 | 55.4 | 42.5 | 216.7 | 42.5 | 265.8 | 41.5 | 471.6 | 50.0 | 440.6 | 46.8 |
| Latin America[b] | 0.1 | 2.0 | 2.4 | 1.8 | 29.1 | 5.7 | 60.7 | 9.5 | 78.7 | 8.3 | 83.0 | 8.8 |
| Asia w/o India | 0 | 0 | 0.3 | 0.2 | 12.0 | 2.4 | 27.2 | 4.3 | 44.8 | 4.7 | 49.9 | 5.3 |
| (India) | 0 | 0 | 4.8 | 3.8 | 25.5 | 5.0 | 32.3 | 5.0 | 42.5 | 4.5 | 40.8 | 4.3 |
| Asia | 0 | 0 | 5.1 | 4.0 | 37.5 | 7.4 | 59.5 | 9.3 | 87.3 | 9.2 | 90.7 | 9.6 |
| Oceania | 0 | 0 | 1.1 | 0.8 | — | — | 19.3 | 3.0 | 31.2 | 3.3 | 31.8 | 3.4 |
| Africa | 0 | 0 | 1.1 | 0.8 | 12.5 | 2.5 | 23.0 | 3.6 | 40.8 | 4.3 | 42.4 | 4.5 |
| World | 5.5 | | 130.5 | | 510.5 | | 640.4 | | 946.5 | | 941.4 | |

*Sources:* A. G. Kenwood and A. L. Lougheed, *The Growth of the International Economy, 1820–2000*, 4th ed. (London: Routledge, 1999), 13. For 1901: *Railroad Gazette*, May 30 and June 6, 1902. For 1910: A. Russell Bond and Albert A. Hopkins. *Scientific American Reference Book: A Manual for the Office, Household and Shop* (New York: Munn and Co., 1915). For 1930 and 1945, figures were calculated from B. R. Mitchell, *International Historical Statistics: Africa, Asia and Oceania, 1750–2005*, 5th ed. (Basingstoke, UK: Palgrave Macmillan, 2007), 713–728; B. R. Mitchell, *International Historical Statistics: Europe, 1750–2000*, 6th ed. (Basingstoke, UK: Palgrave Macmillan, 2007), 675–681; B. R. Mitchell, *International Historical Statistics: The Americas and Australasia* (London: Macmillan, 1983); and Bureau of the Census, *Historical Statistics of the United States: Colonial Times to 1957* (Washington, DC: Bureau of the Census, 1960), 429.

a. Europe includes Russia and the Soviet Union, but not Turkey.

b. Mexico is included with Latin America, not North America.

The railroad's impact up to 1913 is hard to exaggerate. The usually reserved Hobsbawm waxes lyrical: "But by far the largest and most powerful engines of the nineteenth century were the most visible and audible of all. These were the 100,000 railway locomotives (200–450 HP), pulling their almost 2¾ million carriages and wagons in long trains under the banners of smoke."[30] Even if some economic historians such as Robert Fogel cast doubt on railroads' centrality in spurring US industrialization, it is clear that railroads fundamentally altered transport costs and travel time while adding enormous backward and forward linkages (see Table 2.2). They were the largest industrial corporations of the era, with the most factory workers and the largest investment of capital. Moreover, as Alfred Chandler has eloquently demonstrated, they played a significant role in pioneering the managerial revolution of vast new corporations while expanding the white-collar (female as well as male) portion of the workforce. Rail technology not only bound together British markets (which had already been well served by intricate canal systems), but it provided an extremely important export product as well as a basis for British financial investments abroad. In 1913 fully 41 percent of British overseas investment was directly placed in railroad construction, and a good share of its loans to foreign governments also financed railroads.[31]

Over time, exporting the technology undercut Britain's first-mover advantages as other, larger countries with less-developed waterways were better able to take advantage of the iron rail. As a result, Britain's portion had already fallen from nearly half the world's rail in 1840 to only one-sixth in 1870. By 1910 the United Kingdom held only 5 percent of the world's rail network.

That former British colony, the United States, was the first overseas area to apply and adapt British technology and capital. It had surpassed Britain's rail network already by 1840 and in fact had more track than all of the rest of the world combined at that early date. This was done with outside help, particularly that of the British; in 1914 some 57 per-

TABLE 2.2

### Net tons-miles of goods carried, 1871–1939 (in millions of miles)

|  | India | France | Germany | Britain | Russia/USSR | United States |
|---|---|---|---|---|---|---|
| 1871–1874 | 4.2 | 51.6 | — | 181.8 | 21.4 | — |
| 1890–1894 | 27.0 | 96.2 | 219.0 | 308.5 | 76.2 | — |
| 1900–1904 | 45.3 | 83.2 | 378.8 | 435.9 | 166.0 | 650.1 |
| 1910–1914 | 74.0 | 117.8 | 613.1 | 533.4 | 163.0 | 1,075.8 |
| 1920–1924 | 92.8 | 164.0 | 358.7 | 318.3 | 49.0 | 1,233.6 |
| 1935–1939 | 120.3 | 143.6 | 516.8 | 284.8 | 491.0 | 938.8 |

*Sources:* Daniel R. Headrick, *The Tentacles of Progress* (New York: Oxford University Press), 57. For the United States, figures are calculated from Bureau of the Census, *Historical Statistics of the United States: Colonial Times to 1957* (Washington, DC: Bureau of the Census, 1960), 431.

cent of the US foreign debt was held in railroad securities abroad, over half of them held by British capital. Germany also passed England by 1873 in the amount of track laid; France caught up with Britain in 1888.[32] Over time the initial leaders built dense networks, causing profits on new lines to decline; their capitalists sought out other sectors or railroads in other lands.

The new areas with their vast expanses and dispersed populations demonstrated the "relative advantages of backwardness." They were the natural beneficiaries of the railroads and more efficient shipping after 1870. In that year the United States' total of 53,000 miles of track already was more than 50 percent greater than the total combined of Britain, Germany, and France. Sixty years later the US rail network (431,000 miles) was more than four times as extensive as those of the three major European industrial powers combined, and Canada had more than any of the European industrial giants. Areas of older settlement, such as Russia (which joined the Soviet Union in 1922) and India, were rewarded by British and French investments that built up their networks to 49,000 and 44,000 miles, respectively.[33] Even Latin

America, with its sparse population and fertile fields, had some 61,000 miles of track by 1910, more than all of Asia and three times Africa's total.[34] As in the case in North America, these lines bolstered the domestic market for national producers. As Table 2.1 demonstrates, newcomers like the United States, Argentina, Australia, and Canada overshadowed former world powers, like Portugal, Spain, and Turkey. China had virtually no track at the end of the nineteenth century and only 9,000 miles by 1930. Fears that the railroad threatened China's embattled sovereignty, particularly in the interior, undercut official support for track. Given the Japanese invasion and internal civil war, the effective total was probably even smaller in 1945.[35]

## Integration or Fragmentation?

As often as not, railroads were conquering tools of nation or empire building. They as much *created* markets as responded to them. The longest lines early on required state aid because they were not initially profitable. They often passed through areas virtually devoid of passengers, as, for example, did the transcontinental Union Pacific in the United States (1869), the Canadian Pacific that connected Ontario to Vancouver (1886), and the Trans-Siberian Railroad that connected Moscow to Vladivostok in 1905. (The Paris-to-Istanbul Orient Express, 1889, and the Berlin-Baghdad Railroad, finished only in 1940, were more about connecting empires than controlling marginal areas.) Even when the lines remained in only one country, they spurred international trade by permitting goods farther from the coasts to find foreign markets and for imports to have access to ever-denser markets in the interiors. This was particularly true of Western Europe and the United States. Hamburg, Bremen, Amsterdam, Rotterdam, Le Havre, Trieste, Marseille, New York, Chicago, New Orleans, and San Francisco, as well as numerous other ports, connected to land, canal, and sea networks that reached across borders into the interior. Rail lines also served major ports elsewhere, such as Sydney, Melbourne, Buenos Aires, Montevideo, Alexandria, and Cape Town.[36] The railroads also sped up port activities, as rail lines were built right up to the docks and warehouses to reduce bottlenecks that had hindered trade.

Not all rail systems integrated domestic markets, however. Many of the systems built later were designed to service export enclaves—passing through sweltering deserts, as in Arica, Chile, a center for nitrates and copper; dizzying heights, like the Lima–La Oroya–Cerro de Pasco, which climbed the Andes to silver, copper, zinc, and lead mines in Peru; or steaming jungles, like the Madeira-Mamoré Railway that connected the Brazilian rubber forests of Acre to the Amazon River and eventually to the Bolivian highlands. Less of an engineering feat but no less vital were the two rail lines (of differing gauges, of course) in Yucatán in Mexico that connected the port of Progreso, an outlet for henequen fiber, to the state capital of Mérida. These lines often tied their hinterlands more closely into foreign markets than to domestic ones. Some of these were not just successful conduits for exports but engineering marvels, scaling cliffs, tunneling through towering mountains, or snaking through tropical rainforests. But these agents of civilization were built with the blood and on the backs of thousands of laborers, many of them imported from the Caribbean, India, and China.

Other ambitious lines that were intended to integrate neighboring national markets, such as Brazilian railways that passed through Uruguay into Argentina, failed to reorient the overseas export focus. This sadly learned reality would abort the Pan-American Railroad intended to run from Canada to Argentina. The only lines that successfully linked international American markets were those that extended north from the United States to Canada and south to Mexico. Both were intended to exchange raw materials (lumber, grains, and hides from Canada, and silver, gold, copper, and nickel from Mexico) for US finished goods. In the short run they reinforced the export orientation of those two US neighbors and did little to grow domestic markets.[37]

There were important exceptions, however. Monterrey, Mexico, which was conveniently located close to iron deposits on the Mexican National Railroad, became the country's northern industrial center. Mostly specializing in consumer products like cigarettes and a new drink from the Anglo-Saxon north, beer, Monterrey also developed the only advanced steel industry in Latin America during our period. It grew trying to satisfy the demand from the booming railroad sector for rail, bridges, and some moving stock.[38]

Railroads in Argentina and Brazil also succeeded in strengthening their domestic markets, albeit in different ways. In Argentina the rail system reinforced the national dominance of Buenos Aires, won at the cost of repeated civil wars in the nineteenth century and a massive infusion of foreign, principally British, investments. As the country's main port, commercial and financial center, and national capital, Buenos Aires enjoyed the advantages of primacy. In fact, early on it was a global city like New York, London, or Shanghai, with most of its population foreign-born or first generation and many important corporations and banks establishing branches there to serve its prosperous population. As one of the world's richest countries in terms of per capita income on the eve of World War I and with a well-integrated rail system, Argentina's domestic consumer goods factories were concentrated between Buenos Aires and Rosario.[39]

Brazil's coastal settlement dictated that there were numerous competing port cities, each serving different hinterlands. Although the political advantage of Rio de Janeiro city led to an early head start in the railroad age, by the 1890s the coffee boom enhanced the clout of São Paulo (both city and state). Though never becoming the country's political capital, São Paulo became the national commercial, financial, and eventually by the 1920s, industrial center. Its capitalists financed railroads throughout the state and in the adjoining states of Paraná, Goiás, and Mato Grosso, and diverted some of Rio de Janeiro's trade with the country's largest state, Minas Gerais. In São Paulo itself, the booming export economy led to domestic regional integration by 1945. The northeast, Amazon, and southwest regions would have to wait decades for highways to tie them to the prosperous southeast.[40]

Some landlocked capitals were connected to their coasts, but the impetus behind the initiatives was made clear when the railroads *began* at the ports. The line that started in Djibouti in French Somaliland in 1897 did not reach Ethiopia's capital of Addis Ababa until twenty years later because of the wariness of Ethiopia's king Menelik II, who feared French colonial designs. The European-financed railway helped his Shoan government based in Addis Ababa to assert internal colonialism by conquering neighboring peoples such as the Oromo and the Harari. The central Ethiopian government formed a national state by sending out coffee and other goods by rail in exchange for weapons and ammunition. This allowed Ethiopia and Liberia to be the only areas in Africa that remained free of European colonialism (except for a brief Italian occupation).

The Uganda Railroad, which started at the port of Mombasa and reached Lake Victoria in Kenya in 1901, was quite different. A European colonial project, it later completed its 562 miles to Kampala, Uganda, and to Nairobi. But its effects contrasted strikingly with those of the Djibouti line. To make the British line to Lake Victoria pay for itself, English settlers were summoned and given fertile lands in the highlands and a monopoly over coffee production, which was forbidden to native peoples. The one hundred white settlers in Kenya in 1903 became one thousand in 1914 and reached about three thousand in 1942. Small but consequential in number, by the time of World War II they controlled some 6.3 million acres. By the 1920s most of the able-bodied agricultural peoples, like the Kikuyu and the Luo, were working under semicoercive conditions for European settlers. English modernizers disdained their colonial subjects. As Sir Charles Eliot, the British Commissioner of the East Africa Protectorate, blithely observed in 1905: "We have in East Africa the rare experience of dealing with a tabula rasa, an almost untouched and sparsely inhabited country, where we can do as we wish, to regulate immigration and open or close the door as seems best."[41] Indian laborers who were imported there to help build the railroad remained and became important economic actors in both countries. Whites, together with Indian immigrants, came to control the economy and the majority of exports as Kenya became one of Africa's main coffee producers and one of its most racially divided colonies.[42] With racially based marketing and regulatory boards as well as land rights and taxes, this was clearly not liberal, free-trade capitalism. The railroad did not create an imitation England in northeast Africa.

Nor did Uganda come to look like England, but the impetus was to create capitalist labor and land relations and monetized commercial transactions that would benefit the indigenous people. Even the coffee growers and cotton growers were mainly natives. Of course, the revenues raised from the production of these commodities strengthened the colonial state as well.

German East Africa (today Tanzania, Burundi, and Rwanda) also was transformed by the new rail opening to the Indian Ocean, and it, too, became a significant coffee exporter. It was a German colony until the end of World War I, when part of it passed to British control and part to Belgian. Unlike the situation in Kenya, missionaries and then colonial officials sought to incorporate the indigenous population into export commodity production by privatizing land ownership and overseeing peasant production. Coffee and cotton growing remained under majority African control. Because coffee was indigenous in Tanganyika, as in Ethiopia, local peasants undertook most of the cultivation on their own fields.[43]

The railroads, however, were slow to serve internal commerce in Africa. Ethiopia's entire system, which was a mere 193 miles in 1903, reached 490 miles by 1917 and remained at that small number at the end of our period. Goods were still carried by camel and horse caravans, so movement within the country remained slow, expensive, and unreliable. Uganda's system was even smaller, not surpassing 330 miles of track by 1945. Kenya had 640 miles of track by 1916 and increased it to 1,300 in 1945.[44] But paved roads were scarce, in part to protect the railroad's monopoly on long-distance trade. These railways were umbilical cords between the interior and the outside world, not projects for internal development.

The British dominion of South Africa, which Britain seized from the Boers and Zulus in numerous battles after 1877 and officially after a bloody South African war (Second Boer War) and compromise in 1902, received almost a third of the modest 28,500 miles of track laid in Africa by 1914. By 1945 its share had grown to 40 percent of Africa's total of 31,763 miles of track. (No other sub-Saharan colony had one-tenth of South Africa's rail total at the end of our period.) This racially segregated but mineral-blessed colony with abundant diamonds and gold was a prime destination for British capital. By 1913 it received some £370 million (more than US$1.8 billion), almost as much as Australia and New Zealand combined, or India and Ceylon combined, though it had only 2 percent the population of the latter (and was about equal in population to Australia and New Zealand).[45] The railway system had economic and state-building objectives: it connected the diamond and gold mines of the interior with the ports and tied together the Boer interior with the British south. In this it resembled the rail line from the coast to Rhodesia's copper mines. It was also supposed to be Cecil Rhodes's centerpiece to his proposed "Red Line from Cape Town to Cairo"—British railroads that would connect Africa from south to north. But that ambitious plan, like the abortive line from French Algeria to Niger, never became a reality.

This underlines the close relationship between colonialism and railroad building *in certain colonies*. For the most part, the white settler colonies or former colonies, such as Australia, Canada, South Africa, and the United States, received most of the rail. The exceptions were the areas close to Europe (North Africa) or the United States (Mexico and Cuba) and India. In Latin America, which Table 2.1 shows was a major area of railroad building, most of the lines were constructed either in areas closely tied to the North American economy or in countries with large European immigration, such as Argentina, Uruguay, and southern Brazil. The other major exception was India, which by 1920 surpassed the rail mileage of Britain, Germany, and France. Its rather dense rail system was more used for moving passengers, who preferred the cheapest and least profitable seats, than for freight. It also spurred little industrialization, unlike the other major lines.[46]

In almost all countries, rate schedules favored large-scale international commerce over less-voluminous local trade. Fares from the interior to ports were cheaper than between two interior stations and large-scale and long-distance rail shipments received generous discounts and rebates while small, short-distance cargo did not.

Not all state leaders welcomed the railroad. We have already mentioned Chinese imperial reluctance. Similarly, in India some leaders feared the change accompanying domestic development. The Nizam of Hyderabad was appalled that the steel rail would "upset all orthodox notions [and] make the popular mind gyrate or swing backwards and forwards with the movement like that of children at a fair." Despite the fact that he "dreaded the British government and disliked its civilization," he submitted to the British plans for a railroad because he felt that a railroad would provide "the only strong tower where he could in extremity take refuge."[47]

So in certain places and at some times, the railroad maintained subservience and inequality as much as it brought advancement. Historian Daniel Headrick concludes that the railroads in India created "the great transformation of India from congeries of traditional states into something new on the subcontinent: modern underdeveloped nation-states."[48] Similarly, the world's most populous country, China, built a rail system one-quarter the size of India's by 1942, some 19,300 kilometers. For the most part it connected ports with their hinterlands rather than integrating the country, with the important exception of the line from the capital in Beijing to Guangzhou (Canton).

The unevenness of rail growth meant that Asia and Africa, which together in 1913 held over 60 percent of the world's population, in 1945 enjoyed only about 13 percent of the world's rail lines. Vast areas in Asia with hundreds of millions of people were strangers to the rail. Two-thirds of Asia's railway miles lay in India and Japan alone. We must recognize, however, that even in a vast country like China, which built relatively little rail compared to world leaders, the iron track had an enormous impact. Some interior crops like cotton and tobacco could now be exported, and the risks and time for internal transactions was greatly reduced in key areas. The completion of the Beijing-to-Hankou line, for instance, reduced the time it took to travel from Guangzhou to Beijing from 90 days at the turn of the century to 3.3 days by 1936. Even areas not on the line were affected by connections via ship, so that by one estimate the time it took to travel from Beijing to the outer perimeter of the country fell by 84 percent.[49] This, of course, demonstrated the primacy of state interests over export considerations.

In more fortunate areas, the iron connections of ports with the domestic interior were sometimes seen as triumphs of modernization and nation building. Many railway stations, such as Paris's Gare d'Orsay, London's St. Pancras Station, or New York's Grand Central Station, were built as gorgeous and elegant monuments to progress. They were emblems of a modern age that forcefully demonstrated humans' power not only to subdue nature but to erase distance and space. Visitors praised the stations, and the telegraph offices that accompanied them, as the nerve centers of global cities.[50]

Critics, however, saw the steam locomotive as a Trojan horse that permitted foreign capital, technology, and arms to conquer regional politicians, indigenous peoples, and different ways of life. Rail systems were disparaged with epithets such as "suction pumps" or "tentacles."

They also upset and transformed economic calculations, political allegiances, and local and national identities.

## Iron and Steel

In addition to reducing travel time and costs and creating access to places that formerly were out of bounds, railroads had multiplier effects on other areas of the world economy. They reflected and sped the technological breakthroughs in the creation of first iron and then steel. Both metals had long been used by humans, but their modern contributions came first during the First Industrial Revolution. Iron and then steel track, locomotives, and bridges created a huge market and stimulated technical improvements. Iron had served for the first four decades of the railway age, but proved to be too weak and vulnerable to weather. Steel, which was of poor quality until the Bessemer and Siemens-Martin processes were developed at the end of the 1850s, soon transformed transport infrastructure. The connection between the railroad and the steel industry was intimate. In 1848 a quarter of the puddled iron production of England and Wales had gone into rails. In the United States, the connection with steel was even stronger. Until the 1890s more than half of all US steel went into rails.[51]

Although a number of countries made iron and steel by the end of the nineteenth century, few of them could compete with the handful of modern industrial steel producers, such as Britain, Germany, Belgium, Russia, and the United States, who supplied the vast majority of the world's track. With constant technological improvements and great economies of scale, the steel industries were concentrated in the hands of a few enormous corporations (or, as in the case of the Soviet Union, state companies). For example, in 1901 J. P. Morgan bought out Andrew Carnegie and brought together seven steel and tin companies to form the United States Steel Corporation. Capitalized at US$1.4 billion, it was up to that point the largest corporation in the history of the world, producing two-thirds of all the steel in the United States. To demonstrate how significant this was, the United States produced, on average, over 40 percent of the world's steel in 1909–1913 and more than half in 1925 and 1926 as war-driven demand sparked a rapid rise in output. France, Germany, and the United Kingdom contributed another third of world steel production in those years, but destruction brought on by the First World War reduced their share to about 28 percent in 1925 and 1926. By 1938 the United States still produced 35 percent of world steel, which was matched by the combined output of the three main European producers. The Soviet Union and Japan were the only other major steel manufacturers, with Russia jumping from 6 percent of the total in 1909–1913 to 13 percent under the Communists in 1941, which put it third in the world, and Japan producing almost six million metric tons in 1937, making it the world's fifth-largest steelmaker. In both the Soviet Union and Japan, the steel industry was not only fomented by the state but also largely controlled by it for strategic as well as economic reasons.[52] All the other countries in the world combined to manufacture under a quarter of global steel, usually in relatively small, inefficient factories.

India and Mexico were exceptional cases. The former was a British colony and the latter an economic appendage of the United States. India had a long history of steelmaking, but was so inefficient that even the state-run railroads imported almost all their steel from Britain and Belgium. One of India's most famous entrepreneurs, Jamshedji Nusserwanji Tata, who had made his first fortune in textiles, financed the Tata Iron and Steel Company (TISCO), which came to life while World War I cut off competing iron and steel imports. Protected by first the crisis in the world market and then the colonial government, TISCO increased its share of the Indian steel market to 73 percent by 1938, when it was producing virtually all the rail purchased in India.[53] Still, compared to the main steel powers, it was a minor concern. Mexicans in Monterrey, Mexico, developed the Fundidora de Hierro to supply steel track, bridges, and girders for the country's expanding transportation system. It did not export. Financed by local capital, it became a regional growth pole, but again its output was minimal by world standards.[54]

Other countries with major rail lines, like Brazil and Argentina, were slow to build steel industries, though their military leaders and outspoken nationalists called for state-led factories. Brazilian president Artur Bernardes proclaimed in his 1926 message to Brazil's Congress that a steel industry "is the primary condition of our economic autonomy."[55] His successor, Getúlio Vargas, would make the state-run Volta Redonda steel mill a major part of his development policy, though by then the automobile and other steel products loomed more important than the railroad. Because of its rich ore deposits, Brazil would become a major steel producer after World War II. Argentina had to overcome greater geographic disadvantages and was slower to build its steel factories.

Where railroads did not give birth to modern steel industries, they sometimes had other linkages to domestic producers in the form of demand for wood for ties, trestles, and railway cars. Locomotives, the most technologically advanced component of rail systems, still were almost all imported from the United States and Western Europe. The railroad's most important developmental contribution was to build the domestic market, although in some places that just made imports more accessible. But that link to the world economy has probably been exaggerated. Early estimates that most of Mexico's and Brazil's freight traffic was for exports have been reassessed. Even those lines built with European and US markets in mind wound up building up the domestic market for food, clothing, and some durable goods.[56]

Three examples taken from the richest independent successful export economies—Argentina, Brazil, and Mexico—demonstrate the iron horse's varied consequences. Argentina, effectively an honorary part of the British Commonwealth until World War II because of the preponderant influence of British capital and trade, had the most successful of the independent export-oriented economies prior to 1945. Argentines spent extravagantly on imports because of the high wages their sparse labor force commanded, inexpensive imports delivered by the modern port and railroad facilities built at Buenos Aires, and low duties charged by their laissez-faire government. Over time, domestic industries grew, however. Tariffs were set at first to simply raise government revenues for operating expenses. Over time they increasingly financed developmental goals and became more protective as factory owners and workers gained political clout. The same was true for Brazil and Mexico. By World War I, despite pronouncements of fervent faith in free trade, their tariffs were among the highest in the world.[57] From there on out, exports would continuously fall as a share of GNP, reflecting the relative growth of domestic economies.

Just as railroads did not bring free trade to most countries, neither did they guarantee private enterprise. Although the first countries to enter the rail age, such as Great Britain and the United States, relied on private companies, those enterprises had received generous (critics thought, too generous) subsidies, land grants, tax breaks, or guaranteed profits. Latecomers amplified government assistance as railroads came to be seen not only as an economic benefit, but also as a defensive necessity (against either external attack or internal revolt), a lure for foreign investment, a symbol of modernity and civilization, and the glue that held countries together. So essential did they become, that when railway companies faced bankruptcy during recessions, governments nationalized them. This was done not only to keep the trains running and the cities provisioned, but also to maintain the country's international credit and the strength of its currency. As a result, governments dedicated in theory to laissez-faire, such as in Brazil and Mexico, nationalized their principal railways before World War I.[58]

We emphasize, however, that outside of the Soviet Union, state interventions in strategic infrastructure (railroads, shipping, roads, public utilities) were not primarily socialist acts. It is true, though, that there was social pressure for public participation in the infrastructure: railroad workers were sometimes the most vocal and radical sector of the working class, socialists usually advocated nationalization, and urban passengers occasionally rioted about high fares and bad service. Although the nationalization of railroads usually was not socialist-inspired, neither were states acting as public capitalists. Most of the nationalized railroads ran at a deficit in order to subsidize the private sector by providing low-cost services. State interventions were usually seen as temporary remedies intended to shore up the private sector with public funds, though nationalist pique at foreign-owned companies also played a role. Both were involved in Brazil and Mexico, where the federal governments bought control of most of the rail lines before World War I. Even colonial India, certainly no hotbed of radicalism, nationalized its railways to escape the burden of interest guarantees, but allowed private companies to continue to run them. For more strategic reasons, the Turkish government nationalized lines in the wake of the dissolution of the Ottoman Empire after the First World War. The Great Depression later encouraged Germany and other European countries and colonies to assert or expand state control over railroads. Even the British, who had mastered the railroad age with private companies, nationalized their trains after World War II as Labour won power.

## The Automobile

The automobile was to the twentieth century what the railroad had been the nineteenth; emblematic of individual speed and power, it competed with the railroad in the most affluent countries. Numerous inventors in the United States, England, France, Germany, and Italy busily improved the automobile as cheaper fuel for it became more readily available. The growth of demand was astronomical, particularly in the United States, which not only had steel for the chassis and copper and aluminum for the engine, but was the world's leading producer of oil and gasoline at the turn of the century. From 8,000 registered autos in 1885, the number jumped to 902,000 in 1912. As Henry Ford perfected the assembly line in Deerfield, Michigan, the growth really became spectacular. By 1920 the number had grown tenfold to 9.2 million motor vehicles, and continued upward. Then Alfred P. Sloan and General Motors (GM) began to stress mass distribution and offered a choice of models. With yearly changes, they appealed to fashion as well as price and convenience. This allowed GM to surpass Ford as the world's largest producer in the 1920s. Workers in the United States built 2 to 3.7 million new cars a year in the 1920s and 1930s, with the high reaching 4.4 million in 1929, a total that would not be matched again for twenty years. Because Henry Ford had introduced the "Fordist" policy of paying the stupendous wage of five dollars a day (and regimenting workers so they would not unionize) and offered relatively inexpensive cars, the sector created a great swell of consumer and fiscal linkages as well as the backward and forward supplies needed to construct cars and serve them.[59] Despite Ford's efforts to the contrary, autoworkers, along with coal miners, became some of the most powerful and politically influential unionized trades in the United States and Western Europe.

In 1929 the United States had 78 percent of all the cars in the entire world. Almost all the rest were in Western Europe, but there they were far less in use. In 1938 the United States had one car for every 3.9 inhabitants, Britain had one for every 22 people, France one for 28, Germany one for 98, and Italy one for every 151. In Asia, only Japan produced a significant number of autos, and this only after the First World War. They had only one car for every 1,195 inhabitants in 1938.[60]

The overwhelming dominance of North Americans in this new sector was even greater than that astounding percentage indicates, because the major US auto companies exported abroad. The value of US

Model T Fords lining 42nd Street in 1918. Little more than two decades after the first automobiles were manufactured, New York's Manhattan was already experiencing traffic jams. Efficient production by Ford and then General Motors turned the auto into a mass product. As Western Europe joined the automobile age, demand for rubber, oil, and steel exploded. (© Kadel & Herbert / National Geographic Society / Corbis)

auto and parts exports shot up from $11 million in 1910 to $303 million in 1920, making them a leading manufactured export.[61]

However, exports flattened out thereafter because of war in Europe and because the leading firms bought up foreign companies. In 1928, Germany's leading automobile company was Opel, which belonged to GM, while Ford was Germany's third-largest producer. British Ford became a major player in the United Kingdom. Elsewhere the major Detroit companies began to set up assembly plants to circumvent tariffs established to protect domestic producers. In Brazil, Ford had already built an assembly plant in 1920. It was followed quickly by GM.[62]

Most of the world's trucks, buses, tractors, and motorcycles were also in the United States, carrying freight and working the fields as well as moving people. (As late as 1950, 85 percent of Europe's agricultural horsepower was supplied by horses.)[63] The surge of motorized vehicles in the United States not only helped urbanization, but also cemented North American agriculture's position as the most capital intensive and most labor efficient in the world, characteristics that will be more fully illustrated in the section on wheat in Chapter 3.

The sociological effect of the internal combustion engine in our period was ambiguous. In the few countries where it proliferated, the automobile emphasized the individual or family unit over the collective, which the railroad and streetcar served. However, the internal combustion engine also drove a rapidly expanding fleet of buses that served large groups with fixed routes and schedules. Where the auto stressed private ownership, urban bus lines were often municipally owned or at least regulated. And paved roads were a mutual public good.

## The Airplane

The human dream of joining the birds in flight was finally realized in our era. Beginning with (depending on your national loyalty) the Brazilian Alberto Santos Dumont, who brought to life Jules Verne's fiction by flying a dirigible in Paris in 1901 and made the first public flight in Europe in a fixed-wing aircraft in 1906, or the North American Wright Brothers, whose light aircraft had a sustained, though brief, flight in Kitty Hawk, North Carolina, in 1903, air travel captured the public's imagination. Before the 1930s, however, it was more spectacle or military weapon—combatants built some two hundred thousand planes during the First World War—than commercially useful. Its day would come, even more than the auto, after 1945.[64]

As with so many other technologies, the early leaders were North Americans and Germans. The latter had already sent a few planes over the channel to bomb England during the First World War. Longer international distances followed for peaceful purposes as three aircraft succeeded in crossing the North Atlantic to the United States by 1919. Germans developed the radio navigation system in the 1920s to permit flying with minimal visibility.[65] Still, their expense, danger, and small carrying capacity meant that airplanes were little used internationally for commercial purposes until the 1930s, though they were extremely helpful for local flights in vast countries with poor road and railroad networks, such as Brazil, Colombia, and Mexico. Native capitalists initiated many smaller lines.[66] The first aircraft to be commercially viable internationally was in fact the German Zeppelin Company's hydrogen airship, which made 144 transatlantic two-day crossings in the first part of the 1930s. Though the airships were profitable initially because of the considerable cargo they could carry, they were doomed by improvements by their competitors, fixed-wing aircraft, combined with a few tragic accidents when the hydrogen gasbags that kept them aloft ignited.

Airboats replaced zeppelins for international flights; they were hours and days faster than ships. Only a few activities could pay the freight for this more costly means of transport. In the United States and to a lesser extent in Western Europe, airmail was the main customer. Banks in particular were interested in hurrying checks to be cashed so they would not lose interest. Sometimes planes were used to literally drop bags of money to meet payroll in dangerous areas, such as the oil fields of Tampico, Mexico. In certain places time was money, and so money (as well as time) flew. For largely commercial reasons, the US government subsidized airmail. Pan American Airlines in particular took advantage of the 1928 Kelly Foreign Air Mail Act to assemble routes down to and around Central and South America, connecting to Europe via the Caribbean and West Africa, and by 1937 crossing to China via Hawai'i. Because of its size, population, and wealth, the United States was also able to develop the world's densest domestic air industry, just as it had the most developed railroad and road networks.[67] And, as with other US transportation systems, it was private commercial companies, albeit with government assistance, that forged the path for the global aeronautical industry.

Although Germans, the second most active in the air, were interested in the airplane more for military applications, the privately owned Condor Syndicate, a forerunner of Lufthansa, developed air companies in Brazil (VARIG) and Colombia (SCADTA). Until the rise of the Nazi Party, the Soviet and German governments connected Europe with Asia through the Deutsche Russische Luftverkehrsgesellschaft.[68] Thanks to the German treaty port of Qingdao, Lufthansa was also an early leader in China.

The British saw the airplane as a means of tying together their vast empire, but it advantaged the neo-Europes. Unlike the Dutch, who early on encouraged KLM to connect with the Dutch East Indies (Indonesia), and the French, who developed air travel in Indochina through what became Air France in 1933, the British were discouraged from creating a South Asian air network by India's well-developed rail system. As R. E. G. Davies observes: "Throughout the 1920s, India seemed, in fact, to be regarded by Great Britain as a mere staging point on the route to the Far East and to Australia."[69] In fact, the first successful air company in India was planned and financed by an Indian, J. R. D.

Tata.[70] Soviets shared all of these motivations for air travel, but added the symbolic importance of a fast, modern transport for the world's first anti-imperialist, communist country.

Although commerce motivated some of the first private airlines, strategic considerations growing out of both world wars, as well as nation building and colonial impulses, provoked startling growth in aircraft and aviation technology. Headrick has recently pointed out the key role played by airplanes in colonial and neocolonial wars, ranging from the Italians in Libya and Ethiopia to the North Americans in Mexico and Nicaragua. "Air control" gave the colonizers a great advantage up to the end of our period.[71]

State aid was fundamental to the figurative and literal explosion of the air industry and travel. By 1947, the cost of crossing the Atlantic was low enough that a GI sergeant was able to afford to fly Gertrude Topik from Paris to New York, helping to ensure that one of the authors of this book would be born in America a couple of years later.

## Telegraphs, Underwater Cables, and Radios

Just as steamers, locomotives, cars, and planes powered by steam and fossil fuels bound the world more closely together by vastly accelerating the speed with which goods and people moved, the telegraph wire shrank the world via electricity. The "Victorian Internet," as Tom Standage has nicknamed the telegraph, sparked a conceptual revolution, shaking notions of time and space.[72] But it also opened a great gulf between those connected to its hurried and harried rhythms and those who continued to work at the pace of natural time. Communication of news, orders, commodity, stock and gold prices, and interest rates was made possible by revolutionary advances in the use of electricity, which became one of the foundational cornerstones of the Second Industrial Revolution. As with railroads and steamships (and later telephones), the telegraph demanded systems with large capital investments, coordination through private agreements, and government regulations. At first tying together national markets and polities, it soon became the adhesive of the global market, serving commercial, political, and military purposes simultaneously. The dark side of connectivity was discovered in 1873 when the rapidly transmitted news of financial crises in Europe and the United States provoked the first global depression, which affected all countries and colonies that were closely tied into world capital and commodity markets.

The telegraph, like the railroad and steamers, played a vital role in consolidating rival colonial and neocolonial systems. But its high costs and vast range made international cooperation economically advisable. As Dwayne Winseck and Robert Pike observe, the global telegraph system, "like most other capital intensive industries, continued to contain a complex admixture of collaboration, competition, and conflict, self-interest and opportunism, private enterprise and state interventions."[73] International cartels, consortia, joint investments from different countries, and mixed public and private investments capitalized and coordinated these singularly far-flung enormous enterprises. Thus began the modern era of multinational corporations.[74]

Electricity had been known as early as the eighteenth century, but it remained a little-used curiosity until the nineteenth century. Building on the work of many European and American scientists, the Englishman William Fothergill Cooke established the first commercial telegraph in 1837. It was used in London on the Great Western Railway, symbolizing the link between these two revolutionary technologies. Cooke's contemporary, the North American Samuel Morse, developed a more successful telegraph system (and code), which was operational by 1846, connecting New York with Washington and demonstrating its close ties to political and commercial nation building. Soon thereafter, a multitude of telegraph systems based on competing technologies arose. Finally, some order and standards were brought to the fledgling industry in upstate New York and in the Old West with the creation of the Western Telegraph Union in 1856. Traveling largely along the beds of railroads and generously aided by federal funds inspired by the Civil War's strategic needs, the telegraph crossed the United States to California by 1861, driving the Pony Express out of business. Two major private companies, Western Union and American Telegraph Company (which would become AT&T when it added telephones), coordinated and dominated the national network.

Europeans, split into dozens of states and languages, required more strenuous efforts at coordination, because the telegraph was of limited use if it could not tap into neighboring networks in small though prosperous countries like Belgium, Great Britain, and the Netherlands or splintered principalities like Germany before 1871 and Italy before nationhood in 1861. Indeed, international commerce played a large role in stimulating later, denser domestic networks.

Telegraphs eventually stretched over the national territories of Western Europe and North America, followed by Latin America and the colonial areas of Asia and Africa, representing a leap for communications, as the ruling classes of distant countries and continents could remain in contact. The advent of international wire services like Reuters in England, Havas in France, the Associated Press in the United States, and Wolff in Germany provided world news (really the news of the part of the globe they thought was important in Western Europe, North America, and various global cities) to the daily newspapers that were beginning to attract mass readerships in major metropolises.[75] They moved in the direction of homogenizing tastes, prices, and technical and scientific advances, though there was resistance as well as acquiescence. Scandals, riots, and disasters as well as celebrities and fashion became known throughout the Western urbane world, which included overseas outposts such as Rio de Janeiro, Cape Town, Mumbai, and Shanghai. The military joined the intelligence gained from the telegraph with the Maxim gun and rapid deployments on the railroad to subject many formerly autonomous peoples to more-centralized rule.

Both government and private enterprise could expand their reach and concentrate power and surveillance. In addition to spurring commerce and homogenizing market prices, the form of business organization was changed as corporations and cartels could synchronize over distant geographic stretches now that they were wired into the telegraph grid.

As with the other revolutionary technologies, at first the telegraph gave great advantages to Western Europe and North America. In 1870, Western Europeans sent some 40.6 million telegrams (over half from Germany, France, and the United Kingdom) and the United States sent 9 million, while in Africa the telegraph was possessed only by the French colony of Algeria, which sent a mere 263,000 telegrams; the only Asian country to enjoy the telegraph was India, which sent 577,000 telegrams.[76]

By 1913 the gap had narrowed, in good part because, as with the railroad, the colonial powers and their capitalist classes invested abroad. By then Europeans were sending 329 million telegrams, and US residents transmitted about half that number. Though still greatly lagging, Africans sent some 17 million telegrams (three-quarters of them from the Mediterranean countries of Algeria and Egypt, together with South Africa), and Asia 60 million, two-thirds being sent by Japan and its colonies and one-quarter by India. Chinese sent only some 4 million inland telegrams as late as 1935. As with other revolutionary technologies, the Japanese state played a central role in inviting in English technicians in 1869 to build the state-run telegraph system. They were quickly able to adapt the telegraph to Japanese characters, creating a dual Japanese-English, forty-two-character system.[77]

If the Japanese system was built for defensive and state-building purposes, the Indian network was constructed as an instrument of colonial domination. Already in 1858 the British chief commissioner of the Punjab, John Lawrence, had thankfully announced that "the telegraph saved India" (for the British) by allowing them to mobilize troops against anticolonial disturbances.[78]

By 1930 the gap between the first builders and the followers declined because Europeans and North Americans were turning to the telephone and using the telegraph less. Asian telegrams grew some 40 percent in number but remained concentrated in Japan and India. China's telegraph system mainly tied together the European treaty ports, though eventually lines ran into the countryside and smaller cities. Other densely populated areas such as Indonesia and Indochina lagged behind China.[79]

The telegraph did not initially democratize communications, because it was expensive to build, maintain, and protect. In the beginning it was also terribly costly to use, so only the most affluent sent (curt) telegrams. In 1890, when a dollar a day was a good wage, a telegram from London to the United States or Canada cost US$0.25 *per word*. The previous sentence would have cost a worker six days' pay. And that was the cheapest rate! A telegram to India was US$1.00 a word, to Brazil US$1.50, to Australia US$2.37, and to South Africa during its gold rush, US$40 a word![80] Those sending telegrams to South Africa had to literally weigh their words in gold. The telegraph's laggard introduction into many of the most densely populated—and often least affluent—areas meant that local culture and languages retained autonomy longer there.

On the other hand, the telegraph was useful in mobilizing troops of central authorities against local or regional resistance, so in many places the wire reinforced the power of the few over the many. It was not pure coincidence that one of the first acts by local rebels was to cut the telegraph wire. But alas, the wires could be easily strung up again. The first Englishman to oversee Japan's telegraph in 1870 remarked lightheartedly: "Beyond a few of the poles being slashed by fanatical samurai who must find some use for their swords, there was no evidence of hostility on the part of the people."[81]

Underwater cables that bound together continents by erasing oceans were the sorts of modern miracles that so inspired contemporary Verne's science fiction. They represented the greatest conceptual leap in communications until satellites began bouncing back radio signals in the 1960s. Cables connected international markets, leading to commodity exchanges that set global standards and prices while encouraging competition.

Joining areas with underwater cable started small, crossing the English Channel between France and England in 1851. This was made possible by the merging of two nineteenth-century miracle products: copper wire, which transmitted electrical impulses with little loss to heat, and rubber, which insulated the copper and protected it from water. The first form of latex, gutta-percha, had been sent to England as an experimental colonial export from Malaya. In addition to learning that it served as a fine bottle stopper, which advanced the incipient carbonated water industry, and later that it could serve as the core of golf balls, scientists discovered gutta-percha's more important ability to provide electrical insulation while being durable and unappetizing to marine life.

But this was not an easy technology to master, because the early cables often broke soon after being laid on the ocean's floor. That is exactly what happened to the 1857, 1858, and 1865 cables laid across the Atlantic by a steamship specially constructed to lay out cable underwater. Finally in 1866 the first successful transatlantic submarine cable went into operation.

Other submarine cables soon followed. Brazil connected with Portugal via Senegal and the Cape Verde Islands in 1875, with other South American countries joining in to take advantage of the transatlantic cable over the next two decades. The Caribbean was connected to Europe via the North Atlantic cable through the United States and Canada. Wire spreading south from Texas linked up Mexico and Central America down to Peru by 1882, and indirectly reached South America's east coast urban centers.

Already by 1868 London reached Mumbai via telegraph passing through Ottoman and Persian lands and waters, but telegrams took more than seven days and were subject to foreign scrutiny. For political and commercial security, plans for an all-English line (known as "all-red") led to the Eastern Telegraph line connecting with India by 1870. Imperial arrogance also motivated the all-red system. The colonial mindset was blatant in a petition by Mumbai merchants who objected that their connection to London "passes through . . . foreign territory, much of it wild and uncivilized [the Ottoman and Persian Empires!], where European management cannot be brought to bear, and where ignorant and untrained native officers are alone obtainable."[82] "Civilized" British lines continued to reach east to Indochina, China, and Japan and south to Indonesia and Australia.

Sub-Saharan Africa was swept into the world of telegraph by a combination of several forces. Interest in booming Argentina and Brazil had motivated the laying of cable from Lisbon to Senegal and across to Recife. The 1870s diamond strike in Kimberley, South Africa, and the 1880s gold rush in Witwatersrand had whetted the appetite of imperialists like Rhodes. Other European powers developed the same craving that led to unprecedented conferences in Berlin in 1884 and 1885 that carved up Africa, leaving 90 percent of the territory officially under European control. Conquest, at least on the maps in European administrative offices, generated a hunger for control and knowledge. Political, diplomatic, and economic urges led to the connection of the most affluent areas to the European colonial powers beginning in 1886 with the joint-effort African Direct Telegraph Company.

With every continent connected to Europe, the globe was finally girded in 1902 when a submarine cable linked the Americas and Asia. It stretched from San Francisco to the US Pacific territories of Hawaii, Guam, and the Philippines. From there it linked to the Asian mainland and Oceania.

For the telegraph networks to function efficiently, international coordination was necessary. Because early on each country used a different system, messages had to be transcribed, translated, and handed over at the borders. They were then retransmitted over the telegraph network of the neighboring country, causing delays, errors, and additional costs. After numerous bilateral agreements in the 1850s between countries seeking telegraph connections, a conference of twenty European countries created the International Telegraph Union in 1865. It facilitated further standards and procedures as newcomers to the telegraph world joined in. Continents became connected by the submarine telegraph before many countries developed internal networks.

Telegraph wires began to lose some of their usefulness with the wireless inventions of the Italian physicist Guglielmo Marconi. Not only were these a boon to naval communications, they laid the groundwork for the radio on land and later in the air. A Nobel Prize–winning scientist, Marconi was also an astute businessman who quickly commercialized his discoveries, as did other heroic entrepreneur-scientists of this era such as Alexander Graham Bell, Thomas Edison, Ford, Nobel, and Werner von Siemens. By 1901 Marconi's English corporation sent signals across the Atlantic Ocean, and six years later a transatlantic wireless service had been established. By 1906 an international telegraphy conference in Berlin signed the first International Radiotelegraph Convention.

Marconi's invention gave rise to the radio, which would democratize access to information even among the illiterate once electricity and then the battery found their way to poorer countries and once commercial broadcasting began transmitting news and entertainment. In many countries that would happen only after the Second World War. Initially, however, as with the other major inventions discussed, the wireless radio and then broadcasting companies were concentrated in the wealthier countries, expanding the divide in lifestyles by social class and country until the 1930s.

The radio, like the earlier telegraph and telephone, was a communication system that demanded large investments in coordinated networks. This was unsurprising because it was developed by people who sought to perfect the telegraph and the railroad and who had mastered electrical generation and its applications such as lighting and power. Some of the giant electronics corporations that would put their mark on the consumer and industrial advances of the twentieth century were involved in the radio's earliest days. In the United States this included General Electric (GE), which resulted from the 1892 merger of Edison's company with the Thomson-Houston Electric Company; Westinghouse Electric, which began with the air brake for trains; and American Telegraph and Telephone (AT&T).

This was a sector more characterized by collaboration than by unrestrained competition. After Thomson and GE merged, the new GE pooled its patents with Westinghouse, effectively cornering the large and rapidly growing electronics industry. These two firms joined with AT&T in 1919 at the urging of the US government to form the Radio Corporation of America (RCA) to accelerate the diffusion of the radio. RCA bought out the originator of wireless telegraph in the United States, the American Marconi.

Forces were also joined in radio broadcasting. Westinghouse established the first commercial radio station, KDKA in Pittsburgh, in 1920, followed by GE's WGY in 1922 in Schenectady, New York. RCA combined with GE and Westinghouse to form the National Broadcasting Corporation (NBC) in 1926, linking forty-eight radio stations. Two years later the Columbia Broadcasting Corporation (CBS) followed. To regulate them, the Federal Radio Commission was created in 1927. By 1928 Americans from coast to coast could hear *The Lone Ranger* on radios that were created by Westinghouse and GE and distributed by RCA and Western Electric (which had begun the telegraph boom a half century earlier).[83] The radio swept through the United States like a hurricane. Already in 1925, 10 percent of households had radios; five years later nearly 50 percent had one. By 1945 almost 90 percent of US households listened to the radio, as mass production and consumer credit dropped its cost and turned it into a necessity.

But most other countries did not adopt the US radio model based on large private corporations. National governments established major broadcasting companies like the British Broadcasting Corporation and Japan's NHK. France had a combination of public and private broadcasters. In Germany, private companies began broadcasting, but the national Post Ministry had to have a majority share in them. Similarly, in Brazil the *Hora do Brasil* was created, a one-hour time slot during which only a central government program could be broadcast. The Soviet government had complete control of USSR radio.

The radio was used initially for educational purposes but soon was turned to commercial popular culture and to political education. An early student of mass communications and its unfortunate possibilities was the Nazi propaganda minister, Josef Goebbels, who introduced the production of relatively cheap *Volksempfänger* receivers so the country could hear the Nazi version of the "Big Lie." Communication and truth did not necessarily come together. Radios quickly spread through the richer countries. In France, for instance, there were already some five million radios by 1939. Sales of radio equipment in the United States reached $843 million in 1929, a fourteen-fold increase in just eight years![84]

These early radio companies became household names in the United States, Western Europe, and parts of Latin America. They soon became enormous conglomerates producing everything from electrical capital goods to generators and transmission lines, electric trains and trolleys, movie projectors, consumer goods, such as lightbulbs, and by the 1920s refrigerators, electric ranges, and washing machines. These more expensive goods spread more slowly than the radio. Significant international trade goods, their export declined as they were increasingly manufactured in the overseas consuming countries, at first by branches of the European and North American corporations and then, by the 1930s, by protected domestic factories. Still, incomes were too low and the prices too high for electronic domestic goods to enter the mass market in many places outside of the most affluent countries and some major cities. Their heyday would come after the 1950s.

Telephones also were electronic instruments, but they became the monopoly of a different company, Bell Telephone. The Scottish inventor Alexander Graham Bell was trying to improve the telegraph when in 1876 he invented in Boston the device that would speak the telegraph's demise. When it was combined with the mouthpiece invented by Thomas Edison, it could reach the immediate area around the caller. By 1904 there were already three million telephones in operation in the United States. De Forest's triode vacuum tube made possible a phone call from New York to San Francisco by 1915.

But the telephone was slow to bind continents, because the technology to amplify speech sufficiently to send it long distances lagged behind. The first transatlantic call was made only in 1927 from New York to London. A three-minute call, done by wireless radio, cost the then-princely sum of seventy-five dollars, making it economically impractical. Telephone cables were not laid across the Atlantic until 1955. Because telephones required an expensive system to be useful, they were slow to internationalize. They were concentrated in Western Europe and North America, where each had some 26 million telephones in service by 1945. Africa lagged behind with some 400,000 phones for the entire continent, as did Asia, with some 1.7 million, more than two-thirds of them in Japan.[85] Sparsely populated Oceania had 1.1 million telephones.

A few giant companies in Europe also moved away from the telegraph and accompanying electronics into consumer goods. The Thomson-Houston Company that merged with GE established subsidiaries in England and France that became, after mergers there, the largest companies in those two large markets.

Germany experienced the most remarkable advance in the electrical sector, a key to its *Wirtschaftswunder* (economic miracle). Between 1890 and 1913 the electrical industrial sector grew at an astounding

9.75 percent a year. By the eve of the First World War, Germany produced 20 percent more electricity than Great Britain, France, and Italy
combined. (In part to generate electricity, Germans increased coal production almost eightfold between 1870 and 1913, and jumped in industrial production fivefold, so that Germany's primary exports were no
longer raw materials but instead finished and semifinished goods.)[86]

A few gigantic corporations that became world leaders characterized Germany's electrical sector. Edison's German affiliate created what
became the precursor to the Allgemeine Elektricitäts-Gesellschaft
(AEG), one of the largest electrical firms in Germany and in the world.
Also in Germany, another giant corporation, Siemens, had begun
with the telegraph in 1847, then moved to the undersea cable, to the
telephone by 1877, and then power generation. Siemens followed the
same path as US electrical companies by moving downstream into
consumer appliances by the 1920s. It took a more active role than the
other electrical companies in producing instruments of war, in 1944
going so far as to design the V2 rocket, which was an extension of its
experience in the nascent airplane industry.[87]

Initially the large electrical multinationals participated in the public utility companies that arose in major cities in Latin America and
Eastern Europe and to a lesser extent in Africa and Asia near the end
of the nineteenth century. The British tended to invest in stand-alone
companies organized for specific locations, such as the S. Pearson electrical generating company in Mexico and Brazilian Light and Power
in Rio and São Paulo, while US and German investors like GE, Westinghouse, Siemens, and AEG, the Swiss Brown, Boveri & Co., and the
Swedish Allmänna Svenska Elektriska AB (ASEA) won power, lighting, and tram concessions in numerous major cities. Sometimes, as in
Rio de Janeiro, they replaced smaller predecessors that had launched
power companies with local capital. Usually the giant foreign firms
sold off their power companies once they were up and running, because the daily demands of light and power generation and the

political problems of dissatisfied consumers and municipal governments they entailed were too different from these companies' core competencies.[88]

Other holding companies arose to take advantage of their access to European capital—most had intimate ties to large European or US banks—and technology to run public utility companies in many countries. The Belgian Compagnie Belge des Chemins de Fer Réunis, for example, spread its investments in tramways and railroads from Belgium, France, and Greece to as far away as Russia, Turkey, China, Congo, and Egypt, and even to the Americas in Argentina and Chile.[89] The Western European and North American early movers in electricity also were usually the first to win concessions in countries outside the core. The main exception was again Japan, which used mostly national capital supplemented by government assistance. Even in Japan, however, foreign participation in the electrical area was greater than in any other sector because of the systems' bulky demands and the patented technology's sophistication.[90] (In the other major Asian "independent" country, China, modern public utilities were found mostly in the European- and Japanese-controlled treaty ports, where companies from those countries built and ran the light, power, and trams just as they did in their Asian and African colonies.)

Because of their great capital requirements and strategic economic importance, many public utility companies eventually were taken over by national or local public entities. The Soviet Union expropriated foreign power and light companies, and a couple of decades later the Turkish government bought up the French-owned public utilities.[91] Even in the United States, where suspicion of state intervention was strong, calls for public regulation and even operation of utility companies began to resonate. The federally funded and run Tennessee Valley Authority (TVA) began building dams and generators in 1934 to supply light and power to underserved areas in eight states that bordered the valley. Serving mostly as a wholesale provider of electrical power as well as a development program, the TVA became the largest power generator in the country, but it distributed power through municipal, state, and private companies.[92] Only after World War II would state-run public power, light, and transport companies become the world-wide norm.

The site of the greatest gap in inequality for the Americas, Europe, Oceania, and parts of Asia and Africa was not between countries but within countries. Public utilities made the qualitative difference between urban living and life in the countryside much greater than it had been before electricity. Particularly with the rise of public street lighting and movie theaters, the "bright lights of the big city" meant more than the conquest of the night. It meant greater leisure opportunities, perceived "culture," and social standing.[93] With the urban populations being the best educated, most politically attuned, and most socially dangerous because of their capacity to organize and riot, governments concentrated funding for mass public utilities in cities. Of course, their dense residential patterns also made urban dwellers easier to reach with public services. And health concerns over epidemics of contagious diseases made sanitation a generalized concern.

## Copper and Other Metals

So far we have stressed electricity's role in the Second Industrial Revolution's transformation of communications, light, and power. But electricity's newfound roles created demand for other economic activities that stimulated international trade. Employing economist Albert Hirschman's concept of "backward linkages," that is, prior activities necessary for later industrial production, we briefly survey the new needs and possibilities that arose for copper and aluminum.

Humans have found important uses for copper, which nature has widely distributed across the globe, since at least the Bronze Age (bronze is an alloy of copper and tin). Copper is an important raw material for implements and weapons. However, it fell out of favor as harder and more abundant iron took its place. Before the electrical age it was used mainly for coins and jewelry. But copper's ability to conduct electricity made it the logical source for wire (including telegraph and telephone lines) and motors.

In our period copper became essential in the most industrialized and prosperous countries that introduced electricity. Demand was so great that copper production grew twenty-four-fold between 1870 and 1938. One of the leaders in the electrical revolution, the United States, had the good fortune to have the some of the world's richest deposits in accessible areas, such as Michigan's Upper Peninsula and later Butte, Montana, and the Southwest. At the outset of our period the United States produced only one-seventh of the world's copper, barely a third of Chile's or Europe's output. Within fourteen years, US output had grown over eightfold to surpass all other copper-mining countries. By 1913 the United States mined more than 80 percent of the world's copper ore and smelted 60 percent of its output as production jumped another fivefold. Of its competitors, only Chile, Spain, and Russia had mines of any size.[94]

The sector continued to grow rapidly and diversify geographically after the First World War. While US production stagnated so that its share fell to one-third of world output, Canadian and Chilean mines doubled their output. Production in the Belgian Congo (today the Democratic Republic of Congo) and Rhodesia (today Zimbabwe) allowed Africa to become a major colonial copper producer, rising to over 20 percent of world output by 1938.[95]

The European electrical companies had to turn overseas for their necessary copper, because production in Spain and the USSR, which held the richest European copper deposits, could not satisfy demand. Some companies, such as the German giant Metallgesellschaft, invested in US mines through its subsidiary American Metal. Others partnered in colonies or other countries, or imported copper from third parties. In all cases, copper, used for the spread of the mass-produced electrical products, was characterized by oligopoly.[96] This apparent paradox was in fact almost a rule: widespread industrialized products aimed at the masses tended to oligopoly.

Technological advances had created synergies and demanded economies of scale. Vast copper mines became possible in the twentieth century as nitroglycerin was used to blow open pit mines and steam shovels and power drills were devised to exploit them. They built some of the largest mines ever made, usually in remote, sparsely populated areas. The cost of moving workers to these sites, purchasing heavy moving equipment, and laying rail to them meant that only a few companies with close ties to bankers and financiers were able to prosper. For this reason capitalists, like the Rothschilds, J. P. Morgan, and the Guggenheims, and major German banks like Deutsche Bank came to dominate the sector, with interests in numerous countries in the Americas, Europe, and Africa.[97]

Refining technology as well as mining costs led to domination by a handful of firms. Electricity not only needed copper to travel efficiently, it also provided the solution for cheap copper smelting through the "electrolytic revolution." New high-power generators developed in 1891 had to be large to be profitable. As a result, only twelve huge new modern smelters were built in the United States between 1891 and 1910. That was enough to produce a fivefold increase in copper production in the United States by 1914. The five largest copper producers in 1948 were the same as in 1917: Anaconda Copper, Phelps Dodge, American Smelting and Refining, Kennecott, and American Metal. These companies were among the first US multinationals (with the exception of earlier railroads in Mexico, and sugar and fruit in the tropics like United Fruit) to invest abroad; they built vast mines and smelting plants in Mexico, Peru, and Chile.[98]

Although some of the corporations attempted to establish company towns abroad to bring to their workers the "American way of life" (including perceived Protestant morality to order the private lives of their employees), they also unintentionally exported an unsought cultural value: the class struggle. Miners were some of the most politically active and organized workers in Mexico, Peru, and Chile. They created some of the most successful labor unions and helped launch leftist political parties in Chile. The 1906 strike in the Cananea copper mine in Sonora, Mexico, has been seen as a catalyst of the Mexican Revolution. Indeed, the argument has been strongly made by historian John Hart that anti-imperialist sentiments sparked by the flood of foreign investment after the later 1890s was a key to the revolution's outbreak, a position contested by many other historians.[99]

Certainly other copper mines did not explode in violence. But they did sometimes underpin the great divergence in lifestyle that was growing. Dennis Kortheuer has written about this clash of cultures in his study of the French Rothschild-owned El Boleo mine in Baja California. Illiterate miners from Mexico's heartland were brought to tunnel deep into the mountains of Santa Rosalia for copper that transmitted electricity for power, spread the written word through the telegraph, and lit the night in the United States. But the diggers had only dim candles to guide them through the dark caverns, because electricity was slow to reach the mine.[100]

It should be noted that the hunt for copper had the side effect of increased mining of zinc, nickel, silver, and lead. These minerals appeared naturally together with copper deposits, so that miners exploited them all and their worldwide use grew exponentially.

Electricity and copper also led to the expansion of a metal that would become important in the twentieth century, aluminum. To provide electricity in the United States, an enormous generator was built at Niagara Falls, New York. The energy generated by the falls' hydroelectric power attracted to the area some of the largest mineral and industrial processing plants, including heavy industries and food processing. The predecessor of the Aluminum Company of America (Alcoa) with financing from the Mellons, the leading venture capitalists in the United States, built a giant aluminum plant in 1895 at Niagara Falls to exploit the electrolytic process, which had been invented nine years earlier to reduce alumina (bauxite) into aluminum. It allowed the price of a pound of aluminum to drop from twelve dollars to thirty-two cents, turning the formerly costly product into an essential industrial input. This would earn Alcoa a monopoly position throughout the Western Hemisphere.[101] In Europe four firms produced 95 percent of all aluminum before World War I. Still a specialty metal, aluminum would become increasingly important for use in petroleum-based vehicles like the automobile and the airplane, and would find its way into packaging and household appliances, its use skyrocketing during and after World War II.

## Petroleum

Rock oil (petroleum) became a major new source of energy during the Second Industrial Revolution, though its true era of triumph came only after 1945 when it would overshadow coal. Still, already in the first decades of the twentieth century the race to develop and dominate world petroleum products, sources, and markets created some of the largest and most dynamic corporations in North America and Western Europe. It also sparked imperial rivalries among the Great Powers in areas formerly marginal to the world economy, like Central Asia and the Middle East. Petroleum would revolutionize transportation by introducing the automobile and the airplane.

In 1870, however, it was still not of major importance. Though petroleum had been known for thousands of years for its medicinal qualities and as an illuminant, the rather rare and volatile seepage sites where it appeared were too few to make it a major global resource. The breakthrough came when in 1859 an American, Edwin Drake, applied drilling technology initially developed for salt mining to seek pools of oil in the state of Pennsylvania. Turning oil into kerosene created an important international commodity.

One company, Standard Oil, controlled 90 percent of the refining capacity of kerosene by 1879. The company's prosaic name—by today's standards—was taken to connote a uniform, reliable commodity. They sought to set the country's and then the world's *standard* for oil products. Three years later Standard created the first "trust," a legal entity that combined numerous companies under a single management. It produced one-quarter of the world's kerosene. Through pipelines, special arrangements with the railroads, and eventually its own fleet of steamers and sailing ships, Standard came to control much of the distribution as well. Only later did it drill for oil.

Its founder and mastermind, John D. Rockefeller, was an enemy of "unbridled competition," preferring instead organized capitalism. He declared, "The day of the combination is here to stay. Individualism has gone, never to return."[102] Eventually Standard Oil would succeed so well at assimilating or crushing its competition that it became the largest corporation in the world.

That is, it was the largest until muckraker journalist Ida Tarbell aroused public outrage at Standard's market power. Amid an unprecedented wave of trust formation in the United States that witnessed the birth of 234 trusts worth $6 billion just between 1898 and 1904, Standard Oil refined over three-quarters of all US crude oil, four-fifths of its kerosene, and nine-tenths of its railroad lubricating oil. Outcries by Progressives led President William Howard Taft and Congress to take on the Standard Oil "octopus," breaking the trust in 1909 into eight different entities. But that was something of a pyrrhic victory. The successor firms continued to cooperate with each other. They did so well that most of them saw their share values double within a year of dissolution and continued to grow thereafter.[103]

Although most kerosene was used within the United States, the oil industry had an international orientation from its inception. Kerosene became the leading US manufactured export by the 1880s.[104] "Cracking" petroleum also yielded other valuable products: naphtha, asphalt, diesel, fuel oil, lubricants, petroleum jelly, paraffin, and last but not least, gasoline.

Gasoline's rise to prominence proved a godsend. It saved Standard from going the way of whale oil and beeswax producers when the demand for kerosene dwindled in the wake of Edison's 1879 invention of a reliable lightbulb and its diffusion as cities began installing electric lighting. In 1885 there were 250,000 lightbulbs in use; just seventeen years later there were 18 million. The automobile and the navies' and commercial ships' conversion from coal to fuel oil created massive new demand. By 1910 Standard Oil was selling more gasoline than kerosene.[105]

Thirsty vehicles did not drive the international race for oil. After all, the United States, which had by far the most cars, trucks, and planes, was self-sufficient in petroleum because of its rich strikes in Pennsylvania, California, Louisiana, Oklahoma, and Texas. After a brief scare at the end of the First World War, when a survey incorrectly predicted that the United States would run out of oil, there was no fear of insufficient domestic proven reserves. American oil companies looked abroad more because of fear of European competition.

Western European powers found no oil at home. On the continent only Romania had some. But as Churchill had said, the British needed oil, though more as a ship fuel than for cars. Without the navy, he intoned somewhat melodramatically, "the whole fortunes of our race and Empire . . . would be swept utterly away." More pointedly, he warned, "If we cannot get oil we cannot get corn and we cannot get cotton and we cannot get one thousand and one other commodities necessary for the preservation of the economic energies of Great Britain."[106]

Of course, the British, who imported and exported so much, were particularly vulnerable. But in the twentieth century the French, Germans, and Japanese also became concerned about access to oil, not only as a fuel but also as a raw material for so many different products. Initially petroleum was treated much as other commodities, with individual entrepreneurs such as the Nobels staking out the great strikes such as Baku in southern Russia.[107] The Rothschilds soon joined in, as did the Englishmen Marcus and Samuel Samuel. Eventually the major states became concerned with control of what was becoming not only a precious commodity but also a strategic one. The Dutch struck oil in Indonesia and created the Royal Dutch Company, which soon merged with British Shell, which initially had imported Russian oil but then entered Romania. A little later the newly expanded company bought up the Mexican Eagle Oil Company. After the merger the new firm was known as Royal Dutch Shell. In Japan the strategic implications of oil became increasingly acute in the decade before World War II. With no oil production of its own, Japan was largely reliant on supplies from the United States. Japanese engineers unsuccessfully drilled for oil in their new colony of Manchukuo in the 1930s and increasingly dreamed of building a "co-prosperity sphere" in Southeast Asia that would provide reliable access to oil sources.

A British-educated and Turkish-born Armenian go-between, Calouste Gulbenkian, played a crucial role in expanding the race for oil into the Middle East. He secured the concession to oil in Persia (today Iran), where oil was discovered in 1908. The breakup of the Ottoman Empire, Germany's ally, after its defeat in World War I, left the Middle East open to competition between the British and the French. (The German and Japanese dependence on oil from companies flying the flag of competing Great Powers would encourage their invasions of the Soviet Union and Indonesia during the next major war.) Recognizing its strategic importance for India and the rest of the British South Asian Empire, and particularly for supplying the British navy in the Indian Ocean, the British Admiralty and Parliament invested in the Anglo-Persian Oil Company. Later renamed British Petroleum, the corporation came to be an arm of the British government, implementing imperial policy as well as becoming enormously profitable to its other stockholders. Other Middle East kingdoms and emirates such as Iraq, Kuwait, and Saudi Arabia, which came largely under US influence, were only beginning commercial oil production in 1945.

Even before moving into the Middle East, US oil companies like Standard as well as wildcatters like Edward Doheny and the British Eagle Company had found ample oil in Mexico. When the Mexican Revolution broke out and foreign-owned oil concessions were menaced by nationalist regimes, Standard looked south to Venezuela. By 1938 when Mexican president Lázaro Cárdenas decreed the nationalization of oil companies, Mexico was no longer a leading international producer. Its production had been mostly channeled to domestic needs as Mexico's industrialization drive recovered from revolutionary upheaval.[108]

Mexico was not the first country to nationalize a viable oil industry. The Soviet Union had already done so. There the issue was not only one of anticapitalist principle, but also the fact that Communist activist and later dictator Joseph Stalin had gotten his start as a radical organizer in the oil fields of Baku. Elsewhere state takeovers of oil companies became common after World War II. Nationalist populists in Iran, Mexico, and Bolivia would take control of their oil sectors. Others would be undertaken by pro-capitalist and socially reactionary monarchies as in Saudi Arabia and Kuwait. By then the major oil corporations that initially fought the nationalization in Mexico, and later (1954) of BP by Iran, learned that they could live with and profit from state oil companies. The public–private divide has always been hazy in oil, as in many other strategic, capital- and technology-intensive commodities.

## Rubber

For the marriage of the auto and oil to succeed, a third commodity was needed: rubber. Roads were usually dirt and rutted from wagon wheels. For the auto to attract users, the ride had to be more comfortable. Even once asphalt and macadam pavement spread, something else was needed. Rubber, which had been known for thousands of years in Central America for ball games, was turned to broader uses in the early nineteenth century when in 1844 Charles Goodyear invented the "vulcanization" process of removing sulfur from the crude product. Once treated, rubber remained malleable and became stronger and reliable; now it was neither brittle in the cold nor melting in the heat. Rubber had been used for erasers to rub out mistakes (from which its name derived) and for golf balls. Soon it became widely used in overcoats, boots, and even condoms, because of its waterproof properties. But demand and supply were small. Goodyear died a poor man, his name appropriated by others who founded a major rubber company thirty years after his death.

The next invention, which also was the key to an industrial empire and which pushed forward wheeled transport, was the pneumatic tire, invented by a Scottish physician, James Dunlop, in 1888. Dunlop also made little money from his invention of the inflatable tire, as he sold the patent and his name to what became a leading rubber company. The pneumatic tire was instrumental in the bicycle craze of the 1880s and 1890s. Two- and three-wheel human-powered vehicles spread around the world because they were relatively cheap and fast.

However, the pneumatic rubber tire had to wait two decades before it was successfully applied to automobiles. Rubber tires with inflatable inner tubes greatly improved the ride of autos and bicycles, but they faced the continuing problem of wear and tear. The poor construction of the first tires, combined with limited paved roads, meant that the average car needed eight tires a year, quite an expense. Within a few years, though, tire life improved sixfold because of technical advances in production and public investments in better dirt and paved roads. In the United States the surfaced mileage of rural road and municipal streets doubled between 1904 and 1914, reaching over 300,000 miles.

Federal and state highways to connect cities added an additional 250,000 miles by 1938.[109] European paving also advanced rapidly. Petroleum, then, provided not only the gasoline to power autos and the oil to lubricate them, but the asphalt to pave their roads.

The bicycle and automobile revolutions stimulated great appetites for rubber—US imports jumped 25-fold between 1900 and 1929. Although latex is provided by many different plants, the boom centered on a variety of rubber species found in the Amazon Basin. Nature had graced Brazil with a natural world monopoly of *Hevea brasiliensis* rubber until about 1908, which allowed it to enjoy a bonanza as prices doubled between 1900 and 1910 even while the volume of exports continued to climb. Rubber trailed only coffee as Brazil's main export between 1890 and 1920.[110]

This stroke of luck caught the imagination of international observers, with stories of the great tenor Enrico Caruso performing in the elegant Manaus opera house a thousand kilometers upriver from the Atlantic, where the city's elite imported lavishly from Europe and sent out their laundry to France. But Brazil's fabulous experience during its rubber boom wound up an early episode of what later became known as "the Dutch disease." Nature had given Brazil stands of latex-bearing trees but had located them in an inhospitable and sparsely populated area. The boom would be short-lived.

Skyrocketing foreign demand and prices provoked an invasion of the tropics by thousands of rubber *seringueiros* (tappers), mostly men from Brazil's impoverished Northeast, in a hunt for stands of rubber trees. Supplied with hatchets and tin cups, each man collected latex by tapping trees along long roads in the jungle, about a hundred trees to the worker, and then cured it over a smoky fire. This was extraction or hunting and gathering rather than production; the trees soon tapped out because the inexperienced gatherers often cut too deeply into them, and new trees had to be found. Merchants, who had provided advances in the form of provisions and loans to attract many of the tappers, paddled or steamed up the tributaries of the Amazon to collect the scattered bits of cured rubber, but this did not revolutionize the production process. There were no economies of scale. In fact there emerged diseconomies because gathering could be increased only by extensive rather than intensive harvesting, that is, only by expanding geographically. Consequently, the more they produced, the further the *seringueiros* were from their Brazilian depots and European and United States markets. And many of the workers were more indentured servants or even slaves than they were proletarians. Except for frontier trading towns and a couple of modern, electrified outposts of European culture like Manaus and Belém, the rubber trade left little of permanence on the landscape. Its main geopolitical consequences were Brazil's purchase of the Bolivian province of Acre and its diplomatic consolidation of its borders with Amazon neighbors such as Peru, Colombia, Venezuela, and the French, Dutch, and British colonies in the Guyanas.[111]

Brazil's central role in the rubber economy was not a problem for the Americans and Western Europeans craving rubber, as long as auto production grew slowly. But as we have seen, Henry Ford's widely imitated inventions on the assembly line caused an explosion in the number of tire-greedy cars. Synthetic rubber was a complex proposition that defeated Edison's best efforts and yielded only a partial answer from DuPont. A major chemical company that had begun producing gunpowder by 1802, DuPont imitated some of the magic that German chemists were performing across the Atlantic in 1938, creating neoprene and nylon, which, together with cotton and steel, would become the main ingredients of tires. But before 1945 rubber was still so important to transportation that it was considered a vital strategic material.[112] Japanese goals in World War II were, in large part, the conquest of not only oil-producing but also rubber-growing areas.

Asia became involved in the world of rubber by imperial design, not by natural accident. Henry Wickham, a British adventurer and some-

A worker tapping a rubber tree with a machete, probably in Brazil before the bust of rubber's boom in 1912. Hundreds of thousands of migrants from coastal Brazil poured into the Amazon rain forest to use simple tapping techniques to harvest the sap of several latex-producing trees and plants. As the market for bicycle and automobile tires expanded, both foreign demand and prices for rubber skyrocketed, provoking an invasion of the tropics by thousands of rubber *seringueiros* (tappers). (Library of Congress)

time employee of the Foreign Office, managed in 1876 to secretly export from Brazil seeds of the *Hevea brasiliensis* and bring them to Kew Gardens in England. There rubber seedlings were raised and then sent to Ceylon and later on to Malaysia and Indonesia. This was a very dangerous and difficult process, little helped by the minimal assistance offered by the miserly British Foreign Office. Wickham's rewards were as sparse as the vitriol heaped on him by Brazilian nationalists was thick.[113] But within thirty years his scheme had succeeded in fomenting South Asian colonial rubber plantations funded by British and Dutch capital and worked by locals and indentured laborers from India and China. By 1912 their rubber exports exceeded Brazil's and within a couple of years overshadowed Brazilian natural extraction. By 1925 Asian plantations and small farms produced sixteen times more than Brazilian tappers.

Because rubber grew in fertile, populated areas of the East Indies, "native rubber" grown on small family plots of a couple of acres came to surpass plantation rubber. Rubber was the cash crop, but grew alongside food crops like rice, so growers were buffered from international market prices in that they could devote more family labor to consumption crops rather than rubber when prices fell. Political resistance was as important as economic logic in reducing the role of rubber estates and the scale of landholding, however. In Sumatra, Ann Stoler has shown, opposition to the Japanese invasion and seizure of lands led to small-holdings. But, she argues, these holdings ultimately were "brought within the vortex of capitalist control."[114] Auto companies could now buy plenty of rubber and benefit from continually falling prices. Even auto companies in Brazil now imported rubber from Asia.

Perhaps the grimmest episode of the rubber boom afflicted central Africa. Leopold II, king of the Belgians, was awarded a free hand over the Congo Free State by other European powers at the Berlin Conference in 1885, supposedly to squash slavery there and bring civilization.

Rubber (and ivory and mineral) exports certainly increased, but not enough to affect the world market much. The brutal, neo-slave-labor regime under Belgian colonialism, however, may have killed off as many as a fifth of the local population. It provoked international outrage from the likes of the Irish journalist Roger Casement, and it inspired Joseph Conrad's *Heart of Darkness*. Rubber profits built imposing structures in Belgium but brought death and disfigurement to Congolese workers.[115]

North American tire producers like Goodrich, Goodyear, and US Rubber were satisfied with the European domination of rubber supply, but some, like Harvey Firestone, feared that a British-Dutch cartel would drive prices back up. This, in fact, was attempted in the early 1920s under the British Stevenson Plan. The Dutch, however, refused to go along with price fixing, so an open market resumed after 1926.

Concern with British and Dutch control of the world rubber market led to some intriguing, but ultimately failed, experiments. The most famous was Henry Ford's "Fordlandia," a plantation and company town in the Brazilian Amazon. Despite serious efforts, the plan was defeated, not by governments or markets but by tiny pests that feasted on the leaves of the plantation's densely regimented rows of trees. It turned out that rubber could not be grown on plantations in Brazil, not only because of the scarcity of cheap labor but also because rubber was *native*, not exotic. Being indigenous, it was host to native insects and diseases that had developed along with rubber. In South Asia, neither had arisen, so trees could be planted close together. When joined with the large, poor, and accessible peasant populations of Malaysia, Indonesia, India, and China, conditions were ripe for successful plantation monoculture.

Efforts to exploit a different organic source for latex, the guayule bush, had only limited success. Farmers in northern Mexico and, in a little known episode, Japanese-Americans interned in the Manzanar concentration camp in California, cultivated guayule. These experiments were put to rest by political pressures and the success of petroleum-based rubber synthetics.[116]

Harvey Firestone had more success with his rubber plantation in Liberia, and efforts were made to plant in the Philippines. But production never made a dent in US demand. As with other key imports such as sugar and coffee, US policy preferred imports from closer "neocolonial" producers over a concerted effort to establish production in the Philippines colony.

CHAPTER THREE

# Commodity Chains

So far we have taken a rather traditional approach to the economic history of our period by outlining the sinews of the world economy in the period 1870–1945, its transportation, communications, and energy sectors, as well as by surveying the main industrial raw materials of the Second Industrial Revolution. Now to diverge from more Eurocentric studies, we turn to some key international *agricultural* commodities, such as wheat and rice, as well as stimulants, like sugar, tobacco, coffee, and tea. Examining the chains associated with these commodities will illustrate the particularities of change over time, the international variations, and the different effects within producing and consuming countries. We will see that participants in each commodity chain developed their own logic according to a wide set of conditions. Moreover, the nature of the relationships and exchanges in the chain usually changed because of technological innovations and ecological constraints.

The commodity chain approach makes us sensitive to the fact that there was not *one* world market, but myriad, often segmented, and ever-evolving markets. First movers were not guaranteed continued success. They often succumbed at a later moment to rivals. The US automobile industry's loss of dominance to Japanese and European producers in our day is just one poignant contemporary example that head starts were not necessarily insurmountable. Loss of advantage occurred in agricultural and extractive industries as well. Brazilian rubber, Indian jute, Mexican henequen, Chilean nitrates, Indonesian coffee, and even British textiles bore witness to a corporation's rapid changes in fortune. One economic historian has aptly called this merry-go-round of commodity boom and bust the "commodity lottery," underlining the role of chance as well as design.[1]

Moreover, market power, the ability to control the flow and prices of a commodity, rested with different actors along the chain at different times and places.[2] Indeed, the same commodity often participated in several chains with different end uses and destinations. This was the case when the Peruvian and Bolivian coca leaf, which inured Andean peasants to high-altitude sickness when chewed or drunk as a tea domestically, was converted to cocaine (and grown in Java) to become a local anesthesia for surgeries in Europe, the United States, and Japan, to flavor the soft drink Coca-Cola, and later to become a recreational drug in the cities of North America and Western Europe. Social and political attitudes also evolved, from seeing coca as a traditional marker of indigenous identity and an aid to strenuous labor of the working class; to viewing cocaine as a sign of modernity, a heroic medical commodity of the late nineteenth century, and a mainstay of the emerging pharmaceutical industry; to finally labeling the substance as an outlaw and international pariah today.[3]

As pointed out already, we do not assume that the world outside of Western Europe and North America was "peripheral" to the world economy. On occasion Latin Americans, and to a lesser extent Asians and Africans, were the price makers and developed the cutting-edge production technology. The global South—or at least enclaves in it—was sometimes dynamic and prosperous.

We intend to question the agricultural/industrial divide so common to traditional "modernization" accounts of this period. It is a remnant of an Orientalist or tropicalist worldview that implies a sharp break between "the West and the rest." Too often it is assumed that agriculture required sweat while industry demanded mechanization and capital. Agriculture is seen as nature's bounty, as the result of natural resource endowment, a crude raw material, while industry is seen as instead reflecting human innovation.[4] Consequently, agriculture is seen as growing incrementally over time, simply applying traditional methods to wider swaths of land, rainfall, and sunshine; industry, in contrast, develops, invariably bringing something new and creative to the production process.

The divide between agriculture and industry was much narrower than that dichotomy implies. Prometheus inspired both.[5] The processing of agricultural goods took place in the fields *and* in the factories. Steam, electric, and petroleum-driven machines for processing and transporting came to the countryside. There were remarkable botanical, chemical, and mechanical innovations in the rural sector, some of which would shape industrial processes in urban centers.

Indeed, agro-industry, which had existed already for four hundred years in the form of the sugar plantation complex, took firm root in numerous regions of the post-1870 world. Production of primary products almost tripled in the period 1880–1913, accounting for almost two-thirds of international trade by World War I.[6] This swelling of primary products complemented industrialization because Western Europe's urbanization and population growth increasingly led it to turn overseas for food and raw materials. Not surprisingly, then, by 1914 six of the world's richest countries in per capita terms were largely exporters of primary products: Argentina, Australia, Canada, New Zealand, Sweden, and the United States.[7]

At the start of our period, long-distance trade tended to be exchanges of exotics, goods that could be grown, harvested, or mined only in certain ecological niches. To bear transport costs and market transaction costs, they needed to have a high value-to-weight ratio. Before the widespread usage of steamships and refrigeration, and certainly before air transport, the goods had to be durable and relatively imperishable. Table 3.1 shows an estimate for the value of seaborne merchandise.

Although the large share that is not discriminated by item diminishes the analysis, Table 3.1 covers the most valuable transcontinental commodities. Those with high weight-to-value ratios, like coal, iron,

TABLE 3.1

**Seaborne merchandise, 1860–1887, by value**

**(in millions of pounds sterling)**

| Merchandise | Value |
|---|---|
| Coal | 410 |
| Iron | 480 |
| Timber | 660 |
| Grain | 1,050 |
| Sugar | 1,130 |
| Petroleum | 180 |
| Cotton | 180 |
| Salt | 18 |
| Wine | 510 |
| Coffee | 840 |
| Meat | 560 |
| Sundries | 24,982 |
| *Total* | 31,000 |

*Source:* Michael G. Mulhall, *The Dictionary of Statistics,* 4th ed. (London: G. Routledge and Sons, 1899), 130.

timber, and even cotton, were less likely to travel long distances. The world market clearly was not based simply on utility. Otherwise the value of coal, iron, and timber would have far exceeded that of sugar and coffee, and clean water would have been perhaps the leading commodity.

## Grains

The global market for wheat, which was one of the world's most important and geographically far-flung commodities and enjoyed some of the most advanced agricultural technology, provides a major case study of globalization in this period. The sheer magnitude of the wheat trade defies easy description, and the enormous amounts of grain in transit during this era stimulated all kinds of businesses related to transportation, storage, and marketing. This year-round crop developed a dense network of businesses related to transport and storage; it gave rise to standardized grading and a futures market that turned grains (and later many other commodities) into monetary abstractions; it led to innovations in processing, marketing, and advertising; and it brought boomlets to a variety of hard-fiber producers whose products were needed for binder twine. Most importantly, wheat, together with rice, fed cities throughout the world. So successful was it that even historic rice eaters like the Chinese and Japanese and coarse-grain consumers in Eastern Europe and the Middle East turned increasingly to wheat, often imported wheat. The most prominent wheat frontiers had a striking similarity: all were land-abundant and labor-scarce. But each region responded to those resource allocations differently, despite producing for an increasingly well-integrated national and international market. Wheat's central place in the world economy demands that we give it special attention. Its contrast with the other staff of life, rice, leads us to also give the Asian grain detailed study.

"Give us this day our daily bread" took on a whole new meaning between 1870 and 1945, thanks to a revolution in the global grains trade. The diet of millions of consumers worldwide was profoundly altered and enriched as declining grain prices and improvements in modern milling not only permitted consumers to choose from an assortment of bread flours and rice, but for the first time brought to the tables of the middle and working classes a seemingly endless array of pastas, crackers, biscuits, and ready-to-eat breakfast foods.

Pegging the start of a global grains trade is a matter of some scholarly dispute. Some fix it as early as the 1830s and point to falling cereal prices in Europe during that decade as evidence that continental farmers were responding to the distant drumbeat of competition abroad.[8] Although Russian grain exports via the Black Sea port of Odessa had served European markets for much of the first half of the nineteenth century, prior to the repeal of the (British) Corn Laws in 1846 most

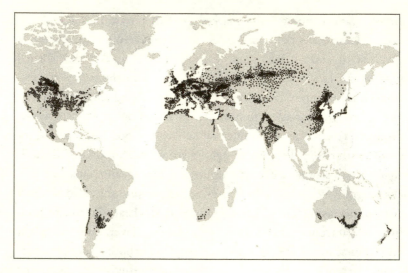

Global production of wheat, ca. 1913–1925.

countries remained largely self-sufficient in bread grains.[9] Grain price differentials between homegrown and imported grains may have been on the decline over the following decades, but it was after 1870 that a veritable tidal wave of cheap wheat, coarse grains (rye, barley, oats, and corn), rice, linseed, and alfalfa began moving across continents and seas, altering what Europe's proletarians ate while sending its farmers clamoring for relief.

Always a bastion of protectionism, continental Europe refused to go down without a fight. Determined to defend their tradition-bound farmers from the onslaught of cheap cereals from temperate settler societies on the Canadian and US prairies, the Argentine pampas, as well as the fields of Russia, Romania, India, and Australia, Western and Central European governments imposed stiff tariffs to stanch the flow of imported grains and to cushion the impact of falling prices on their farmers.

France's response was typical. Always a family affair, as late as 1921, 85 percent of its farms were twenty-five acres or less. French farmers were generally reluctant to embrace change or adopt new technologies, yet they insisted on government protection to insulate them from more efficient competition from abroad. And they were a very effective lobby. Politicians invariably came to their rescue: one observer wrote, "There is no tolerance by the French government of the proposition that wheat might be more cheaply imported. Every reduction of the wheat area is regarded as a national disaster."[10]

Interestingly, doubts about the relative merits of the trade were voiced not just in Europe. Even experts in countries dedicated to grain exports expressed reservations. Writing in 1867, an Australian extension agent pointed out: "To produce cereals largely beyond our own requirements for home consumption . . . will prove an extremely hazardous speculation . . . sending grain out of the country . . . is like selling a portion of our birthright—the soil's fertility."[11]

Doubting Thomases and populist protectionism, so prevalent for much of the 1870s and 1880s, however, were powerless in face of the onrushing market revolution. The continent's breadbasket increasingly was outsourced as population growth in Europe outpaced cereal production during the late nineteenth and early twentieth centuries. Once proudly self-reliant, Central and Western Europe by World War I were importing more than 30 percent of their wheat needs.

In Great Britain, where the dogma of free trade was not just empty rhetoric, little prompting was required. In 1883 *The Economist* did not seem troubled in the slightest by a growing dependence on imported grain:[12]

People think of the old days when the British harvest really fed the British people. Now we have to go further afield. A good wheat harvest is still as much needed as ever to feed our closely packed population. But it is the harvest already turning brown in the scorching sun of Canada and the Western States—the wheat already ripe in India and California, not the growth alone of the Eastern counties and of

Lincolnshire, that will be summoned to feed the hungry mouth of London and Lancashire.

Wheat acreage dipped from three and a half million acres to under two million acres in a little more than thirty years. By 1914, 80 percent of the United Kingdom's wheat and flour consumption came from abroad. Britain may have built tariff walls around its Commonwealth to keep other commodities out after World War I, but it arguably did more to sustain the global grains trade than any other nation, just as it was at the center of the tea and sugar trades. Between 1909 and 1937 Great Britain alone absorbed 30 to 40 percent of the world's wheat exports. That gave British grain importers, as one expert opined, "commanding importance" in the setting of international grain prices.[13]

Reduced transportation and insurance costs, low land and labor costs, the mechanization of agriculture, and a host of technological and scientific improvements in the cultivation, harvesting, transport, and marketing of grains all contributed to what economic historians refer to as "dramatic price convergence" in the global grain market. Improvements such as the standardization of grain varieties, inspection protocols, the increased usage of commercial as well as natural fertilizers (such as animal manure and clover), the periodic rotating in of crops that restored nutrients to the soil, like alfalfa and maize, and the adoption of early-maturing and hardier, drought- and rust- (or mold-) resistant varieties all prompted greater market integration and heightened productivity.

Plant breeders scoured the world in search of varieties that met local needs and created hybrids that combined the best attributes of different strains. As a recent study of biological innovation has demonstrated, specimens from the old periphery of cereal producers in Eastern Europe, Russia, and North Africa became the genetic building blocks for new varieties that then flourished in the settler societies of the Americas and Australasia. But scientific experimentation traveled no predictable path, as new hybrids moved in multiple directions. "By the early twentieth century the new generations of successful European wheats—distinct varieties tailored for the United Kingdom, France, Germany, or Italy—often contained germplasm introduced from North America and Australia." Plant breeders were celebrated for their accomplishments; for instance, the likeness of Australia's William Farrer, the nation's foremost wheat scientist, who experimented with "130 varieties of wheat under cultivation and had made approximately 1,500 crosses," appeared on Australia's two-dollar bill.[14]

Beginning in the 1830s, revolutionary advances in labor-saving farm implement machinery replaced the scythe and sickle. Cyrus McCormick's mechanical reaper, John Deere's steep plows, the twine or self-binding harvester that automatically gathered the grain up in sheaves, and the combined harvester-thresher (or combine) all increased productivity. The combine, powered by the internal combustion engine and petroleum, which first made its appearance in the 1890s, could cut a ten- to fifteen-foot swath through grain fields, lopping off the heads of the yellow stalks and sweeping "through miles upon miles of ripened grain." One knowledgeable writer waxed enthusiastic about this new machinery.[15]

> [It is] the most wonderful of modern harvest machinery; it not only cuts, gathers, threshes, and cleans the wheat, but even sacks the grain without a touch from man's hand; the only human labor is sewing up the sacks . . . one man can easily operate this machine, with a boy to ride the lead horse, and in one day it is possible to cut and thresh the grain from six to ten acres.

Estimates had the combine saving 3.6 to 5.4 cents a bushel.[16] The tractor, which followed soon on its heels, continued the mechanization mania.

These new machines made economic sense only where large areas of grain could be harvested, privileging land-extensive, labor-scarce regions like the North American prairies, the Argentine pampas, and southern and western Australia. As late as 1914 only 270 combine harvesters were manufactured in the United States; fifteen years later, 36,957 had been built. Similarly, the numbers of tractors on North American farms skyrocketed from 30,000 in 1916 to 850,000 twelve years later. Cereal production, as a result, became a much more capital-intensive undertaking. Fewer workers and draft animals were needed, the per-acre cost of harvesting was slashed, but much larger acreage was required to justify the expense.[17] Traditional grain producers, who had an abundance of labor or lacked an open frontier or the necessary infrastructure, chose not to mechanize, putting them at a decided disadvantage with their competitors.

Thanks to the telegraph and the transatlantic cable, international sales "that were formerly awaited for two or three months are now flashed by electricity over the whole world during the same day on which they are made."[18] Farmers, dealers, and speculators in the Americas or Australia had at their fingertips specialized and detailed data on how much wheat was in storage worldwide, what and how much was "afloat" on the oceans, and what their Russian or Indian competitors' prospects were for the next harvest (or harvests). Price differences between the home market and the grain exporter, which might have been ignored prior the advent of the cable, now presented golden opportunities for merchants and speculators.[19] As one observer noted in 1912:[20]

> If a telegram is received saying that the monsoon in India is overdue; that the drought in Kansas has been broken; that a swarm of grasshoppers has been seen in Manitoba; that a hot wind is blowing in Argentina; that navigation on the Danube is unusually early; that bad roads in the Red River Valley are preventing delivery; that ocean freights to China have risen; or that Australian grain "to arrive" is freely offered in London, prices rise or fall to a degree that corresponds to the importance attached to the news.

On one level this made farmers and traders more vulnerable to price fluctuations around the globe, but that susceptibility, as we shall see, would lead to the creation of futures markets that (at least in theory) spread risks and helped diminish the volatility of cereal markets. A new class of professional speculators emerged, willing to assume risks previously considered unacceptable to local and regional grain dealers or farmers.[21]

As a result, the price differential between British and American wheat tumbled from 54 percent in 1870 to zero at the onset of World War I, while barley and oats price gaps dropped from 46 percent to 11 percent and 138 percent to 28 percent, respectively, over the same time frame. Small- and medium-size European grain farmers, unlike their North and South American counterparts, may have been more reluctant to invest in American-made McCormick reapers and Deering binders, but they realized that their productivity had to improve and their costs had to be cut if they hoped to meet the competition and remain solvent. Rather than emulate their mechanized competitors, many European peasants either voted with their feet and headed across the seas to seek employment out on the burgeoning grain frontiers or switched to other cash crops, which, thanks to the liberal adoption of guano and nitrate fertilizers imported from Peru and Chile, respectively, were more remunerative.[22] The Americas benefited either way. The immigrants went mostly to the United States or South America, and until German chemists synthesized nitrates at the end of the nineteenth century, Peru and Chile enjoyed enormous windfall profits from their guano and nitrate exports, which for a while strengthened both states and gave a push to economic development. It also radicalized labor and introduced nationalist politics.[23]

Clearly this global cereal market did not exist in a vacuum; a rise in one grain's prices could trigger a corresponding increase in the price of another, especially in locales where the markets for different cereals converged. Given the enormous size of the wheat market, it became, in effect, the price leader of the trade in all grains. Under normal market conditions there was a correlation between its price and that of other coarse grains, such as barley and rye. But the same appeared to be true about wheat's relationship to rice, two grains that heretofore had catered to different clienteles. It may be an overstatement to argue, as one scholar does, that "rice and wheat were not separate markets, but together formed a basic market for food grains," but more so than in the past, price and availability, rather than preference, dictated what people ate.[24]

Improvements in water-powered milling during this period not only resulted in the grinding of more flour but improved the taste and extended the shelf life of certain varieties of wheat, opening the eyes and palates of German and Russian peasants, who were now more willing to supplement their customary allegiance to rye. The same could be said for Japanese and Chinese consumers, who continued to express a cultural and gustatory preference for rice but now were complementing their diet by producing and importing vast quantities of wheat for noodles. As anthropologist Sidney Mintz notes, preferences in diet and food habits are unpredictable and shift and change over time. "These addings-on and gradual eliminations are often hard to explain, for they proceed against a substantial, persisting stability of diet at the same time."[25] Prior to World War I, China imported 2,000 metric tons of wheat; by 1930 it was purchasing 580,000 metric tons a year; during the same time frame Japan almost quadrupled its imports from 93,000 to 350,000 metric tons. Japanese policy makers were so alarmed at this influx that they made food self-sufficiency a priority, and by 1935 domestic wheat production had increased by 60 percent.[26]

Wheat was the most valued and easily shipped of the boxcar lot of grains, and during this period wheat and rice became staples of preference for four out of five of the earth's inhabitants. Remarkably adaptive to heat, cold, and different soil types, wheat could be grown just about anywhere, from Sitka, Alaska, to Patagonia, save for the hot, low-lying regions of the tropics. Wheat even prospered at the equator; Ecuadorian and Colombian farmers successfully raised the crop in upland regions. It was almost indifferent to soil type, so long as the ground retained moisture. One expert was only slightly exaggerating when he opined, "It is as much at home in the sands of North Africa as in the 'black lands' of Russia."[27] The only region where wheat was un-growable was the lowland, monsoon belt in Asia, where it was shunted to highland areas.[28]

Wheat farming was not without its challenges. Susceptible to in-clement weather, winterkill, blight, rust, and insects, it encouraged farmers in temperate regions to diversify their holdings. Even so, fron-tier production would not be denied, as farmers overcame each of na-ture's challenges and world exports surged nearly sixfold from 130.5 mil-lion bushels in 1873–1874 to a peak of 747.9 million bushels in 1924–1929. Ultimately, with the notable exception of many parts of Latin America and Africa where maize still held sway, wheat's transcendence would relegate the other coarse grains to animal fodder (although barley was used to make beverages).[29]

By the end of World War II, more than forty countries were pro-ducing the ubiquitous grain, but, perhaps surprisingly, only a relative handful were active participants in the global grains trade.[30] China was the exception that proved the rule. Although statistics must be used with care, one estimate of China's annual wheat crop in the early 1930s was five hundred million bushels, making it one of the three largest wheat producers at the time. Yet little of that entered in-ternational trade markets. So production was not always synonymous with exports.[31]

It was, more than anything, the rise of an urban, industrial working class during the Second Industrial Revolution in Europe and the United States that helps explain this surge in demand and the export of enor-mous quantities of wheat from the grain frontiers. One might expect that falling wheat prices would eventually discourage producers in neo-Europes, but such was not the case. The worldwide growth of demand for bread flours, fueled by population growth and lower grain prices, meant that except for certain moments in the 1870s and then again in the early 1890s, the demand for wheat and flour continued to outstrip supply up until 1930. As a result, neo-Europes continued to increase acreage throughout the period. Prior to World War I, enhanced yield per acre best explains increases in productivity, but after the war a spike in planted acreage accounts for the increase in world wheat production.[32]

The Great Depression would put an end to this era of expansion, as gluts, production quotas, and higher tariff walls prompted a time of reckoning for grain farmers. Protectionism was back in vogue, as government or quasi-governmental control boards monitored transactions, provided farmers with subsidies, and established strict rules to limit the acreage planted with certain grains. Moreover, European colonials gave preference to their dependencies. In 1933 an International Wheat Agreement was reached by eighteen European countries and the big-four exporters to set export quotas and reduce acreage. But the best efforts of diplomats to regularize production were for naught, undermined by the absence of an enforcement mechanism. It was the mid-1930s dust bowl in North America, not international agreements, that (tragically for some) reduced the glut of surplus grain.[33]

It may be surprising that government regulation in some cases spurred greater productivity and capitalization though its intent was to insulate farmers from depressed markets. During the New Deal, economic historian Sally Clarke contends, farm sector productivity soared. American farmers, taking advantage of stable grain prices, new sources of credit, and changes in marketing by farm implement manufacturers, invested increasingly in tractors, combines, and trucks. Regulatory agencies gave farmers much-needed breathing space by providing long-term security against price fluctuations in the grain market. With prices stabilized, farmers were not as concerned about savings and more willing to assume debt.[34]

At a time when increasing numbers of rural Americans moved to urban areas in search of employment and the number of farms diminished, the size and scope of the remaining farms increased significantly. By investing in biological and chemical inputs, such as hybrid seeds, insecticides, herbicides, and chemical fertilizers, US farmers, despite operating under the constraints of bad economic times, were more willing to invest in costly machinery than they had been during the 1920s. Of course, taking on such heavy debts was a complex calculus. As Clarke notes, farmers not only replaced their horses and oxen with machines, but when they invested in a tractor, farmers made not one but a series of decisions.[35] Now they needed to buy fuel, lubricants, and repair parts rather than raise feed for horses. Horses no longer supplied manure; the farmers had to switch to commercial fertilizers. Moreover, they often needed to purchase additional land to better realize the machinery's cost savings. Thus, the capital-intensive, mega family farms that Americans are so familiar with today were the product not only of market forces, but also of calculated governmental strategies to bolster grain prices, credit, and productivity.

Given the ebb and flow of business cycles and wars, it is not surprising that there was a shakeout in the export trade during this period. Prior to World War I, Russia, Argentina, Australia, Canada, and the United States dominated grain exports. The Russian case illustrates just how difficult it was to maintain market share in such a competitive market. Before the war, Russian peasants continued to produce and consume rye for the domestic market. But wheat and barley were cultivated for export on the southern steppes on large estates and by wealthier peasants (who supplemented their holdings by leasing lands) on modest properties on the northern shore of the Black Sea where the black soil, even without the benefit of manure or fallowing, was so rich that it sustained higher yields. "Production for export, in competition with young countries of extensive farming," according to an agricultural economist writing in 1930, "did not contribute to intensification, especially in a country of small peasant farmers which, owing to the scattering of its production, was at a disadvantage with its competitors on the world market." The railroad gradually usurped river and canal transport, and storage elevators began to pop up at railheads in the late 1880s. But inspections and grading were not mandated, resulting in dirtier, damaged grain that fetched lower prices on the market. As a result, samples had to be sent abroad before foreign buyers agreed to the transaction. By the onset of World War I, exports of wheat were in decline, while lower-value barley exports were on the rise—not a harbinger of future success. Just as significant, Russian wheat exports to England, always its principal market, were losing out to competition from the Americas and Australia.[36]

Even so, Russia maintained its position as the world's largest wheat exporter in the years leading up to the First World War. But it had to rebuild its agrarian sector from the ground up after the 1917 Bolshevik Revolution and subsequent civil war, as production fell by almost half, prompting a virtual cessation of Soviet exports. The Revolution and its aftershocks also prompted a massive agrarian reform; large estates were broken up and turned into cooperatives and state farms, and the number of peasant households increased dramatically—from twelve million in 1905 to twenty million by 1924.

Desperate for foreign exchange and anxious to regain its preeminent position in the grains trade, the Soviet Union went so far as to collaborate with a New York–based capitalist philanthropy, the American Jewish Joint Distribution Committee, to move more than 150,000 Russian Jews from towns and cities in the Pale of Settlement in western Russia to the rich, black soils of the Crimean steppes and the southern Ukraine. From 1924 to 1938, the Soviets made available nearly two million acres of land, while the philanthropy provided $17 million in aid, tractors, and water-drilling equipment as well as their expertise in crop rotation and high-yield seed varieties. Although initially successful, the partnership between these strange bedfellows foundered during the 1930s, a casualty of Stalin's collectivization and industrialization impulse, the purges of the mid-1930s, and growing Stalinist xenophobia.[37] In the short term, collectivization proved profoundly disruptive to the wheat sector. Significant deficiencies in infrastructure, animal power, and farm implement machinery, coupled with a growing domestic population that consumed ever-greater quantities of grain, hamstrung the Soviet Union's effort to recapture its export markets.[38]

The Soviet Union's dislocation and devastation during and after World War I would be a windfall for the other four principal exporters, who during the interwar period collectively gobbled up Russia's prewar share of the market. During the War to End All Wars, the six great European powers had lost sixty million men, and the continent's soil fertility had been impaired. The result was a precipitous decline in continental cereal production and a fundamental reordering of the international grain market. Cereal producers untouched by the fighting leaped to the forefront. By 1929, Canada, the United States, Argentina, and Australia had cornered more than 90 percent of the market (see Table 3.2). European and Soviet agriculture did recover somewhat, although the latter would never regain its prewar position in the trade. But European cereal producers could not match their rivals when it came to yield, scale of production, capitalization, mechanization, or infrastructure. Still, economic nationalism and self-sufficiency continued to be championed across the continent, despite (or perhaps because of) their competitors' considerable comparative advantage.[39]

The United States had such a massive domestic market that it—along with China, among the major grain producers—was not reliant on exports. The population of the United States grew from 50.1 million in 1880 to 131.7 million sixty years later; more significantly for US

TABLE 3.2

**The principal wheat-exporting countries, by market share, 1909–1929**

| Country | Market share (%) |
|---|---|
| **1909–1914** | |
| Russia | 24.5 |
| USA | 16.4 |
| Danubian countries[a] | 16.2 |
| Canada | 14.2 |
| Argentina | 12.6 |
| Australia | 8.2 |
| India | 7.5 |
| **1924–1929** | |
| Canada | 38.8 |
| USA | 22.4 |
| Argentina | 19.4 |
| Australia | 12.1 |
| Danubian countries[a] | 4.6 |
| Soviet Union | 1.6 |
| India | 1.1 |

*Source: World Agriculture: An International Survey* (London: Oxford University Press, 1932), 75.
a. Principally Romania, but the figure also includes exports from other Eastern European countries.

farmers, during the same period urban centers grew from 14.1 million to 74.4 million. By 1940 more than 55 percent of the population lived in urban areas, a fivefold increase since 1880. In fact, as urban demand and population increased, the US domestic market garnered an increasingly larger share of the country's wheat sales. Exports fell accordingly from 23 percent of production in 1922–1927 to a mere 0.3 percent in 1932–1937.[40] That, coupled with high tariffs, made it difficult for competitors to crack the protected US market. By contrast, sparsely populated Canada and Argentina had much smaller home markets and had little choice but to ship their wheat and flour greater distances across the Atlantic, thereby incurring higher costs.

And distances mattered. Even though the US grain producers turned inward during this period, they and their Canadian neighbors had a powerful advantage over other wheat producers. Whereas Canadian and American producers only had to ship their grain exports 3,000 miles, it was 12,000 miles from Sydney to Liverpool and 6,500 miles between Buenos Aires and Great Britain. Grain shipments on clipper ships from California to England traveled 14,000 miles around Cape Horn and took four to five months. Even factoring in the time it took to ship wheat from the prairies to the Eastern Seaboard, Southern Hemisphere wheat, whether from the Southern Cone or from Australia, could take two to three times as long to reach market as wheat from its North American rivals. Australia could not have been a major player in the trade if not for improvements in shipbuilding techniques, the opening of the Suez Canal, and the adoption of the Great Circle Route in the 1850s, which took advantage of more favorable winds and currents between England and Australia, reducing the trip from 120 to 90 days. Steamships with larger carrying capacities replaced clipper ships in this long-distance trade after the 1880s.[41]

Despite such handicaps, expanding grain frontiers found ready markets in Western, Central, and Northern Europe, the Far East, Egypt, South Africa, and New Zealand. Unlike for most commodities, demand for wheat, as a necessary staple, was remarkably inelastic and remained predictably consistent despite frequent price swings; per capita consumption, with some minor variation, hovered around 2.5 bushels even during the depths of the Great Depression. The wheat market may have been susceptible to sharp fluctuations in price and periodic gluts, but that did little to affect overall production levels from year to year. Wheat was not immune, though, to the generalized slump in commodity prices during the mid-1870s, the early 1890s, and after 1920. As one agricultural survey noted in 1932, it was not overproduction but the importers' lack of purchasing power that precipitated the crisis; "the root of the farmer's difficulties lay in the general financial situation and in the general dislocation of international trade."[42]

The sheer magnitude of the wheat trade defies easy description: the average carrying capacity of boxcars in the United States during the late nineteenth century was eleven hundred bushels, and it was not unusual for trains to "haul sixty such cars." Minneapolis, which milled more flour than any other US regional distribution center, received upward of ninety million bushels annually, but that paled in comparison to its northern neighbor Winnipeg, which regularly handled more than double that amount.[43]

Great Lakes whaleback steamers, resembling Viking longboats, transported flour from Minneapolis or grain from Duluth or Chicago, carrying cargoes containing as much as three to four hundred thousand bushels. Transatlantic sailing ships, which once dominated the grains trade, gradually gave way to steam liners and tramps during the last few decades of the nineteenth century, because it was so much more cost-effective and efficient to move the vast quantities of grain by steamship. Tramps could carry the harvest of fifteen thousand acres of wheat land, while ocean liners could hold twice that. Within the Americas, however, the iron horse soon eclipsed water transport. In the United States alone, by 1876, 83 percent of all the grain transported to the Eastern Seaboard was sent by rail.[44]

More than any other improvement, the railroad opened up grain frontiers in settler societies, giving wheat farmers a cheaper and more efficient way to get their product to market and making it cost-effective to open up new lands for development. In some cases, development-minded politicians gave railway companies vast expanses of frontier lands as a subsidy, which the companies then made available to would-be farmers. Now instead of having to farm near fertile river valleys, farms sprung up along recently opened railway corridors. Farmers' expectations were raised as costs fell. Grain producers now thought in terms of filling boxcars instead of sacks of grain. "By the Civil War," as environmental historian William Cronon notes, railroads "could pull enormous loads at better than twenty miles per hour on end—far longer than horses or people could move a tiny fraction of that load at less than half that speed." Because railroads had such high fixed costs and because the costs of loading and unloading grain were the same whether the boxcar was hauled a short or a long distance, railway companies stood to realize larger profits (or smaller losses) on longer journeys. To encourage such long-distance shipments, railways offered discounts to more-distant grain farmers.[45]

Railway companies became just as reliant on hauling grain as wheat farmers were on the railroad. In Argentina alone grain was nearly 40 percent of total freight tonnage. This transport revolution also redirected the flows of grains. In the United States, Chicago became not only the gateway to the West, but the point of departure for midwestern and western grain shipments to the Eastern Seaboard and beyond. The same phenomenon developed over the next few decades, with minor variations, in Canada, Argentina, and Australia. In some cases governments proactively assisted their farmers by pressuring railway companies to cut freight charges. In Canada, where grain had to be transported great distances, policy makers drove down freight rates so that their farmers' wheat remained competitive, but in Argentina, where grain was carried hundreds rather thousands of miles to the ports of Rosario, Bahía Blanca, and Buenos Aires, the state was reluctant to pressure its British-owned railway companies.[46]

Given the enormous amounts of grain on the move, methods of storing and transferring the grain from rail to ship became indispensable. In the United States, railway companies, grain dealers, cooperatives, and in some cases individual farmers built massive wooden elevators at local and regional markets, at railheads, and at primary distribution centers. They not only loaded and unloaded the grain from and to wagons, boxcars, and the holds of ships, but stored, cleaned, dried, and gathered the wheat. Cronon has called the steam-powered

Unloading grain at the Great Northern Railroad elevator in Buffalo, New York, ca. 1900. Given the enormous amounts of grain on the move, methods of storing, cleaning, drying, and transferring the grain became indispensable. Major flour corporations built multiple manufacturing plants closer to the sources of production and sought out sites that reduced their transaction costs. Thanks to the rise in importance of the Great Lakes as a conduit for western US and Canadian wheat, and the abundance of cheap electrical power from Niagara Falls, by 1930 Buffalo was the world's leading milling center. (Library of Congress)

elevator, which got the grain "off the backs of individual workers and into automatic machinery," the most important innovation "in the history of American agriculture." Henceforth, grain entering primary markets like Chicago had to be sackless—"in this way corn or wheat were more like liquids than solids, like golden streams that flowed like water."[47]

Chicago became a first mover in the construction of terminal elevators, giving it a tremendous advantage over its rivals. "They [Chicago's distribution centers] can receive and ship 430,000 bushels in ten hours . . . in busy seasons these figures are often doubled by running nights." Public and private warehouses in that city could hold upward of fifty-six million bushels of grain, a study of wheat reported in 1912. Once it was inside the giant elevator bins, "workers could deliver grain to a waiting ship or railway car simply by opening a chute at the bottom of the building and letting gravity do the rest of the work." The cost of moving a bushel of grain from railroad to ship was half a cent.[48]

The advent of the elevator, railroad, and the steamship (and the resulting fall in freight charges and insurance costs) meant that land considered marginal at best for wheat cultivation was now considered ripe for expansion. In North America the frontier moved ever westward, as Minnesota, the Dakotas, and Kansas replaced Illinois, Indiana, Wisconsin, and Ohio as the top wheat-producing states. Across the northern border, Saskatchewan replaced its more eastern neighbors as the premier provincial producer on the Canadian prairies.[49]

## Breadbasket Variations

The new grain frontiers were by definition land-abundant and labor-scarce, historically considered unattractive backwaters before their future was synchronized to the wheat boom. At first glance, two of these new breadbaskets, Argentina and Canada, appear to have much in common. Both recently had achieved nationhood; each sought to replicate the path followed by US grain farmers; each had at its disposal vast public lands well suited for cultivation once indigenous groups had been summarily pushed out of the way, put on reservations, or annihilated; both featured highly speculative land markets that drove up prices; in each case, the railway system, which was initially paid for, built, and managed in the main by British companies, proved indispensable, not just in getting grain to market but in opening up new lands for cultivation; each enticed European immigrants to populate their rural hinterlands; they welcomed mechanization; and for the most part both fed the same market, Great Britain.

Yet even though they shared similar resource endowments, these temperate frontier societies are a study in contrasts, evolving in markedly different ways. Ever since Frederick Jackson Turner, scholars have debated whether frontiers, acting as a kind of demographic escape valve, fostered the yeoman farmer and a more egalitarian ethic. Theorists have posited that a tradition of family farms that took hold on the Great Plains and the Canadian prairies helped to inculcate a democratic and populist ethos. But not all grain frontiers were created alike, nor did they evolve in the same way. Argentina privileged large landed estates, tenancy, and an authoritarian tradition (as did Chile, Romania, Russia, and India). Argentine dependency theorists and some Canadian staples theorists contend that external forces (in Argentina's case, often in collusion with native landholding oligarchs) provide the best explanation for the failure of these vast regions, over the long haul, to live up to their potential. But Argentina and Canada were both reliant on British capital and markets, yet they took demonstrably different paths. It is the internal dynamic—land tenure, labor relations, infrastructure, and government policies—that best explains why and how different settler societies responded the way that they did to the global grain market.[50]

Pastoral pursuits—cattle and sheep farming—had dominated rural life in Argentina prior to the 1880s boom in cereal production. Fresh off a successful military campaign against Indians in the late 1870s that added 175,000 square miles to the national domain, the Argentine state moved aggressively to open up its great plains, or pampas, which extend in a large semicircle three hundred to four hundred miles south, west, and north of the national capital, Buenos Aires. Even though Argentina tried to emulate the US yeoman-farmer homesteading model, its bureaucrats had little appreciation for the value of regulation and oversight. Because of official negligence, coupled with easy credit and out-right fraud, a speculative land market emerged on the pampas that privileged large landholdings at the expense of family farms.

Some elite families, who initially had catered to the hides and jerked beef markets and then switched over the course of the nineteenth century to wool and beef production, gobbled up tens of thousands of hectares of land on the pampas. They were responding to the dramatic expansion of the international chilled mutton and beef market made possible by *frigorificos*, refrigerated steamships that brought relatively good-quality meat to Europe and especially England beginning at the end of the nineteenth century. So valuable did this become that some of the largest packing companies in the world, like Chicago's Armour and Swift, built plants in Argentina. They took advantage of new canning technology that used tin containers to preserve meat. Ultimately the packing industry would transform politics in Argentina as meat packers became some of the most unionized and militant workers in the country and a foundation of Peronism.[51]

But in 1924 the rural elite still ruled. In Buenos Aires Province, fourteen families owned more than 100,000 hectares each; one family alone acquired 412,000 hectares. As historian Jeremy Adelman writes, "the Argentine frontier, unlike its North American counterpart, was not an empty land on which the State could create a society of owner-producing agrarian units. Grazing antedated the movement to enclosure, and was a lucrative enterprise."[52] Because the State did not impede the concentration of land, cattle barons sold off their sizable patrimonies only when land prices were on the rise. Yet even if property relations precluded homesteading, that did not mean that Argentine ranchers were irrational or inefficient. Cereal production always had to compete with a prosperous cattle economy.[53]

Wheat would have to earn its pride of place on the pampas; skeptical cattle ranchers only grudgingly turned portions of their holdings over to agriculture in response to rising world grain prices. In their eyes, farming was always a secondary activity, a safety valve to turn to when beef prices were depressed. This prioritizing of ranching is perhaps also explained by the greater capitalization and labor inputs required by grain. And even after it became the nation's chief source of foreign exchange, wheat still had to vie with a number of additional rivals, including sheep, maize, alfalfa, and flax or linseed. Despite this crowded field of competitors, attractive wheat prices, state-sponsored European immigration, and government subventions for railway construction led to a surge in wheat production in the 1890s. Between 1890 and 1910, wheat acreage increased nearly fivefold from 3.2 million to 15 million, and by 1914 no settlement on the pampas was more than twenty miles from a railroad, making the region competitive with the US Midwest wheat bowl. Despite the considerable revenues wheat generated, the nation's skewed land-tenure regimen and the oligarchy's political clout made certain that this precocious newcomer never challenged ranching for primacy. No presidential administration between 1880 and 1930 enacted any substantive policies to aid wheat agriculture; land reform for smallholders was out of the question.[54]

Breaking the pampa sod was so labor intensive and costly that, to contain labor costs, cattle barons leased portions of their ranches to tenants. This reliance on tenancy was highly unusual; the wheat produced by its principal competitors was predicated on family farms.[55] Startup costs for Argentine tenants were modest. They, in turn, hired seasonal workers at harvest time, not infrequently "swallows" *(golondrinas)* who had emigrated from Italy or Spain to seed the crop or work the harvest and then return home. Government policies were redesigned to address the labor market, rather than to encourage immigrants to become settlers on the land. *Golondrinas,* who earned three to six times the wages of Argentine peons, traveled to Argentina after the fall harvest in Europe, worked through to February, and then returned home in time to plant in the spring. One should be careful not to overstate the importance of *golondrinas* for agricultural production; recent scholarship has documented the increasingly important role played by the domestic urban and rural labor sectors, which complemented imported labor on the pampas.[56] Nonetheless, the Argentine model of seasonal international labor migration for agricultural workers would not be imitated anywhere else until Mexican workers were hired in the United States under the US government-sponsored Bracero program during and after World War II (though temporary—if not seasonal— workers were brought a shorter distance overseas from India to work in tea in the neighboring British colony of Ceylon, as also happened with Haitian workers in Cuban sugar). Only in Argentina was agricultural labor sufficiently remunerative, because of labor shortages, and transport sufficiently cheap, because of vast exports, that this system of interoceanic commutes could work.

It may seem counterintuitive, but immigrant tenants turned out to be tough negotiators; they demanded land at low rents, and if ranchers did not comply, they had several good options. They could pack up after a few years and seek out lease arrangements on other ranches, return home, or seek employment in Argentina's urban centers. But tenancy also was beneficial to ranchers, giving them the flexibility they desired to respond to the vagaries of the market. During the 1920s, when beef prices collapsed, many ranchers converted their properties into grain farms, while others rented out parts of their cattle ranches and carried over their tenants' lease contracts.[57] When beef prices rebounded, however, more land reverted to pasture.

Argentines also eagerly embraced mechanization on the wheat frontier; 1,112 combines were imported in 1921, and by 1929 imports had reached 15,000. But a snapshot of "modern" Argentine wheat farming offers some jarring inconsistencies. A Canadian traveler writing in 1938 noted: "Among these southern and southeastern European tenant farmers one finds the paradox of a mud hut with a bench, a table, and a bed for furniture, but outside a combine harvester, a tractor and a motor truck of the latest models." To tenants, machines were mobile assets they could take with them if or when their current contract ran out. By 1936, combines harvested more than 65 percent of the wheat crop.[58] In fact, the Argentine pampas mechanized faster than its northern rival; Canadian family farms were slow to adopt the combine-harvester. The Canadian government actually worsened matters for its own farmers by setting extremely high tariffs on agricultural machinery to protect its farm implement manufacturers. That kept the costs of mechanization artificially high at home. But farm implement manufacturers, anxious to export their wares abroad, sold their machines overseas for well below what Canadian prairie farmers had to pay. The result was that Ottawa was "subsidizing the Argentine or Australian wheat farmer to assist him in competing with the Canadian wheat farmer in world markets."[59]

The absence of granaries in Argentina meant that marketing began right after harvest. The grain was transported in jute bags and then hauled along pitted country roads by enormous two- or four-wheeled carts with eight-foot wheels. Two-wheelers were hauled by up to twelve to fifteen horses or mules or by eight to sixteen oxen. Only the largest grain dealers had warehouses, so small farmers had to be content with piling wheat outside where it was exposed to the weather.[60] The inability to build an effective marketing system would plague Argentine grain farmers for decades to come.

The pampas had a warmer climate (with little danger of frost or snowfall except in the southernmost districts of Buenos Aires Province) and more fertile soil than the Canadian prairies, and lower labor costs, and its farms had the added advantage of being within two hundred miles of the nation's principal port, Buenos Aires. Their farmers did not have to absorb the cost of transporting their grain by rail across the continent, as their North American rivals did. But Argentines did not make the most of their natural advantages; unlike Canadians, they neglected to invest in agricultural research and education, and so their infrastructure lagged behind that of their competitors.[61]

Unlike in Argentina, where landowners had so many options about what to produce, wheat was king in Canada, the source of 50 to 75 percent of prairie farmers' cash income during the interwar period. A turn-of-the-century Canadian economist estimated that wheat was three times more important to Canada than it was to Argentina or Australia.[62] The fundamental difference between the two breadbaskets was that family farms predominated in Canada. To understand why such different paths were taken in what were in 1914 two of the world's richest countries, we must consider what each region looked like on the eve of their coterminous wheat booms. Unlike the pampas, where ranching on a large scale was a well-established way of life dating back to the early 1800s, the Canadian prairies offered thousands of square miles of open lands that ambitious policy makers were intent on populating and developing with white farmers.[63]

Canadian lawmakers thought they had an imaginative solution to the problem of populating the frontier in which the risks as well as the rewards could be shared with private interests. Ottawa doled out huge chunks of national lands to two companies, the Canadian Pacific Railway and the Hudson's Bay Company, which would in turn sell off that land to homesteaders. But the companies could not entice enough settlers to move to the prairies. Despite the railways' arrival in the western prairies, a raft of liberal land legislation, and a variety of inducements to colonists, Canadians and foreign immigrants were initially reluctant to take advantage of the public and private lands made available to them.

Cheap land was not enough. The principal problem was that the United States was a much more attractive option to European immigrants. Settlers did not begin to flock to the Canadian prairies until the mid-1890s, when a bevy of scientific and technological enhancements persuaded immigrants from abroad and migrants from the United States that grain farming north of the border was viable.

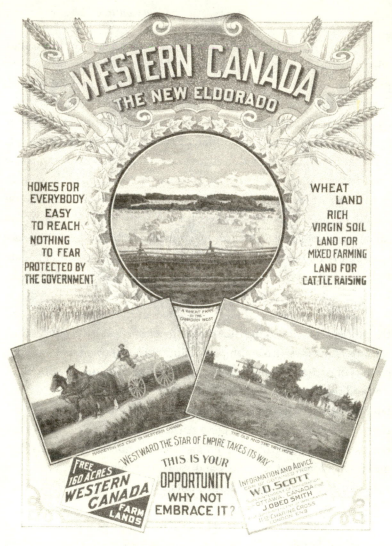

"Western Canada, the New El Dorado," a promotional poster produced by the Canadian Department of Immigration, ca. 1890–1920. The Canadian prairies were considered a veritable *tabula rasa*—thousands of square miles of open lands that ambitious policy makers were intent on populating and transforming into wheat farms. The government made extensive public lands available to the Canadian Pacific Railway Company and the Hudson's Bay Company, which in turn sold the tracts at low cost to Canadians and European immigrants. (Library and Archives of Canada, C-085854)

First, there was discovered a new strain of hard wheat, Red Fife, that matured twenty days earlier than the next earliest maturing variety—no small matter to prairie farmers who had to cope with the persistent threat of frost in late August and early September. At the same time, innovations in milling techniques made it possible to grind heartier, quicker-ripening varieties like Red Fife into flour.

Two additional innovations clinched wheat's rosy future on the prairies: surface mulching, a moisture-conserving technique that inhibited evaporation on the arid prairies; and dry-farming, which coupled summer fallowing with spring soil compaction to prevent "the passage of the moisture from the sub-surface to the surface by capillary action, thereby trapping the moisture on the soil, so that while the land lay idle, its moisture content would rise—theoretically to a level to sustain crops for at least two successive years."[64]

Recent arrivals from the States were more interested in obtaining a quick return on their investment and took advantage of surging land prices to flip their wheat farms rather than patiently waiting to build up livestock herds. The capital needs for a mixed regimen of livestock and grain were too great for most family-owned farms to bear on the prairies. Moreover, unlike in Argentina, government policies consistently privileged farming at the expense of ranching. Coupled with a speculative land boom that attracted American migrants from the Dakotas, Montana, and Wisconsin to move across the border, wheat farming took off. Interestingly, speculation did not concentrate land in the hands of a few, as it did in Argentina. Once locked in, wheat farmers found it disadvantageous to shift out of wheat.[65]

Canadian farmers were well aware of the pernicious effects of monoculture, but they felt they had good reasons for sticking with wheat. As one defensive Saskatoon farmer put it:[66]

I know perfectly well that continuous wheat-farming exhausts the soil, but I know that stock-raising, or at any rate dairy-farming, means continuous and hard work, and I know too wheat-growing requires less capital and less labor and gives bigger returns, and though there is a disadvantage in having all one's eggs in one basket, I am to take the risk and go on growing wheat until the soil will grow it no longer, and then I shall sell out to the tenderfoot and move west.

As a result, wheat became the engine driving Canadian exports. Between 1890 and 1916, the number of farms on the prairies increased from 31,000 to 218,000, while improved acreage soared from 1.4 million to 34.3 million acres. Ultimately, after the frontier had reached its limits, the ecological consequences of monoculture would become all too apparent, but from 1890 to 1945, sowing wheat on the prairies made good economic sense.

Although the Argentine and Canadian governments both aggressively sought European immigrants to populate their hinterlands, their objectives and policies were very different. Argentina's immigration policies were much less selective, because they were not predicated on creating a permanent rural landholding class. Initially Argentine policy makers wanted to attract northern European immigrants, but they quickly settled on southern Europeans, who came cheaper and were willing to work seasonally. Canada's immigration policies were much more restrictive and ethnically discriminating. Ottawa was less interested in creating a fluid and efficient labor market and was more intent on creating family farms on the prairie.

Another salient difference between these two large wheat producers was the cooperative ethic that crystallized on the prairies. The Scandinavian, British, and Central European immigrants who established family farms on the prairies had experience with consumer cooperatives in Europe and, being capital-poor, were willing to pool their resources. By the 1920s the cooperative movement, which pooled members' grain sales, stored their grain, and functioned as a mutual aid association, was firmly entrenched in the wheat-growing districts of western Canada. In contrast, ephemeral tenancy arrangements on the pampas did not lend themselves to collaboration. As a result, Canadian farmers' standard of living and quality of life improved markedly during the 1920s, far exceeding any improvement for their Argentine counterparts.

This brief comparative sketch of these twin breadbaskets illustrates that not all grain producers were created alike, nor did they evolve in the same way. Despite similar resource endowments, domestic forces—such as land tenure, labor systems, and state policies—shaped how Argentina and Canada responded to a highly competitive global grain trade.

Imperial ambitions also tried to shape the grain sectors of colonies. British India's wheat producers on the dry plains of the Punjab were greatly aided by the opening of the Suez Canal in 1873, but railways were slow to make headway across the subcontinent and "the traveler still saw the long lines of camels that were silently and majestically treading their way through the night across the plains to the seaports, in successful competition with the railroads as grain carriers."[67] Although India never satiated the United Kingdom's appetite for grain, it was not for lack of trying. British entrepreneurs invested heavily in railways and canals in the Ganges and Indus River valleys where wheat had been grown for centuries, but much of the wheat they produced stayed at home to feed India's burgeoning population, and the trains mostly carried Indian passengers.[68]

The planting and harvesting of wheat may have been a seasonal preoccupation for farmers, but the trade itself barely enjoyed a respite. Somewhere around the globe farmers were harvesting wheat each and every month of the year, making it possible to stagger the arrival of wheat and flour shipments to ensure that Europeans and other importing nations would not go hungry (see Table 3.3).

One observer of the trade writing in 1911 described when and from where Europeans got their daily bread.[69]

TABLE 3.3
**The global wheat harvest calendar**

| Month(s) | Harvest area |
| --- | --- |
| January | Australia, New Zealand, Chile |
| February–March | Upper Egypt and India |
| April | Lower Egypt, India, Syria, Cyprus, Persia, Asia Minor, Mexico, Cuba |
| May | Texas, Algeria, Central Asia, China, Japan, Morocco |
| June | Western, midwestern, and southern USA, Turkey, Greece, Italy, Spain, Portugal, southern France |
| July | Midwestern USA, northern Canada, Romania, Bulgaria, Austria, Hungary, southern Russia, Germany, Switzerland, southern England |
| August | Midwestern USA, southern Canada, Colombia, Belgium, Netherlands, Great Britain, Denmark, Poland, central Russia |
| September–October | Scotland, Norway, northern Russia |
| November | Peru, South Africa, northern Argentina |
| December | Argentina, Burma, Australia |

*Source: The Crop Reporter, 1899, cited in Peter Dondlinger, The Book of Wheat: An Economic History and Practical Manual of the Wheat Industry (New York: Orange, Judd Co., 1912).*

For the greater part of the year there is surplus wheat awaiting shipment on some port on the American coasts, by January and February the wheat exports from the Pacific coast of the United States have begun to arrive in Europe in considerable quantities; in March, the wheat ships from Argentina and Uruguay are arriving in Europe with their first cargoes of importance; winter wheat of the United States first reaches the ports of Western Europe in August; U.S. spring wheat begins to cross the Atlantic in considerable quantities in October, and Canada spring wheat in November.

To the serendipitous constellation of forces that propelled the transformation of the international grain market, we must add one more critical enhancement that arguably was more critical in propelling the expansion of the trade than any other single factor—the futures market.

## Hedging Futures

Futures not only greased the wheels of credit, they sustained a continuous, year-round market, thus making possible the sale of much larger quantities of grain than ever before.[70] The principal innovation was to facilitate future delivery of grain through standardized contracts. Now farmers, millers, jobbers, and exporters had an incentive to store grain throughout the year. By buying a bushel of wheat that did not yet exist, a merchant was not only taking a risk, but also reinventing the concept of property rights. As we shall see, commodities like wheat became useful tools to gamble on, whether or not that bushel of grain ever left the farm. Along with its contemporary, the cotton exchange, the grains futures market laid the foundation for a dizzying array of commodity futures markets, for everything from pork bellies to orange juice and coffee. Multimillion-dollar transactions among strangers continents apart soon replaced a handshake between a farmer and a wholesale jobber. Moreover, futures contracts also acted as a hedge against volatile prices, always the bane of grain markets.

To accomplish this, private grain exchanges, like the Chicago Board of Trade (CBT), imposed a uniform system of weights and measures (with penalties prescribed for offenders) to bring order to what had been a very decentralized and unregulated market. As one expert put it in 1911, without futures markets "the grain trade would be chaos."[71]

In 1856 the CBT set quality standards for three types of wheat. That seemingly simple step proved revolutionary. If a shipment of grain received a certain grade, it could be mixed in elevators or boxcars with other shipments of the same grade. For all intents and purposes it was considered identical. Now when farmers or grain dealers shipped their grain to market, they obtained a receipt that they or anyone else could redeem for payment. These contracts allowed farmers to secure credit from their local bank by simply presenting a "to arrive" contract to the lender, specifying that a certain amount of grain would be delivered at a specified date in the future. These markets proved so successful at increasing sales of grain, raising capital, and managing the trade that a futures market was added in Liverpool in 1883 and in Buenos Aires in 1908.

A futures market could not have come about if warehouse, boxcar, or elevator receipts for specific lots of grain did not mean the same thing in Liverpool as in New South Wales. When an elevator receipt was as good as the bushels of wheat it represented, then and only then was it possible to buy a contract for the future delivery of a good and be reasonably certain that the buyer would get what he was promised. By 1860 the CBT had identified ten different grades of wheat; quality standards were soon mandated for other coarse grains. By the mid-1880s, the volume of Chicago's futures market was fifteen to twenty times as large as the city's actual grain sales, strong evidence that it was the pieces of paper, not wheat or corn, that speculators were buying.[72]

Because futures contracts had less to do with the sale of the commodity and more to do with the price of those goods at a future date, speculators gambled on whether or how much grain prices would rise or fall. Such arbitrage and fungible grain receipts, of course, could not have become a reality unless sufficient storage capacity, financing, and the necessary transportation and communication infrastructure existed to permit continuous deliveries of grain year-round. Whereas in the past, grain dealers had to build in a substantial margin of five to ten cents a bushel to guard against prices dropping, now, thanks to the opportunities for arbitrage and the standardization of the trade that made it possible, margins were reduced considerably to perhaps a penny per bushel. By trading in futures, at a certain price for a certain grade of grain, risks were shifted theoretically from the farmer and dealer to the speculator, who then offset his exposure by hedging transactions to insure against losses.

Justice Oliver Wendell Holmes welcomed this innovation, noting that, although "speculation does result in evil consequences," governments should be prudent about if and when they meddled in the operation of these markets. In his mind, these self-regulating institutions were proof positive that capitalism had matured.[73] Farmers on the plains likely would find much to disagree with in Justice Holmes's survival-of-the-fittest mentality. Holmes's assertion that "the success of the strong" induced "imitation by the weak" was, however, more than just elitist rhetoric. It reflected a liberal worldview that held that markets control people rather than the other way around.

Unfettered markets, however, invited abuse. After all, the two markets—the actual grain market and the futures market—were, in fact, linked to each other, as tenuous as those ties might seem to be. This became all too apparent when bulls, speculators confident that prices would rise, attempted to "corner" the market. A corner might begin harmlessly enough with bulls quietly buying up futures contracts just before the harvest season, when supplies were at their lowest. Then they would move into the actual grain market, buying up sizable quantities of "spot" wheat as well. Now bulls had control of both present and future supplies of grain. If this was accomplished surreptitiously enough, unsuspecting bears, those who believed that future prices would fall, could be caught unawares. If a bear speculator could not make good on his futures contracts and deliver the grain, he had little choice but to buy grain from bulls who now dictated prices. If bears failed to fulfill their contracts, they could be subject to legal action, their reputations ruined.

Corners, however, entailed significant risks for bulls too. Those stockpiles of actual grain had to be disposed of eventually; holding on to such large quantities of grain indefinitely was costly, but selling them off was risky because putting all that grain up for sale meant that high prices could not be sustained. If bulls could not sell off their grain before prices fell below what they bought the grain for, they faced major losses.

At first glance, the winners or losers of a corner appeared to be confined to speculators playing the futures market. But there were residual effects that could either help or harm all those connected to the grains trade. Any time a market was intentionally distorted, it undermined confidence up and down the grain chain. Successive corners so infuriated the German government that it banned futures trading on the Berlin Exchange in 1897. Most efforts to regulate the trade, however, proved ineffectual; speculators simply picked up and moved their business to another exchange. Meanwhile, farmers and dealers watched helplessly as prices fluctuated up and down with little apparent connection to supply and demand.[74]

With so much out of their control, it is understandable why growers organized to defend their interests by establishing cooperatives like the Grange and by backing populist politicians. They had little faith in the market and little trust in bankers or railroad tycoons. Grading was a subjective matter at best. Farmers were convinced that unscrupulous speculators, railway and elevator operators, and state grain inspectors were conspiring to lowball their grain.

## Sealing and Resealing Boxcars

Given the daunting scale of the trade and the relative speed with which it covered enormous distances, oversight to maintain standards and inhibit fraud was essential and increasingly sophisticated. The time and money spent on the maintenance of these protocols were a testament to the cereal trade's budding professionalization and the potential for abuse. Unscrupulous jobbers invariably tried to hide "plugged" (inferior, dirty, or damaged) grain underneath better-quality grain in railway cars or in grain elevators. Too much was at stake for farmers, brokers, millers, railway and elevator operators, shippers, millers, futures traders, and consumers to allow any one of the principals too much latitude.[75]

The linchpin of protocol enforcement in the United States was the state inspector. Walking encyclopedias of wheat minutiae, inspectors had the exacting task of evaluating grain for "color, soundness, and the plumpness of the kernel" in each and every boxcar that arrived at major distribution centers. They tested the weight and determined the grade, providing written justification for their assessment.

Invariably there were complaints from both sellers and buyers about the grades assigned. Elevator operators and railway companies were the usual suspects, accused of mixing grades and tampering with weight scales. Grain making the long forced march across the heartland might be inspected anywhere from three to six times. During a busy time of year, it was not unheard of for a million to a million and a half bushels a day to be inspected and weighed at the Duluth, Minnesota, distribution center. In general, inspection delayed the shipment of grain by one day, so inspection was clearly not too meticulous.[76]

Elsewhere government oversight was lacking. In Argentina, for instance, no state inspection protocol was in place; instead, representatives of buyers would appear at railway stations and personally inspect the jute bags hauled by peons to railway cars "by means of a 'tryer,' a pointed tube that is thrust into each bag bringing out a section of its contents." Buyers often would fix their own standards to the grain, guaranteeing greater variability and more complaints.[77]

The absence of standards put outliers at a competitive disadvantage, as uniformity was prized. But there were limits to this drive for standardization. Wheat may have dominated the diet of much of the world during this era, but certain regions asserted their preference for one or more of its rivals. Barley was king in North Africa; maize the staple of choice in much of the Americas and Africa;[78] rye held sway despite inroads made by wheat in Eastern and Central Europe; and, of course, rice, with the exception of some parts of China and India, had no peer in South, Southeast, and East Asia. With the exception of rice, wherever wheat was preeminent the grains that were its competitors were consigned largely to livestock fodder.

## From Millstones to Minneapolis

Consumption of flour increased dramatically during this period, thanks to a slew of innovations that altered the production, distribution, and marketing of bread. Sadly, there were casualties. Millers in particular became an endangered species, as the mass production of flour transformed what had been craft into an industry.

For centuries the making of flour rested in the hands of experienced millers. To mill wheat, skilled artisans furrowed their sandstone millstones with sharp edges, set the stones close together, and ran them at a very high speed. The objective was to grind once through as fine as possible. Popular wisdom had it that millstones were quirky and temperamental, supposedly feminine traits.[79] Only the most practiced millers, who understood their particular stones' idiosyncrasies, could coax sufficient quantity and superior quality out of such finicky machinery.

Beginning in the 1870s a series of innovations was introduced in flour mills springing up along the banks of the Mississippi River near Minneapolis, Minnesota. Taking advantage of the thunderous waterpower cascading down the Falls of St. Anthony, Charles Pillsbury and Cadwallader Washburn's mills refined and improved upon Hungarian and French techniques of milling, and in the process radically transformed how flour was produced worldwide.[80]

In this case, necessity was the mother of invention. Minneapolis millers had ready access to hard spring wheat in their home state and the neighboring Dakotas. This variety, although higher in protein and more gluten-rich than its chief competitor, winter wheat, was harder to grind and more difficult to sift to remove impurities. The most notable change the Minneapolis manufacturers made was to switch from millstones to automatic steel rollers, a modification that produced superior, cleaner, and more uniform flour in greater quantities at reduced costs. The corrugated rollers did 30 percent more work but required 47 percent less power. Where millstones had to be redressed twice a week, the steel rollers ran for months without the need for adjustment.[81]

New techniques were developed to recover valuable elements of the kernel left on the mill floor. Termed "gradual reduction," these extra steps necessitated additional machinery, oversight, and, of course, expense, but gains in productivity more than offset the added cost. Milling now was entirely mechanized and automatic; "from raw material to finished product the stock is treated without the direct intervention of human hands."[82] Gradual reduction demanded copious amounts of energy. New sources of power—first steam and then electricity—were adopted over a period of time to sustain the more complex industrial plants.

At first critics ridiculed Cadwallader Washburn for sinking the unheard of sum of one hundred thousand dollars into his first mill. Even though "Wash-burn's Folly" experienced some costly growing pains, it was the entrepreneur who enjoyed the last laugh.[83] The innovations were a revelation, especially for farmers in Minnesota, Dakota, and Canada; formerly unpopular with millers and bakers, hard spring wheat was now the bread flour of choice at home and in Europe. Flour produced in Minneapolis by the "New Process," as it was called, produced 12.5 percent more bread, on average, than the best winter wheat flours on the market. Milling capacity skyrocketed. In 1870 a large mill might produce two hundred barrels of flour a day; two decades later, three out of four Minnesota mills were producing more than a thousand barrels a day.

Better-capitalized, high-capacity mills bought their wheat in bulk from farmers and elevator operators and benefited from rebates and an array of transit privileges from railway and shipping companies.[84] Economies of scale also enabled big mills to better service the burgeoning overseas market. By the turn of the century, Minneapolis millers were shipping out sixteen million barrels a year and the city could lay claim to being the greatest flour producer in the world.

Critical to Minneapolis's ascendancy was its commitment to export its flour abroad, especially to Great Britain. By 1880 the United Kingdom absorbed three-fifths of US flour exports; Minneapolis exports alone rose from one million barrels in 1881 to 4.7 million barrels in 1900, much of it to the United Kingdom. In addition Minneapolis flour found its way to Western Europe, Hong Kong, the Philippines, Cuba, Brazil, Haiti, and Jamaica.[85]

The New Process consigned the age-old craft of artisanal milling to the dustbin of history. It also led to a fundamental reorganization of the flour-milling industry. Experienced millers now found work in large factories as mill managers, while captains of industry with no prior experience in the business took control. Over time Pillsbury's and Washburn's flour mills became two of the world's largest manufacturers, and their brands of flour (Pillsbury and Gold Medal, respectively) not only became mainstays in North American pantries, but were aggressively marketed abroad.[86] Not surprisingly, the high costs associated with mass production and the smaller mills' inability to compete with industry giants at virtually every phase of the commodity chain signaled the death knell for smaller flour mills. In Minneapolis alone, by 1890 four corporations had secured 87 percent of the city's milling capacity.[87]

Foreign investors thought they knew a profitable undertaking when they saw it. Pillsbury, already a well-known brand in England, attracted the interest of a British syndicate in 1889. The syndicate had invested heavily in US railroads and breweries and now turned its attention to flour milling. The investors took control of three of Pillsbury's mills, two additional Minneapolis flour mills, two waterpower companies, and the Minneapolis and Northern Elevator Company. Charles Pillsbury did retain managerial control of the flour mill itself and held significant stock in the new company. As with other Gilded Age industries, however, combinations in the flour business met with considerable resistance and sometimes collapsed under their own weight. Overbuilding, gluts in production, price cutting, low profits, and fierce competition undermined the conglomerates' efforts to corner the market. The British intervention in the Minneapolis flour market proved relatively short-lived. In 1924 the Pillsbury family and other American investors refinanced and absorbed the British holding company.[88]

Despite the obstacles, the lure of consolidation proved irresistible for Washburn's successors at Washburn-Crosby. In 1928 General Mills was born in a massive merger of milling companies in the US Midwest, Southwest, and far West. The conglomerate absorbed twenty-seven companies from sixteen states, making it for that time the largest flour-milling company in the world.[89] (In the United States the name "General" came to signify dominant rather than ordinary, as enormous corporations such as General Motors, General Electric, and General Foods arose.)

Although economic historians disagree on why these combinations occurred during the Gilded Age and what their relative impact was at home and abroad, they generally concur that such consolidations were part of a "managerial revolution"—a revolution that would effectively alter the structures of all kinds of businesses throughout the world.[90]

These capital-intensive industries proved effective only if they fashioned an efficient managerial hierarchy that coordinated purchasing, pricing, production, and marketing. Salaried managers developed long-term and short-term strategies to integrate their enterprise vertically. Integrating "backward," they secured access to raw materials; linking "forward," they created a modern, responsive sales organization to market their goods and services efficiently.[91] General Mills' predecessor, Washburn-Crosby, went national as early as 1882, opening up a sales office in Boston, and it was the first to buy advertising space for its product—in the *Ladies Home Journal* in 1893.[92]

Competition reared its head abroad as European governments turned increasingly protectionist and raised tariffs, while making a greater effort to import more of their flour from their colonies, or, in the case of the United Kingdom, from Commonwealth nations. Nor did it take long for English millers to adopt the New Process; by 1905 Great Britain, always the United States' best customer, was importing only half as much flour as it had in the previous two decades. Canadian manufacturers like Ogilvie Flour Mills moved into the British market. Indeed, the heyday of US flour exports proved short-lived, as exports declined from twelve million barrels a year in 1911–1914 to a low of less than five million barrels during the Great Depression.[93]

Branding and packaging became two cornerstones of the flour industry's efforts to beat competitors. Pillsbury and General Mills' determination to brand their own flours met with success, proving that they could market their products directly to the consumer. In this way, they bypassed nettlesome jobbers who heretofore had promoted their own brands and dictated their needs to the manufacturers. The goal of branding was to connote uniformity and reliability to the consumer. Pillsbury's xxxx brand, for instance, was consciously chosen to invoke medieval bakers who had marked their flour for communion wafers with crosses. Packaging size was reduced over time to 2.5-pound bags to better service retail customers. Wholesale and retail markets became more segmented over time, owing to the growing demand for different types of flour (e.g., whole wheat, cracked wheat, oat flour, cornmeal, and buckwheat flour) destined for home use and commercial baking. Increasingly, manufacturers were asked to blend flours to precise bakery specifications.[94]

The massive amounts of wheat processed meant that science became the new standard of expertise. Whereas flour buyers in the past had judged the raw material by color, odor, and appearance, now flour's chemical properties (especially its gluten content) were subjected to rigorous testing in factory laboratories. Large batches of wheat ema- nating from different sources, even if they were of the same general quality, varied in moisture and protein content. Ensuring uniformity under these conditions was not without its challenges. The wheat first had to be tempered or conditioned by adding or subtracting moisture, and then impurities were removed before grinding could begin, all under the watchful eye of experienced technicians.[95]

Technicians also were preoccupied with the flour's color, because dealers and customers apparently judged quality by its whiteness. Arti- ficially bleached flour first made its appearance in England in 1879 and then in the United States in 1904, as nitrogen peroxide was applied to the flour to make it appear whiter.[96] It soon became the industry stan- dard, despite protests from critics who claimed it was unfit for human consumption. Although the milling industry spent vast sums to rebut the charges and publicized their technical reports, which insisted that bleaching did not alter the flour's basic properties, Progressive-era re- formers passed the Pure Food and Drug Act in 1906, which mandated that bleached flour had to be so labeled.[97] Gadfly journalist Dorothy Thompson did not hold back, lambasting the white-flour bread mar- keted by commercial bakers as "a sickly, bleached-blonde, airy, quick- staling, crustless, sweetish, sticky mass."[98]

Mass production was unkind to millworkers, as conditions inside the mills were straight out of Dickens's *Hard Times*. A labyrinth of conveyers, elevators, chutes, and clattering machines, the new flour mills were an assault on the senses. The noise was deafening, "the per- sistent sweetish smell and taste cloying," working in the summer was especially stifling, and the flour dust lingering in the air not only made it difficult to breathe but proved hazardous to workers' health.[99] Mul- tiple operations in succession generated vast quantities of flour dust inside the factory walls. In one of the largest Minneapolis mills, "three thousand pounds of dust were collected every day from two dust

rooms on a floor underneath the millstones." Unchecked, flour dust—
"air so thick that one often could not see a light bulb ten feet away"—in
the poorly ventilated factories prompted a host of pulmonary and re-
spiratory problems for workers, including shortness of breath and a
chronic "miller's cough," better known as mixed dust fibrosis.[100]

Under the "right" conditions, the New Process mills could turn
deadly in the blink of an eye. To address the dust problem, initially
mill owners placed exhaust fans in the different rooms of the factory,
but this solution proved lethal because the dust "under favorable conditions will ignite and burn so rapidly that the gases released have explosive force."[101] This increased the potential for mill fires so much that
insurers were reluctant to underwrite policies for flour mills.

On May 2, 1878, the Washburn "A" mill in Minneapolis blew. The
force of the explosion was so great that it blasted the roof hundreds of
feet into the air, leveling the building and razing three neighboring
mills as well. Eighteen men were killed in the explosion, fourteen in the
Washburn mill alone. The explosion destroyed half of the city's milling
capacity, but within a year Washburn had built a new mill, adding specially designed dust-collecting machines to "minimize the fire danger."
The entrepreneur kept adding new plants, and by 1881 flour production
in his factories had doubled.[102] But it did not take long before Minneapolis's hegemonic position in the industry was challenged. With
wheat farms scattered all over North America and beyond, by the
1920s it was no longer cost-effective to ship grain to one central point.
Mills sprang up in regions where consumption was greatest. Moreover,
railroads, increasingly under criticism for cozying up to manufacturers, raised rates to flour mills, making lake shipping a more attractive
option.

In response, the major flour corporations branched out, building
multiple manufacturing plants closer to the sources of production. They
also sought out sites that reduced their transaction costs. Thanks to
the rise in importance of the Great Lakes as a conduit for western US

and Canadian wheat and the abundance of cheap electrical power from Niagara Falls, by 1930 Buffalo, New York, was the leading milling center in the world.[103]

Despite the periodic upheavals in the flour industry, manufacturers, farmers, merchants, and speculators all shared a common goal—consumers needed to eat more grains. They invested copious sums in education and marketing to convince global consumers that it was in their enlightened self-interest to alter their diets.

## Uneeda to Eat More Crackers

The age of industrial capitalism implied a never-ending stream of mass-produced goods.[104] As scarcity gave way to abundance and factories churned out ever-greater numbers and varieties of finished goods, patterns of consumption and methods of encouraging that consumption changed as well. Progress was at hand; gluts and overproduction, advertisers argued, could be overcome simply through their formidable powers of persuasion. Advertising agencies were on a mission "to compose a new chapter of civilization." As an arrogant copywriter explained, "It is a great responsibility to mold the daily lives of millions of our fellow men, and I am persuaded that we are second only to statesmen and editors in power for good."[105]

According to cultural historian Jackson Lears, advertisers, who sought national and increasingly international markets for their corporate clients, promised the public a "magical self-transformation through the ritual of purchase."[106] In this vein, not-so-subliminal messages were spread that grains and flour meant much more than just sustenance; their daily consumption augured well for an individual's self-worth. Those consuming the right product would work harder, be more efficient, and set themselves apart from their peers. A turn-of-the-century Quaker Oats advertising campaign promised their product would "put its whole strength into your system," while a later advertisement insisted in intense alliteration that "lovers of Quaker Oats" were "wide-awakes, active and ambitious, whether they were seven or seventy. . . . Lovers of life eat them liberally. Lovers of languor don't."[107] Although the rest of the world was slow to adopt American innovations in the branding and marketing of food products manufactured by massive corporations, these trends would reach worldwide by the 1960s.

Consumption habits also changed remarkably during this period as diets, especially for urban dwellers, diversified considerably. As early as the 1890s in the United States, food-processing companies "single-handedly destroyed the traditional American breakfast."[108] The rise of Kellogg's "Corn Flakes" and Post's "Toasties" meant less bacon and beans in the morning and more carbohydrate-carrying grains in American diets. These products were initially marketed to the middle class as more healthful; in fact, Corn Flakes were created as a vegetarian alternative at a religious sanatorium in Battle Creek, Michigan. Charles W. Post, who created his own breakfast cereal company to challenge the primacy of Kellogg's, was a former patient at that same sanatorium and was so enamored with the concept of healthy breakfast foods that he began marketing his "Grape-Nuts" as "brain food." It did not take long before cereals were touted as cures for everything from malaria to consumption, and even loose teeth. Post preyed on concerned mothers, asking them, "Are you bringing up your children properly?" Not to worry, Post informed housewives, Grape-Nuts contained "iron, calcium, phosphorus and other mineral elements that are taken right up as vital food by the millions of cells in the body."[109] Breakfast cereals, a dietary marker of American identity, would also begin to spread internationally both before and in the decades after World War II.

In their efforts to spread the gospel that grains were good for the body and the soul, flour manufacturers were aided by advancements in packaging, especially the industry-wide transition from paper bags to paperboard folding boxes. The latter were less likely to rip during ship-ment, thereby minimizing spoilage. Cardboard boxes also protected their contents better, making them much more attractive for products like crackers. Finally, they were well suited for printing and were at-tractive for store displays. It was the Quaker Oats Company that pio-neered the concept of selling its products in "small, clean, distinctive packages," which today is in evidence worldwide.[110]

American and European per capita consumption of flour, however, nosedived after the First World War. The average American consumed only a little over two-thirds as much flour as he or she did in 1900. The decline was triggered by a number of factors—wartime conservation edicts that educated consumers to save wheat and eat different foods; increased consumption of milk, sugar, and vegetables; commercial bak-ers' doctoring of flour with nonflour ingredients; dieting; and mechan-ical bread slicing. One study published in 1952 concluded that "over the last fifty years, almost no factor worked in the direction of increasing flour consumption."[111]

Even though nutritionists were well aware by the 1920s of the in-herent deficiencies of white flour, and consumers were informed of the need to supplement their diets accordingly with fruits, vegetables, meats, and dairy products, it was very difficult for health officials to overcome the impact of huge advertising campaigns by the food-processing in-dustry. A heady mix of vitamin scientists and Hollywood celebrities sold Americans on how wholesome white wheat flour was. An indus-try consultant came before a congressional committee to rail against "the pernicious teachings of food faddists who have sought to make people afraid of white flour bread."[112] The companies went so far as to ingratiate themselves with the public school systems and women's or-ganizations by hiring teams of home economists to give demonstra-tions, buy up ad space in the *Journal of Home Economics,* and provide educational materials that testified to the wholesomeness and nutri-tional value of their products.

Baseball superstar Babe Ruth eating Puffed Wheat breakfast cereal in a publicity photograph, 1930. Prodigious advertising budgets of companies like Quaker Oats and Pillsbury made new products household names, especially when nationally known celebrities, like the "Sultan of Swat," George Herman Ruth, trumpeted their value. While many ads targeted housewives, others, like this one, were geared to their husbands and children. (Getty Images North America)

No matter the contradictory health claims, what these mass-produced foods had going for them, of course, was convenience, catchy packaging, and advertising. Companies initiated the sort of market research that would become accepted practice around the world. They conducted studies of the "instinctive likes and dislikes of buyers" as their marketing departments labored over the shape, color, and the texture of the packaging and how it would be displayed in stores.[113] Slogans that were "easily read, easily remembered and distinctive" sold these brand names to the American public. For instance, Washburn-Crosby implemented an aggressive advertising campaign featuring the slogan "Eventually—Why Not Now," which was plastered on countless billboards along railway routes. Not to be outdone, their rival Pillsbury shot back a response to Gold Medal's rhetorical query on its own billboards, "Because Pillsbury's Best."[114]

Manufacturers realized that their market was gendered. They reached out to housewives to sell their flour and one only had to glance at the data to understand why. By the 1920s, researchers were estimating that women purchased at least four-fifths of the total products acquired by families. To better target them, market researchers distributed questionnaires and took surveys to assemble "a portrait of the housewife." Advertising agencies sought answers to all that transpired in the home, pioneering "the statistical surveillance of private life, a practice that would become central to the maintenance of managerial cultural hegemony."[115] Who better to watch and then sell their wares to than the "average" woman? But as historian Jennifer Scanlon has noted, for advertising agencies in the United States, typical was synonymous with female, white, and middle-class.[116]

Washburn-Crosby came up with the ingenious gimmick of the larger-than-life persona of Betty Crocker, a fictional character who answered questions and shared recipes with American housewives. Soon the ubiquitous Crocker, "the embodiment of old-fashioned neighborliness," was a fixture in newspapers and magazines and on the radio, validating women's place in the domestic sphere.[117] Cooking schools were launched across the country, and twenty-one home economists were hired to work in Betty Crocker kitchens to test and demonstrate Gold Medal Flour. "Betty" would respond to up to four thousand letters a day from housewives about the intricacies of baking, and her radio show, *Betty Crocker School of the Air*, was a hit.[118] Small wonder that General Mills' Betty was once voted the second-best-known woman in America, taking a backseat only to Eleanor Roosevelt.[119]

In the 1920s the radio eclipsed print journalism and billboards as the preferred mode of transmission. Catchy singing radio commercials were unveiled; the lyrics of an early jingle for Wheaties was short and to the point:[120]

> Have you tried Wheaties?
> They're whole wheat with all of the bran.
> Won't you try Wheaties?
> For wheat is the best food of man.

With women won over, marketers turned their attention to husbands and children. General Mills not only sponsored action-packed radio shows like *Jack Armstrong, All-American Boy* to better appeal to male listeners, both young and old, but they produced and wrote the serials, all the while shamelessly plugging their products. Even so, Wheaties really did not become a household word until the company strategically associated its product with sports to appeal to consumer masculinity. The coined slogan "Breakfast of Champions" was advertised by sportsmen, such as heavyweight champion boxer Jack Dempsey, Olympic swimming champion Johnny Weissmuller, and tennis star Don Budge.[121]

Some of the industry's first movers were enormously successful and used their monopsonistic position in their markets to buy out their competitors and establish market dominance. The National Biscuit Company (NABISCO), for instance, thanks in large part to its flagship Uneeda Biscuit soda cracker, was one such corporate heavyweight, accounting for an astonishing 70 percent of industry sales. A clever name was not enough, however; the company wrapped its crackers in colorful, hygienic packaging and then cut out the wholesalers by building its own sales team and selling right to grocers. The cracker's taste was secondary to marketers. Advertisements featured a rain-slicker-clad boy carrying his prized package of crackers in a downpour, safely protected from the elements by a double-sealed package. That plus a prodigious advertising budget made the cracker a household name as Americans were persuaded they had multiple reasons to need large quantities of Uneeda Biscuit crackers.[122]

Food-processing companies, however, soon came to realize that there were limits to what consumers would eat and that an increase in consumption of one item often came at the expense of others. In this zero-sum game, industry magnates had to get the attention of consumers, no matter the cost. A flour millers' trade association, which trumpeted the virtues of grains, called on consumers to "Eat More Wheat" during the 1920s. This far-ranging campaign, which sought to arrest the decline in per capita consumption of flour, was as imaginative as it was multifaceted.[123]

Advertising and corporate research and development departments worked synergistically; the former, for instance, provided timely data to the latter, which was constantly in search of new product lines. Millers began grinding a drought-resistant, rust-resistant durum variety grown initially in Eastern Europe and then transplanted to the Dakotas. By 1919 the durum wheat crop averaged forty million bushels annually in the United States alone, and flour manufacturers were not far behind in trumpeting the virtues of macaroni products. Manufacturers touted the nutritional value of their pasta products in their trade publication *Macaroni Journal* and crusaded nationwide for a Friday "Macaroni Day." As a flour company president self-servingly noted: "Such new products represent an increase in the consumption of grains as food; they actually compete less with other cereal products than with types of foodstuffs outside their own field."[124] European companies were not far behind their American counterparts in conjuring up catchy ad campaigns to sell their products.

Not all grain products during this era experienced such a revolution in marketing and advertising. These techniques were little used, for instance, in selling rice. But in other respects, rice's commodity chain complemented rather than competed with the wheat trade. The rice chain demonstrates that the existence of technological and infrastructural innovations during this period did not in and of themselves guarantee that growers would embrace such changes.

## Rice as Contrarian

Unlike grain farmers in settler societies, rice growers in South, Southeast, and East Asia, with few exceptions, chose not to substitute machines for human and animal power, nor did they adopt chemical fertilizers or allocate funds for agricultural extension services.[125] Given the choice to invest in labor or machinery, rice farmers chose the former. It is not that rice and mechanization were or are incompatible; in this period, rice cultivators in the United States, Australia, and southern Europe adopted the latest farm machinery to sow and harvest their crops. In the United States rice was cultivated in the same highly mechanized manner as wheat and other grains; farmers employed combines, tractors, and even airplanes. Japanese rice farmers also were quick to adopt beneficial technology, replacing treadle irrigation wheels with small diesel and electric pumps when they were first made available in the 1920s. In fact, the pumps dramatically transformed rice production in Japan, reducing labor requirements on the Saga Plain from seventy worker-days per hectare in 1909 to twenty-two worker-days in 1932 while doubling production. But the great majority of rice farmers had very plausible reasons for eschewing new technologies and investing their energies (and profits) elsewhere.

The difference in ecology, the idiosyncrasies of wet-rice growing, and the diminutive size of the large majority of rice plots in monsoon Asia best explain why peasants stuck with the traditional tools of the trade and looked for other ways to enhance productivity. Much of the prime wet-rice land was in deltas, along coastal strips and river basins. Such land was boggy at best, usually silts and silky sands, soils where the wheels of machines could not gain traction. The machines that best tolerated such muddy conditions were those that floated and did not require adhesion.

Rice, like wheat, prospered in different ecological zones; for instance, it could be grown on hills or mountains without the need for irrigation or surface water. Upland rice, however, was cultivated in sparsely settled regions and constituted only a small proportion of the world's rice crop. Roughly 90 percent of global production during this period was lowland rice, which thrives in the hot lowland tropics with abundant rainfall and enough water to either naturally or artificially flood fields.[126]

Lowland rice, unlike wheat, had few competitors in the tropics and subtropics; only millet, sorghum, and maize would tolerate such heat and moisture, and then only in areas of modest summer rainfall. Paddy rice in monsoon Asia also had another intrinsic advantage over its rivals: it grew "under water," so it was relatively impervious to pests, disease, and, of course, drought.[127]

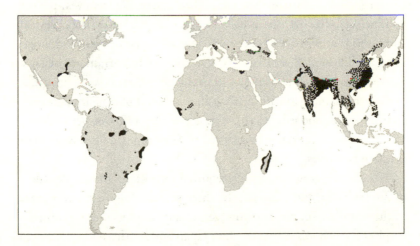

Global production of rice, ca. 1913–1925.

Unlike settler societies where labor was scarce and emphasis was placed on substituting machinery for labor, Asian agrarian economies had the luxury of drawing on an abundance of skilled manual workers. Instead of mechanizing, growers focused on improving rice yields. When sufficient labor was available, wet-rice growers in well-watered areas often could realize two or three crops a year. As a recent survey of rice economies noted: "It is no coincidence that the most densely populated agricultural regions of the world, Java, the Tonkin delta (present day Vietnam) and the lower Yangtze provinces of China, all have a centuries-long tradition of intensive wet-rice farming. No wheat growing areas can sustain such numerous populations."[128] Multicropping also enabled farmers to grow different varieties in any one season, to minimize risks and cater to niche markets. Moreover, rice had a higher yield-to-seed ratio than wheat, barley, or rye, so conserving seed grain at the end of harvest season was not as much of a hardship for peasants as it was for European and American wheat growers.

Another striking contrast between wet rice and other grains was that yields could actually increase in the same paddy from year to year and then stabilize over time "because water seepage alters the chemical composition and structure of the different soil layers in a process known as pozdolisation."[129] Soil type was much less important to wet-rice farmers than proper irrigation and drainage. Whereas soil from grain or dry-rice farming lost its fertility after a period of time if manure or fertilizers were not utilized, the reverse was true with wet-rice farming. Small wonder rice farmers preferred to farm old paddies rather than break in new ones.

Not all rice-growing regions required irrigation. The fertile deltas of Burma, Siam, and Vietnam, the three principal rice-exporting areas of the world during the late nineteenth and early twentieth centuries, employed much less irrigation than Japan and southern China, where land was scarce and population pressure demanded that yields be maximized. Rivers overflowed the delta banks at least once a year, depositing rich alluvial silts that replenished the soil and permitted rice to be grown year after year with little need for fertilizer or the rotation of crops. Unfortunately, these three prime exporting regions in Southeast Asia were on the same marketing schedule. With harvests occurring simultaneously, the result was "intensified competition and consequent (downward) pressure on prices, with adverse effects upon returns to growers and government revenues."[130] Because more than fifty million peasants' livelihoods were tied to rice production, price fluctuations or declining yields often had dire consequences.

Even where irrigation was in vogue, methods of addressing constraints varied. Chinese rice farmers focused on multicropping and early-maturing varieties of rice. Their Japanese counterparts adopted varieties that responded well to fertilization, as Japan "coaxed" farmers in its colonial possessions in Formosa and Korea to plant in new lands for cultivation after World War I.

Rice was produced and circulated largely within Asia during this period. India and China were the largest producers, but almost all of their production fed domestic consumption. Because most rice was consumed locally or regionally, and because rice milling was far simpler than milling wheat into flour, the transport, storage, marketing, and milling of rice did not follow the pattern of wheat. Harvested or paddy rice was transported to mills by oxcart or on workers' backs; rice that had to be conveyed longer distances was shipped by water transport. Railroads, such stalwart conveyors of wheat and other coarse grains, were utilized to carry rice in Japan and India, which as we have seen had Asia's best rail networks, but other rice regions made the most of water transport. Storage facilities were rudimentary at best, so rice was milled soon after harvest.

Rice-milling establishments varied considerably, "[ranging from a] farmer's hand-operated 'woodpecker,' which merely removed hulls to a large power-driven establishment employing many laborers and

equipped with machines that hull, skin, polish, and coat the rice."[131]
Suffice it to say, even the largest rice-milling factories in Rangoon,
Burma, paled in comparison to the size and output of Pillsbury's mas-
sive Minneapolis flour mills.

The establishment of a uniform set of weights and measures proved
elusive. Even where varieties were categorized, price quotations were
limited to the nominal classifications high-, middle-, and low-quality,
with considerable variability found at different rice exchanges. According to a study published by the Stanford University Food Research Institute in 1940:[132]

> The buyer of paddy rice . . . must learn to know as best he can from ex-
> perience the quality of rice grown from one region to another and by
> many individuals. In the absence of marketing standards, trading nec-
> essarily becomes a highly individualistic matter. Trading risks are
> therefore large . . . [and] the spread between producers and retailers
> prices tends to be high.

Prior to World War II, Asia accounted for 93 percent of global rice
exports, but the continent also absorbed three-quarters of the imports
and, taking into account subsistence rice farming, probably consumed
over 90 percent of the world's rice. Just as there were a few prominent
exporters in the wheat trade, Burma, French Indochina or Cochin
China, Siam (present-day Thailand), Korea, and Formosa dominated
the rice trade. Exports steadily grew throughout the late nineteenth
and early twentieth centuries. By 1940 Burma was exporting 3 million
tons of rice annually, while Indochina, Siam, and Korea shipped out 1
to 1.3 million tons a year. Japan imported the most rice—on average 1.7
million tons annually, with almost all of it after the mid-1920s coming
from its colonies in Korea and Formosa. Japan privileged these colonies by placing import restrictions on "foreign" rice imports. British
India was the next-largest importer, taking in 1.5 million tons annually, with the British colonies of Ceylon and Malaya each garnering

half a million tons of foreign rice a year. Chinese imports fluctuated greatly from year to year, owing to the unpredictability of domestic rice harvests.

Just as Western national governments became increasingly protectionist as commodity prices declined in the 1920s and 1930s, nationalistic Asian governments also promoted food self-sufficiency at home to preserve favorable balances of payment and to protect domestic rice production. In some cases governments even encouraged their citizens to consume less rice to promote self-sufficiency. Because the level of urbanization—outside of Japan—was low in Asia, imports were less crucial than in much more urbanized Western Europe. Despite the growing tendency toward protectionism, rice exporters, with the notable exception of Burma, which saw its European market shrink precipitously, held their own during the Great Depression, especially when compared to wheat-exporting countries. As one comparative study noted:[133]

> Rice exports increased more rapidly than wheat exports in the period before 1930, declined relatively less on impact of the world depression, and ... [from 1936 to 1938] rice stood moderately above their immediate pre-Depression level while wheat exports fell by nearly a fourth. With rice, enough import markets expanded to offset those that contracted; with wheat, the policies of self-sufficiency were much more general and more restrictive upon world trade.

The rice trade's ability to weather the volatile interwar period is especially noteworthy given that wheat was becoming progressively cheaper in relation to rice (see Table 3.4). Asian demographic growth, which far outpaced rice production and ensured demand, partially explains the rice trade's resiliency under such difficult conditions. Perhaps another reason was that up until 1935 one of its major importers, China, acted as a stabilizing influence by importing more heavily when rice prices were lower and buying up less from external markets when

TABLE 3.4

Indexed wheat and rice prices on British markets, 1867–1939

|           | Average wheat price | Average rice price | Ratio of wheat to rice |
|-----------|---------------------|--------------------|------------------------|
| 1867–1877 | 100                 | 100                | 1.00                   |
| 1878–1887 | 75.5                | 80                 | 0.94                   |
| 1890–1899 | 54                  | 63                 | 0.86                   |
| 1904–1913 | 61                  | 77                 | 0.79                   |
| 1922–1930 | 89.5                | 152                | 0.59                   |
| 1931–1939 | 48                  | 93                 | 0.57                   |

*Source:* V. D. Wickizer and M. K. Bennett, *The Rice Economy of Monsoon Asia* (Palo Alto, CA: Stanford University Food Research Institute, 1941), 137.
*Notes:* Indexed average for the period 1867–1877 = 100.
Average wheat price represents the British and American price for the period.
Average rice price represents the average price of cargoes arriving from Rangoon, Burma.

prices shot up. Because China was such a major force in the rice trade, such elasticity kept rice prices worldwide in check. This held true until 1935, when the Chinese government moved aggressively to protect its home market, causing rice imports to decline significantly.

Each of the principal exporters serviced a discrete market and by and large stuck to it. Burmese rice went to England, where a portion of it was re-exported to the rest of Europe, the West Indies, and Africa. Prior to World War I, rice from Burma, which was part of India from 1852 until 1937, was sold only in Asian markets during times of famine. After 1937 most of its "exports" went to other Indian ports and were then re-exported to East Africa, British Malaya, and Ceylon. But the rice seldom flowed to East Asia. On the other hand, exports from Siam and Cochin China (later southern Vietnam) were earmarked for Japan, China, the Philippines, the Dutch East Indies, the Malay Peninsula, and Java, although the French market bought up rice produced by its colonials, especially during years when East Asian markets contracted.

Interestingly, as the period wore on and as ever-larger amounts of wheat and coarse grains went to the European continent from grain frontiers, less rice was shipped to Europe from Asian exporters. Instead, rice was shipped from the ports of Rangoon, Bangkok, and Saigon to growing Asian markets or it now bypassed England and was exported directly from the rice frontiers to the West Indies and Africa. Before paddy rice was exported, it needed to be cleaned and polished because this made it keep better. Owing to the dearth of storage in producing countries, rice was bagged for overseas transport, rather than shipped in bulk the way that wheat and the other coarse grains were.

The focus on the export trade, however, obscures a lively domestic rice trade that existed in some countries, mainly flowing from countryside to the city. Bengali rice, for example, was shipped largely westward in India, while surplus rice from southern China was shipped to China's northern provinces.

Although it is true that rice was cultivated globally—Spain and Italy were Europe's largest producers, the US South and Brazil dominated production in the Americas, and Egypt and Sierra Leone monopolized African rice production—taken together, non-Asian rice never amounted to much; less than 5 percent of world production was grown outside of monsoon Asia on the eve of World War II. Or to put it another way, the output of the United States and Brazil together was less than that of the smallest Asian producer, Formosa. It was not until the 1930s that Africa and the United States began to export significant quantities of rice.

It may seem counterintuitive, but the three deltas in Southeast Asia—the Irrawaddy-Sittaung (Burma), the Chao Phraya (Siam), and the Mekong (Vietnam)—dominated the export trade to Europe and China, even though rice yields in these regions were historically low (and showed no upward trend until after World War II). Compared to other major rice producers, their double-cropping and fertilizer use was minimal, agricultural education and infrastructure lagged, and what irrigation existed was qualitatively inferior to methods used in East Asia. On these new frontiers, however, rice was grown on larger farms for export.

What these Southeast Asian delta frontiers had in common with settler societies in the Americas and Australia was an abundance of new lands available for cultivation and significant in-migration. These expanding rice frontiers also were characterized by colonial interventions, often with unintended consequences. A fascinating illustration was Lower Burma. Colonial administrators immediately recognized the untapped economic potential of the Irrawaddy-Sittaung Delta region. What had been a sparsely populated, underdeveloped backwater of the British Empire would become over the course of the next fifty years the world's largest rice-exporting area. Colonial authorities invested considerable sums to improve rail and water transport and to establish technical education, credit institutions, and public works projects.

But imperial plans did not go according to script. British officials initially encouraged the development of small landholdings in the delta region, in the belief that independent peasants, many of them transplanted from the "dry" districts of Upper Burma, would improve and extend their properties in a way that large landowners, who were, in the minds of the British, little more than glorified rent collectors, would not. Because this was relatively untouched territory, where no preexisting land tenure system had established roots, officials believed it would be possible to develop a rural economy that favored independent proprietors who received the profits and where the "rent surplus went to the state rather than to intermediaries."[134] To promote this, squatters, taking advantage of familial labor, were given titles to lands after they had occupied and paid taxes on their holdings for twelve years. Hundreds of thousands of Burmese migrants, making the most of their opportunities, made a successful transition from subsistence farming to export production. Marketing of the trade, for most of the part, stayed in Burmese hands, although increasing numbers of southern Indian immigrants moved to Rangoon and began to participate in all aspects of the export trade.

Peasants dominated rice cultivation in the Irrawaddy-Sittaung Delta until well into the first decades of the twentieth century as production grew exponentially. But as yields stagnated and the rice frontier closed after World War I, land values increased. Moneylenders, rice brokers, and millers who had advanced credit to smallholders in return for their paddy rice, began to acquire properties, often as a result of foreclosures on mortgages. Debt burdens mounted, and peasants lost their lands and became tenants on large estates. As historian Michael Adas explains, "the social and economic position of a small segment of Delta society, the large landholders, improved substantially, while the solvency and wellbeing of the great majority of persons engaged in agricultural production was gradually undermined."[135] A system designed to promote economic growth, rice exports, and imperial revenues, and in which Burmese farmers, middlemen, and entrepreneurs were all active participants, became progressively less balanced. During the Great Depression the delta region was especially hard hit. Rice monoculture left landless tenants in desperate straits. Rural unrest and the Japanese occupation only compounded their plight.

Cochin China presents a different model of colonial economic development. Although the region was sparsely populated when the French first arrived in the mid-nineteenth century, over the next seventy years under French rule, rice cultivation increased fourfold as peasants flocked to the region from the northern provinces. The colonial administration invested heavily in water control, constructing a sophisticated system of canals. To recoup some of their costs, colonial administrators sold large expanses of land to French nationals and companies. By 1930, rice lands were concentrated in the hands of some 120

French colonists who among themselves held approximately one hundred thousand hectares of land. Recently arrived tenant farmers were given ten-hectare plots on these estates in return for a portion of their rice.

In Cochin China and other delta regions, cultivated rice lands were owned by landlords who advanced money and supplies to tenants at usurious rates of interest in return for a portion of their crop. Much of the rice crop was mortgaged out even before it was planted. Soon after the harvest, growers had to settle up with landlords or merchants to meet their obligations. Unlike wheat farmers, rice farmers were all too often in the dark about market prices, rates of interest, the cost of supplies advanced to them, and the weight of their crop.

In Japan the government took an active role in marketing and financing the crop. Rice exchanges were established in all of Japan's major cities, but in this case it was the government, not the private sector (as in the West), that administered the trade. In stark contrast to the Chicago Board of Trade and other Western commodity exchanges, speculation was discouraged.

The rice trade, then, in virtually every meaningful way, ran counter to the other grain trades. Export markets were more regional and remained remarkably consistent over time. South and Southeastern Asian exporters serviced Asian markets first and foremost; although countries in North and South America, Africa, and Europe produced rice, much of it was destined for home markets. Because several of the largest exporters essentially planted and harvested rice on the same timetable, and because storage facilities in the principal exporting regions were remarkably underdeveloped, large quantities of rice flooded the market at the same time, inevitably depressing prices. The business of rice trading was much more rudimentary than the grains trade; there was much less standardization, processing functioned on a much smaller scale, markets were not as integrated, transportation and storage infrastructure were glaringly deficient, and speculation, which had such a dramatic impact on investment, capitalization, and price differentials in the West, was a nonfactor in Asian rice markets.

Although not averse to new technologies, fertilizers, or scientific experimentation, rice growers understandably invested more time and capital into increasing yields through multicropping than through mechanization. The presence of dense populations and the ability of rice to reward ever more workers by increasing yields mitigated the need to embrace costly machinery. Rice had been and continued to be a peasant-cultivated crop. Even in the southeastern deltas, where large farms predominated, tenants, who leased lands from large landowners or companies, cultivated rice.

Still, there were some significant similarities that warrant mention. Open rice and grain frontiers prompted migration and the concentration of land and wealth in the hands of a few (though in other, less export-oriented areas, rice permitted the continuation of small peasant plots.) But given how fertile the deltas were, there was less need for substantive investment in irrigation or other technologies. As we have seen, formal and informal colonial relationships mattered in both trades; mother countries privileged their dependencies. Interestingly, consumers preferred their grains, whether rice, wheat, or other coarse grains, "white"—nutrition be damned!

## Ripple Effects

The growth of a global grains trade had multiplier effects that facilitated the growth of other products and industries vital to the production, processing, marketing, and consumption of the trade.[136] Some of these products, and the processes needed to transform them into useful inputs, dramatically transformed those regions of the world that cultivated and manufactured these items. Hard fibers proved indispensable to the grains revolution and in turn became creatures of that trade. The life histories of several hard fibers illustrate how commodity chains were forged, how and why they flourished, and ultimately how each one proved unable to sustain its position in its respective market during this tumultuous age. The fates of entrepreneurs and peasants in such disparate regions as the Bengal region of eastern India, the Yucatán Peninsula in Mexico, and the East Indies were tied not only to the world market price of their commodities and to those of their chief competitors, but to the roller-coaster, boom-and-bust cycles of the grains and rice to which they owed their existence.

A competitive hard-fibers trade developed during the nineteenth and twentieth centuries as new fibers were introduced to manufacturers—each with its own strengths, weaknesses, and particular applications. Each new fiber jockeyed with more established rivals, and eventually the market became more segmented. Some versatile fibers had multiple applications and benefited from the growing complexity of the global market; others were confined essentially to a specific submarket. Each new fiber was first subjected to intense chemical scrutiny, followed by controlled cultivation investigations at agricultural experiment stations, before a lengthy apprenticeship in the market. In general, each hard fiber gained ascendancy in the market for the better part of a century, as each enjoyed a brief Ricardian comparative advantage. Although in some cases new uses were found or new cultivation or processing techniques were employed to postpone the inevitable denouement, bona fide development for the regions that produced these crops proved illusory. These export economies simply did not generate sufficient forward or backward linkages to prompt sustained economic growth. Hard-fiber sectors in Africa, Asia, or Latin America never acted as growth multipliers, nor did they prompt economic integration for the host countries. This was particularly serious because, unlike rice and grains, one can't eat hard fibers.

One inexpensive fiber useful for the storage and transport of grains and other commodities was jute (*Corchorus capsularis* and *Corchorus olitorius*). Although not so strong, durable, and elastic as other hard fibers, Indian jute was more plentiful, cheaper to produce, and easier to manufacture. It soon conquered the bagging market. Handwoven jute bags (called hessian or burlap) produced on looms in the Bengal delta region (present-day Bangladesh) had been an important cottage industry as early as the sixteenth century. Although too rough for apparel, jute found its niche as a preeminent packaging material of the age. The Dutch were the first to use the coarse fiber for coffee bags from their Java plantations in Indonesia in the 1830s. When the Crimean War cut supplies of Russian hemp and the US Civil War caused a shortage of cotton bags, the jute industry responded.

Inexpensive labor costs contributed to jute's popularity with fiber buyers. Peasants and tenants interspersed plantings of jute with rice paddy in northern and eastern Bengal, but its cultivation placed heavy demands on the labor force. The cash crop required deep plowing, weeding, hand-cut harvesting, and then the retting of the fiber in ponds to separate the stem and the outer bark from the fiber. Brokers extended credit to growers at usurious rates—one estimate fixes the rate at never less than 36 percent—and then shipped the raw product in bales, first by boat and later by railway, to the port of Calcutta in West Bengal. By 1910 production had soared to nine hundred thousand tons a year and by the end of the Second World War, India had a virtual monopoly on the raw material. When the chairman of the Indian Jute Mills Association stated in 1915, "We want cheap jute, and lots of it," the implication was obvious: Indian jute's comparative advantage lay in its exceedingly low labor cost—in the field and in the factory.[137]

Jute was made into burlap and gunnysacks for everything from sandbags to sugar, and fertilizer to animal feeds. (Devotees of rock-and-roller Chuck Berry may recall that even "Johnny B. Goode" carried his guitar in a gunnysack.) By the mid-nineteenth century, power-driven jute mills in Dundee, Scotland, had overtaken the Indian handloom industry. The fiber's popularity soon attracted a rash of competition from manufacturers in France, Germany, Belgium, Austria, and Italy. By the end of the nineteenth century, however, Calcutta bagging manufacturers, benefiting from cheap labor and proximity to the raw product, stepped into the fray and offered serious competition to European mills. The process was relatively simple: first, raw fibers of varying length, thickness, color, and tensile strength were spun into a uniform yarn; then the yarn was woven into cloth. As early as 1875, the US consul general in Calcutta reported that local jute manufacturers were a force to be reckoned with: "There seems to be every reason to expect that Calcutta will become the great jute manufacturing center of the world."[138]

Located in and around Calcutta along the banks of the Hooghly River, jute mills were managed by Scotsmen imported from Dundee, but capitalized by a melding of British expatriate and indigenous entrepreneurs who established holding companies. Initially they catered only to domestic markets and the rice trade in nearby Burma, before marketing their bags internationally. Over time Indian capitalists increasingly assumed command of these holding companies. By the turn of the century, Calcutta and its environs had thirty-five mills with a capacity of 315,000 spindles and 15,340 looms, turning out 440,000 tons of gunny and burlap sacks.

Angry Dundee jute manufacturers pleaded with their members of Parliament to implement tariffs or quotas, fully expecting that "an upstart competitor in a dependent part of the empire could be brought to heel."[139] They were sadly mistaken. Dundee's jute makers never recaptured their preeminent position; all of their politicking could not keep Indian jute out of United Kingdom and its dependencies. The reason was that jute paid its way; after the turn of the century, sacking was frequently India's largest export earner, which helped pay for the administrative costs of empire during the Raj. This tale of two cities is an instructive example of the limitations of empire. Manufactured jute may have gotten its start near the imperial center, but it reigned triumphant in the colony. One could think of this as India's revenge. Where the First Industrial Revolution in England had undercut India's textile industry, the Second—and the growth of agricultural (rice) exports—had allowed Indian manufacturers to outcompete British rivals.

Between 1870 and the First World War, Indian gunnysack production increased from 1.8 million to just under 370 million bags annually.[140] At their zenith, the Calcutta mills employed between 250,000 and 300,000 workers, and jute constituted just under 30 percent of India's total exports. By World War I the Calcutta factories had even founded a cartel, the Indian Jute Manufacturer Association, which regulated production by buying up raw material when prices were low and storing it in warehouses until prices improved.

By the early twentieth century Calcutta's cheap and coarse gunnysacks and its higher-quality burlap bags had captured the market in Australasia, the United States, South Africa, and the Southern Cone of South America. Calcutta hegemony proved short-lived, however. During the Great Depression, European governments revived their jute industries by imposing high tariffs on imported bags. Together with the transition to bulk transport of grains and competition from paper and cotton sacks, this led to a crisis in India's jute industry. Peasant and tenant producers, by definition not well capitalized, were particularly hard hit. An economic historian, writing about the litany of ills of Bengali jute growers during the depths of the depression, painted a discouraging picture: "With no relief in sight, increasing indebtedness, consumption loans at exorbitant interests, distress sales, short-changing, debt default, land appropriation, proliferation of pauperized sharecroppers and agricultural laborers were the mileposts on the road to debt peonage."[141]

Producing jute inexpensively became an industry-wide mantra. Producers and manufacturers had good reason to be concerned about the revolution in bulk storage and transport, newfangled synthetic substitutes, and old-fashioned protectionist strategies employed by their chief competition in Europe. The subsequent introduction of synthetic fibers, like nylon, patented by DuPont in 1934, sealed the industry's fate.

If jute found a niche in the bagging market, Philippine-grown manila *(Musa textilis)* proved to be a more than worthy adversary for Russian- and US-grown hemp *(Cannabis sativa),* which had been the raw material of preference for the making of cordage. Whalers, clippers, and eventually steamships required a seemingly endless supply of rope for rigging, cable, and towlines. The smallest schooner carried a ton of cordage; a frigate used one hundred tons. Even the advent of steamships did not curtail demand, as they still required large amounts of cordage for towlines, warps, and auxiliary sails.

By the late nineteenth century, manila, a member of the banana family, overtook hemp in the cordage trade. Extracted from the plant's bark, it was naturally resistant to saltwater, so that it did not have to be tarred like hemp. This clean fiber, introduced and tested by North American cordage manufacturers in 1818, was more durable and 25 percent stronger than tarred hemp, had greater flexibility and elasticity, weighed a third less, and carried a lower price tag. By 1860, manila, which was grown in the Kabikolan Peninsula in southeastern Luzon, was firmly entrenched in the US maritime trade, and consumption by British and other European manufacturers steadily increased. Production doubled between 1870 and 1880 alone.

The cordage industry's infatuation with manila overshadowed the introduction of a new tropical fiber. Although henequen *(Agave fourcroydes)* had been cultivated in Mexico's Yucatán Peninsula since pre-Columbian times for clothes, shoes, and hammocks, only in the late colonial period did Spanish entrepreneurs begin to recognize its broader commercial potential. Commonly, but incorrectly, known as sisal—the name of a Gulf of Mexico port from which the fiber was shipped—henequen was earmarked for low-end cordage and rigging purposes because it lacked tensile strength for heavy-duty usage.

Twice as strong, more rot-resistant, and smoother than the Yucatecan fiber, manila merited its higher price and remained the fiber of choice in the maritime market. Henequen justifiably gained a reputation as an inferior but inexpensive substitute for manila. Blends of manila and henequen were marketed as such and priced midway between the "pure" twines. Hence, the prices of these commodities were inextricably bound. Abundance or a shortage of one commodity invariably affected the rival's price.

Demand was ensured as technological advancements continued to find new industrial applications for the erstwhile rivals. Tests determined that rope offered the most economical means of conveying power. With new factories springing up throughout North America and Western Europe, manila proved ideally suited for power transmission cables and the expanding oil-drilling industry. The new application of greatest consequence for henequen (and, to a lesser extent, manila) was binder twine. Labor-intensive hand-binding had been supplanted in the early 1870s by mechanical wire binders attached to reapers. When bits of wire clogged the machinery and found their way into flour mills and animal feed, inventors built a mechanical twine knotter in the late 1870s that substituted biodegradable twine for wire, thus revolutionizing the farm-implement industry. Now a harvesting machine with two men to pick and shock the sheaf could reap twelve to fourteen acres of wheat a day, effectively doubling previous output with a substantial labor savings. The North American Deering Company and the McCormick Harvesting Machine Company, the world's largest producers of mobile agricultural machinery, quickly built their own twine binder harvesters in 1879 and 1881, respectively. Sales of mechanical grain binders soared, and by the turn of the century, henequen and manila production grew exponentially to meet the insatiable demand.

When fiber prices were high, growers and merchants made bountiful profits. Local business leaders in the Philippines and Yucatán served as conduits for British and North American brokers and manufacturers, realizing sizable profits, usually in the form of commissions and kickbacks but also from the usurious loan practices that access to foreign capital allowed them. Ideally, just as foreign investors sought to carve out a durable monopoly or "corner" on the trade, local collaborators wished to enjoy exclusively the benefits of a monopoly over communication with foreign interests controlling the market. With these limitations, it was difficult for local producers to adjust productivity and to predict prices; so local landholders were vulnerable to the repeated boom-and-bust cycles that afflicted the trade. Chronic price instability, coupled with the producers' inability to diversify, meant that these regional economies experienced severe dislocations amid sustained growth.

Yucatán was one of the economic jewels of Mexico; its henequen plantations enjoyed a dominant position in the hard-fibers market, supplying upward of 85 to 90 percent of the fiber used to make binder twine in North American cordage and twine factories. Over the last four decades of the nineteenth century, the peninsula's colonial-style haciendas were transformed into bustling modern plantations; contemporaries chronicled how cornfields and pasture had been replaced by rectilinear rows of bluish-gray spines of the agave plant. Fortunes were realized by enterprising landowners, fiber merchants, and North American cordage and binder twine manufacturers, who secured bountiful profits from the turn-of-the-century fiber boom. Locally, a "divine caste" of thirty families and a smaller subset of prosperous landowner-merchants dominated the henequen economy, transforming the state's capital city of Mérida into a beautiful showcase, while constructing opulent homes for themselves in the state capital and on their haciendas. State and national governments came to rely on tax revenues generated from this profitable export.

Like many staples, henequen was hamstrung by cutthroat competition and a fickle marketplace that constantly sought out more cost-effective supplies of hard fibers. But hard fibers did enjoy some notable advantages over other tropical commodities. Fibers were nonperishable, so production, transportation, and distribution did not have to be systematically coordinated as they did for other tropical goods. Moreover, unlike some staples, henequen was seasonless; the absence of a prescribed harvest season had important ramifications for marketing, distribution, and the labor regimen.

By 1902 the International Harvester Company, a combination of five of the largest harvesting machine companies (including McCormick and Deering), had become the world's principal buyer of raw fiber. Binder twine, manufactured in Harvester's Chicago twine plant, was an important secondary line for Harvester, as farmers needed a regular supply of twine to operate their binders. The company made its profits by selling binding machines rather than from twine sales, so Harvester and its agents sought to keep twine prices low to make its farm implements more attractive. Historians debate the leverage that Harvester enjoyed over the market, but local agents such as Olegario Molina y Compañía in Yucatán benefited greatly from access to foreign capital. This enabled Molina to acquire mortgages, purchase credits outright, and consolidate its hold on regional communications, infrastructure, and banking—all of which guaranteed control of local fiber production and generally worked to depress the price. In the short term, the boom enriched a small group of foreign investors, merchants, and local elites in Mexico and the Philippines while the greater majority of producers and tens of thousands of laborers found themselves tied to the whims of an unforgiving market.

Inputs like land tenure patterns, labor relations, technological improvements, and marketing and credit practices were either overhauled or fine-tuned in the wake of the boom. Henequen was highly inelastic to price changes in the market. Because landowners had to wait seven years to begin harvesting their crops, they invariably based their decision to expand or contract their holdings on their ability to acquire capital. Faced with such a lag between planting and first harvest, landowners could predict neither future prices nor world market demand. As a result, supply in the short run was usually out of phase with demand.

The henequen estate had some physical resemblance to a commercial plantation—with modern machinery, narrow-gauge tramways, and land-intensive cultivation of the staple crop—but familial ownership, management, and *mentalité* continued to imbue the institution with characteristics of the pre-henequen cattle and maize hacienda. Emblematic of a rural society in the middle of a complex transition, the henequen estate is best viewed as a hybrid that illustrates some of the traits of its predecessor but reflects inevitable adjustments in land, technology, labor, and infrastructure. Moreover, a full-fledged plantation society's emergence was inhibited by lingering vestiges of the earlier institution, particularly the way in which *hacendados* confronted their labor problems.

Just as the syncretic henequen estate combined characteristics of both the traditional hacienda and the commercial plantation, its labor relations were also an amalgam of various modes of coercion. Underwritten by the assistance of the state political apparatus, three complementary mechanisms of social control—isolation, coercion, and security—allowed *henequeneros* to maintain the disciplined work rhythms of monocrop production. These three strategies worked in unison to cement the structural relationship that not only suited the production requirements of management but also served the subsistence needs of workers, at least until the eve of the Mexican Revolution.

Designed by *henequeneros* to limit the workers' mobility and autonomy, the three mechanisms were often so mutually reinforcing that it is sometimes difficult to delineate where one began and the other left

Women workers operating twine-balling machines at International Harvester's mill in Chicago, Illinois, April 26, 1939. Raw henequen, manila, and sisal fiber, produced on plantations in such tropical locales as Mexico, the Philippines, and East Africa, were shipped to cordage and twine factories in the United States, Canada, and Europe. These modern, mechanized plants manufactured binder twine from these natural fibers and then sold the inexpensive product to North American and European farmers, who used it to bind sheaves of wheat. (Wisconsin Historical Society, WHi-8897)

off. Institutions like the hacienda store, for example, served many functions. On one level, the store gave *henequeneros* a surefire mechanism for raising workers' debts (coercion). On another level, by providing basic foodstuffs and household needs, it diminished the need for resident peons to leave the property to purchase goods, thereby minimizing the chances of potentially disruptive contact between resident peons and neighboring villagers and agitators (isolation). Finally, through the sale of corn, beans, and other staples, it ensured subsistence for resident peons (security). In sum, the hacienda store was a perfect vehicle for appropriating labor in a scarce market, as it facilitated dependency and immobility while conveying a measure of convenience and security for landless peons. Henequen monoculture's fundamental security of subsistence throughout the boom, coupled with the economic demise of nearby village communities, enlisted workers for, and harnessed them to, the disciplined work rhythms of fiber production.

Gender relations on henequen estates only reinforced these complementary mechanisms. In fact, masters and peons found common ground in their perceptions of the role Maya women should play on the estates. First and foremost, they agreed on a rigid division of labor. Male debt peons toiled in the fields, performing all tasks related to planting, harvesting, and processing the fiber on the estates. If the daughters or wives occasionally worked in the fields to remove the spines from the henequen leaves after cutting (just as they had helped in the past with harvesting corn), they were accompanied by their fathers or husbands and were never paid in scrip for their labors.

Not surprisingly, women on henequen estates were relegated to the domestic sphere. Their tasks centered on rearing the family, cooking, cleaning, retrieving water from the well and firewood from the forest, bringing lunch to their husbands and sons in the fields, and tending the family garden. Ledger books occasionally listed women as domestics who worked in the landlord's "big house" or as hammock and sack makers and corn grinders, but they were not identified as henequen workers. Indeed, it appears that the fiber boom brought little change to the *campesinas'* regimen, for this strictly observed division of labor on the estates was consistent with preboom patterns. Even at the height of the fiber boom, when planters were desperate for workers, Maya women were not used in the fields.

Why did planters, who regularly complained about the scarcity of labor in the henequen zone and who did not shrink from using coercive strategies when it suited their purposes, not employ *campesinas* in the fields? By permitting the male peon to earn "wages" to provide for his family through access to corn plots and hunting and to exercise power over women in his household, the *hacendado* was securing the "loyalty" and limiting the mobility of his worker. As a consequence, families were rarely separated in the henequen zone nor does it appear that *hacendados* used the threat of separation to ensure loyalty.

This thin veneer of reciprocity formalized gender relations on the estates. When *henequeneros* arranged weddings for their peons, they provided grooms with a loan—the couple's first debt—to pay for the religious and civil ceremonies and a fiesta. The result was a complicit arrangement among males on the estate in which the master permitted the peon to preside over his own household as a subordinate patriarch. If this led to cases of domestic violence, more often than not they were handled circumspectly on the estate; rarely did grievances find their way to the local courtroom. Typically, *hacendados* and overseers put gross offenders in the hacienda jail.

Such *campesino* patriarchy, however, had limits. Often enough the *henequenero* or his overseer, exercising the humiliating "privilege" of the "right of first night," invaded the peon's hut and violated his spouse or daughter. Even though such an affront undermined the reciprocal nature of the shared sense of patriarchy, it did provide the peon with one more object lesson in where power ultimately resided on the estate. The servant would seldom take revenge on his boss; more often, we learn of unfortunate cases of misdirected rage, as peons abused their wives to reassert their dominion in the home.

Planters were reluctant to tamper with the peons' patriarchal control of their families because in the long run it suited their economic interests. As far as the *hacendado* was concerned, the principal task of

Maya women was to procreate and rear the next generation of henequen workers. To permit women to work in the fields would under-
mine that role and upset social relations on the estate—relations that
reflected the acculturated Maya's evolving cultural identity as well as
the requirements of fiber production.

Thus a grim irony emerged from the henequen commodity chain:
capitalistic North American wheat farmers, embedded in a democratic
political system, using advanced technology on their family wheat
farms, created demand for henequen in Mexico that spread and intensified coerced grueling manual labor and disrupted families in an oli-
garchic polity. In effect, the labor that was saved in the Midwest by
mechanization was expended in Yucatán by Maya peasants working to
exhaustion in the henequen fields. Ultimately the success of midwestern farmers, made possible in part by low wages in Yucatán, led them
to modernize corn production and begin to export south. That, in turn,
would undercut and drive down corn prices in Mexico, where maize
was first domesticated.[142]

After World War I, henequen and manila found their comfortable
niche challenged by a new fiber. Yucatecans were well acquainted with
sisal *(Agave sisalana)*, which was indigenous to the peninsula and had
long been used by artisans to make hammocks and bagging. This true
sisal reached German East Africa in the 1890s, and by the 1920s sisal plantations flourished in Tanganyika and Kenya. Later Java, in the
South Pacific, would commit to sisal. A formidable competitor, sisal
was stronger than henequen and, unlike manila, lent itself well to
defibering machines. Labor costs in these areas were even lower than
in Yucatán and the Philippines; another race to the bottom. By 1927,
Asian and African nations accounted for nearly half the world's hard-
fiber production.

The Great Depression and the invention of the combine, which did
not use twine, hurt the henequen and manila trades. Production fell
precipitously; henequen exports reached a low in 1940, when they were

less than one-fourth the six hundred thousand bales exported during World War I. The introduction of low-cost synthetic fibers after World War II would devastate all hard-fiber economies; indeed, reports of their demise were not exaggerated as polypropylene harvest twine gradually replaced both sisal and henequen-based baler twine as the industry standard.

To add insult to injury, the economic multiplier effects of these primary commodities were limited. The local economies were too small to transfer earnings to other productive enterprises. Hard-fiber exports, despite the great wealth generated for some in the short run, were unable to lead to self-sustaining economic development in Mexico, the Philippines, Africa, Bengal, or Java. In this, hard fibers were much less generous than wheat, whose sophisticated commodity chain helped foment industrialization by technological invention, important backward and forward linkages, labor-saving devices, and a lowered cost of living in the booming cities. The fibers were also more injurious than rice because of the widespread use of coerced labor in henequen and manila and their intense market orientation. Rice continued to mainly be for subsistence; it fed the same people who worked the paddies, though its role was more developmentalist in industrializing countries like Japan.

## Stimulants

Last we include a category of goods that has usually been given insufficient attention in this period: stimulants. They are often dismissed as luxuries, "non-necessaries," or "drug foods." Some of them, such as cocaine, are even denounced as outlaw goods on the margins of booming world trade. Other stimulants, like kava, the kola nut, mate, or khat, while permitted, were popular only locally. Even when goods important to the world economy, such as sugar, coffee, and tobacco, are included, they have been derided as the "big fix" and "the big drain."[143]

Most are psychoactive, or mind- and body-altering. At certain times and in certain places they were considered illicit (sugar would have to be converted to alcohol to win such a dubious honor). Ingested for purposes other than nutrition, initially they were thought of as medicines, drugs, or spices, and soon they became associated with food and even replaced the hunger for food (though not the body's need for nutrition). In fact, they played a central role in feeding international and transcontinental trade. Some began as luxuries and ended as necessities or even industrial inputs. Others became medicines essential to health and to military operations. They were closely attached to the development of the food and pharmaceutical industries.

The goods that were important in the last third of the nineteenth century still had in common characteristics necessary for the era of slow-moving and expensive trade, loosely institutionalized markets, and incipient chemistry labs. Given the risks of oceanic travel, however, they also had to be potentially quite profitable to encourage traders to engage in long-distance commerce. They had to travel well—that is, not spoil easily—and have a high value-to-weight ratio to support transport costs. Moreover, these stimulants could be cultivated only in a limited geographic area, otherwise they would simply be grown in the country of consumption. Finally, they operated in varied cultural and religious contexts in which they played many different roles.[144]

The sometimes radical difference in climate between growers (often tropical) and consumers (mostly temperate) was usually also reflected, at least in 1870, in the strikingly distinct social and cultural settings of the people involved in the trade. By 1945, however, some of the difference between the two ends of the various commodity chains had declined as export-led growth brought development and urbanization to the most successful agricultural countries and at least urban pockets of development in the places less enmeshed in the world market.

The post-1870 period experienced new uses even for products that, like sugar, had been consumed for a long time: this was the era of urbanization, intensified labor, longer workdays, and market-oriented workers who could occasionally afford to buy imported goods. Although these goods often began as markers of distinction and status to separate the wealthy and privileged from the masses, they became necessities sometimes as important as food itself where factories and electricity imposed work discipline over laborers' biological clocks. Stimulants both induced pleasure and dulled misery.

We concentrate on sugar, tobacco, coffee, tea, and chocolate because they were among the first commodities to tie together the continents, as early as the sixteenth century, and became some of the most valuable internationally traded goods in the years 1870–1945. They highlight the contrasting and changing roles of colonialism, slavery, immigration, mechanization, and botanical improvements in cultivating areas. They also demonstrate the industrial, marketing, and financial transformations, and the growing mass appeal in consuming countries as well, allowing us to contrast production systems on different continents. Cane sugar was grown in tropical Caribbean and South American colonies but was challenged by beet sugar production in more temperate zones. Coffee in our period was overwhelmingly grown in independent countries in Latin America after an initial success in South Asian colonies; tea grew almost exclusively in Asia, at first in China and Japan but mostly in colonies by the twentieth century; and chocolate was first cultivated in independent Latin America but increasingly in African colonies after the First World War. The global reach and cultural interactions of the international economy are underlined by the fact that the word *coffee* is derived from Arabic, *tea* from a Chinese dialect, and *cacao* from the Olmecs of southern Mexico. (*Chocolate* is a corruption of the Aztec name for the beans.)

The impact of these commodities cannot be measured solely in monetary terms. Their social and political impacts were also registered in their strategic importance and the roles they played in people's everyday lives, from the crushing labor in the fields to the delight of a sweet candy, a good smoke, or a fresh brew of coffee, tea, or chocolate. Some stimulants were particularly prized during wartime.

## Sugar

Sugar remained one of the most valuable commodities on the world market. Its cultivation and production were spread around the globe, because in addition to the more traditional tropical cane sugar, beet sugar started flourishing in temperate lands during the late nineteenth century. Competition between the two types of sugar provoked technological and institutional improvements that reduced the price to consumers while progressively broadening the market for both. Both types of sugar delivered cultivars, capital, migrant labor, new business forms, and new products all over the world. The economist W. Arthur Lewis notes that sugar was the only tropical crop to undergo a scientific revolution before the First World War.[145] Still, the circumstances of its production in different areas varied widely.

Characterized by innovation and dynamism, sugar was not a crop that lent itself to freedom, even though overt slavery was abolished in our period. By and large, neither labor nor commodity markets were free. Generating some of the most advanced capitalist cultivation and processing complexes in the world, sugar also relied on various forms of colonialism: international, internal, and neocolonial; coercion through a variety of means from slavery and debt peonage to indenture; corporate monopoly of land and monopsony of harvested cane; and cartels and trusts in consuming countries. Not surprisingly, sugar labor relations played a large role in inciting revolution in Haiti (1791–1804), Cuba (1860s and 1896–1898), and Mexico (1910–1917) as well as inducing radical politics in the Caribbean and elsewhere. For consumers, sugar—formerly a luxury—became an everyday spice and fuel that provided sweetness and calories. Not only were its cultivation and processing industrialized, sugar became an important ingredient in the burgeoning processed-foods industry as a sweetener and a preservative.

Sugar, specifically the species *Saccharum officinarum,* was one the first transcontinental commodities to mobilize world trade and colonialism while moving laborers across oceans. Domesticated by humans perhaps twenty-five hundred years ago, it remained of minor importance until the early modern era. Restricted by nature to areas free of frost, it was the quintessential tropical crop. The spice that had begun probably in New Guinea or Indonesia, then India, in the early modern era was moved to the Mediterranean area, where Arabs adapted processing techniques first developed for olive oil. Although sugar continued to be cultivated in India, China, and Persia, it was grown on such a small scale that it did not replace other sweeteners. In the Western world, especially in Europe, it would become what by the seventeenth century could convincingly be called, along with silver, one of the first two transatlantic commodities. Sugar replaced honey, syrups, and tree saps to become the dominant sweetener. It enjoyed the advantage of not changing the flavor of the food or drink to which it was added, and it was cheap to transport once processed, relatively imperishable, and easy to store.[146] It was also the raw material for highly coveted products like molasses and rum.

Sugar's inherent botanical characteristics were certainly responsible in part for its enormous popularity and extensive economic consequences in Europe. But demand was as important as supply. Changes occurring in Europe set the stage for the explosion of demand that started in the seventeenth century and became full-blown in the last quarter of the nineteenth century.

Sugar evolved from a spice and medicine to a marker of status.[147] Demand for it in Europe grew at a stunning 10 percent per year in the nineteenth century. The British had the greatest cravings for sugar, or at least the greatest capacity to buy it—and Europe's worst teeth. On average, each Briton ate eighteen pounds in 1800 and ninety pounds a century later.[148] Because Great Britain ended its protection of colonial sugar imports by 1846, it became the largest free import market in the world as its colonial production declined. This reflected the victory of domestic sugar refiners and candy makers over colonial and foreign planters. As historian of sugar Noël Deerr ruefully admonished: "During the whole three hundred years of the British sugar industry there has been a clash of interests between the producer and the refiner, and it is not going too far to say that there has been a tendency to reduce the former to the position of a bond servant to the latter."[149]

British duties were low or absent on low-grade sugars but high on better, more profitable sugars. Hence, colonial planters sent an industrial input that the protected refiners in Britain turned into a more profitable finished sugar product. It turned out that free trade meant the colonial grower was not protected but the home refiner was. Continental European countries like Germany and Austria as well as the United States followed the same policy, privileging the home industry over those overseas.

Sugar in the years 1870–1945 is given less scholarly attention than in the colonial slave era, but world sugar production expanded tenfold in our period, growing four times as fast as the world's population. Even once the last major cane sugar growers abolished slavery—Cuba in 1886 and Brazil in 1888—world sugar output continued to mount, quadrupling from 3.8 million tons in 1880 to 16 million tons at the outset of World War I, and as high as 27.8 million tons in 1942. The continued upsurge in production occurred not so much because sugar now relied on free wage labor, but because new forms of coercive labor, such as debt peonage and contract labor, were introduced, and the fields and mills were increasingly mechanized.[150]

The ability of the sugar trade not only to survive but to grow vertiginously after emancipation would have shocked principals of the sugar trade who had for centuries assumed that sugar required slavery. (They did not know that in Asia, free peasants grew and cut the cane.) Clearly, planters in the Americas were able to make adjustments to this radical change in the labor regime. This should not have been surprising. As historian Manuel Moreno Fraginals has shown for Cuba, some of the planters were agile capitalists, not hidebound feudal traditionalists committed to precapitalist labor forms.[151]

Despite the multitude of reformers and historians who have argued that slavery impeded industrialization, that was clearly not the case for sugar. Sugarcane was not simply a "raw material" that would be refined by factories in Europe. In one sense it was an industrial good, processed initially in situ on the plantation. But it could be considered an intermediate good because it more often than not was added to other foods and often underwent further processing in consuming countries. The processing in sugar mills to extract sucrose from the cane and then purify it—sometimes in a different installation—had required some of the most advanced chemistry, which was practiced in mills that were some of the largest enterprises of the early modern and nineteenth-century worlds. A good case has been made that sugar mills were the first modern factories in the field with large disciplined labor forces and integrated, time-sensitive processes. These factories were developed by local and often immigrant landowners and merchants as well as by absentee investors in the purportedly backward Caribbean and South America, not in the advanced centers of the Industrial Revolution.[152]

After 1870, abolition, electricity, foreign capital, and modern transport would inspire a new technical revolution. The industrial nature of sugar production meant that demand for sugar could rise at the same time that prices of cane and processed sugar *fell*. In the restricted markets of mercantilist Europe, growing demand usually had been answered by soaring prices and restricted trade. But after 1870 the competition of empires changed almost everything. As historians Bill Albert and Adrian Graves observe: "By World War I, the only aspect of sugar production which remained unchanged from the early decades of the nineteenth century was cane cutting. In all other respects there had been a complete and radical transformation."[153] The transformation was brought about not only by changes in technology and labor regime, but also by the organization of sugar firms. Economic historian Alan Dye notes, "In most instances, the industries affected by the technical changes of the second industrial revolution and the organizational innovations of the accompanying managerial revolution centered in Europe and the United States. In one industry they did not—sugar."[154] The market widened beyond the aristocracy and bourgeoisie and spread out from the largest cities to towns and villages. In England, even servants were given a weekly sugar allowance.[155] The downtrodden sailors of Her Majesty's navy received a generous rum allotment. Sugar, even when it relied on slave labor, was, as Adam Smith recognized, a capitalist enterprise that increasingly reached a mass market.

Capitalism and slavery had gone hand in hand; many of the most capitalistic of planters invested the most in slaves.[156] But sugar plantations proved to be a hybrid. In Cuba they had started using the railroad to move sugar on plantations within thirteen years of its first public use in England. Steam-powered, and then electrically powered, machines moved out to the ever-larger sugar mills in the countryside.

While welcoming technological innovation, planters did not want to dive straight into a world of free labor. Part of the solution to the end of slavery for growers was some years of "apprenticeship" of ex-slaves adopted throughout the Americas to ease the transition for planters (and extend it for laborers). With the end of the Atlantic slave trade in the first half of the nineteenth century, the colonial powers encouraged the movement of technically free but often indentured peoples from one colony—and ocean—to another. Importation of Amerindians from Mexico (in Cuba) and immigrants from India as well as Chinese and Pacific islanders (in Fiji and Australia) provided some of the hands that had previously come from Africa.

Some of the most important changes came in the last decades of the nineteenth century when slavery's demise became evident to even the most successful sugar producers. Large central mills were installed that employed the centrifugal process using vacuum pans to separate the crystals from the molasses. They greatly sped up the process and permitted undreamed-of economies of scale if provided sufficient cane to keep the boilers and centrifuges operating at full throttle. The new machinery would demand greater coordination between the harvest in the fields and processing in the mills.

In Cuba, technological innovations, combined with the devastation of the smaller mills caused by the pro-independence Ten Years War (1868–1878) and the closing of the transatlantic slave trade in midcentury, led to the establishment of large mill-plantation complexes. They were neither agricultural enterprises nor factories, strictly speaking, but rather, in the words of sociologist Fernando Ortiz, a complex "system of land, machinery, transportation, technicians, workers, capital, and people to produce sugar. It is a complete social organism, as live and complex as a city or municipality, or a baronial keep with its surrounding fief of vassals, tenants, and serfs."[157]

Until official colonialism ended in 1898, these complexes were financed mostly by Spaniards, though with growing US investments. Then, under neocolonial independence, large US sugar corporations built giant central mills. They required fewer workers to process far more cane much more quickly and extract more sucrose. The central mills were not only more efficient; they exercised local monopsony control over the smaller sugar estates. The smaller-scale sugar landholders, known as *colonos,* began to specialize in cultivation while sending their cane on a much improved rail system to be processed by their giant industrial neighbors. Increasingly, the US mills moved to the east end of the island where they dominated landowning. *Colonos* became their tenant farmers. Before Cuba's 1895–1898 war for independence from Spain, the slightly less than three million acres of sugar lands had been divided into ninety-one thousand estates that averaged just thirty acres each. Afterward land became so concentrated that by the 1920s, 180 huge sugar mills owned almost twenty-three thousand square kilometers of land, 20 percent of Cuba's territory! The voracious sugar sector came under the sway of US capital just as Cuba bent to North American military and political might. Already in 1896 some three-fourths of Cuba's sugar went north to the United States. By 1913 almost 80 percent of Cuba's exports went to North America.[158] Most of the economy, not just plantations but also the railroads, public utility companies, banks, and even hotels, were owned by Yankees. Sugar saw the creation of enormous foreign-owned estates, modern agro-industrial factories in the fields. The mill owners were not only factory bosses and planters, but also virtual sovereigns issuing laws and money and overseeing housing.

The botanical nature of cane sugar, with one or at most two harvests a year, and the fact that cane had to be processed within a day or two of cutting or its sugar content fell drastically, meant that factories had to process *local* cane—the cane could not be imported from elsewhere during the local off-season. As a result, the industry faced idle capacity and unemployed laborers during the dead season. Seasonal instability was exacerbated by cyclical fluctuations of world prices caused by rain, drought, and hurricanes. This was in the context of a secular price drop by half between 1870 and 1910 and then, after a spike during World War I, back down to one-quarter the 1870 price by 1930.[159] Because so much capital was invested in the sugar mills, members of the mill complex could not convert to another crop to compensate. They had to find a means to improve efficiency in processing and transport,

A sugar mill near Havana, Cuba, ca. 1904. Cuban sugar barons became world leaders in sugar production by combining the most advanced technology of the Industrial Revolution in their large steam-driven mills with efficient railroads that brought cane from huge plantations and exported processed sugar to the world. These factories in the field were serviced by the back-breaking labor of machete-wielding rural proletarians. (Library of Congress)

which brought further debt and reliance on external markets. Not surprisingly, some of the first literature stressing the "dependence" of exporting countries on overseas markets and capital focused on sugar and was published in this period.[160]

Cuba and to a lesser extent the Dominican Republic and the newly won US territory of Puerto Rico were the Caribbean success stories of the first part of the twentieth century. The other European former sugar colonies stagnated or lowered their sugar production while Cuba's production grew two and half times just between 1904 and 1914. By 1929 it had doubled again, though output would fall rather sharply once the Great Depression hit.[161]

The solution to reducing production costs and attending to the rapidly growing markets of North America and Western Europe was not only better machines. Agronomy also contributed. Experimental stations in Cuba, Java, and England developed through "nobilization," breeding new types of sugarcane that had higher sucrose content, were more resistant to disease, could flourish in different climates, and were easier to harvest.

In addition to both intensifying and extending sugar planting and processing in the Spanish Caribbean, the colonial regimes stimulated new areas of cane cultivation in the Indian Ocean. The more dependable and larger ships, driven by steam and the Suez Canal's opening, allowed such an inexpensive, bulk product as Indian Ocean sugar to compete with Caribbean production in the markets of Europe.

The Dutch turned to sugar once Java's coffee economy was devastated by leaf rust disease in the 1870s and 1880s. By the 1920s, Java was the second most important sugar exporter in the world, though it declined sharply with the Great Depression and a change in British sugar import duties in India. Java's sugar success stemmed from a system quite different from the Caribbean's. Using what anthropologist Clifford Geertz calls "agricultural involution," a mounting population invested increasing amounts of labor in their sugar and rice terraces to maintain food at a "minimal level."[162] Geertz viewed this as more than a colonial relationship:[163]

There never really was, even in [Dutch East India] Company times, a Netherlands East Indies economy in an integral, analytic sense—there was just that, admittedly highly autonomous, branch of the Dutch economy which was situated in the Indies ("tropical Holland" as it sometimes was called), and cheek-by-jowl, the autonomous Indonesian economy also situated there.

Elsewhere in the East, the British applied their own capital and workers from Pacific islands to Queensland, Australia. Having assumed control of the continent from the indigenous Aborigine population in the late eighteenth century, white settlers and British capital began the sugar industry in the mid-nineteenth century. The extent to which these initial workers were voluntary or "kidnapped" is disputed, but that they were indentured seems clear. However, racism and broader imperial goals soon reshaped the Australian sugar industry. Seeking a land of small-scale *white* farmers rather than the more typical plantation model using foreign capital and brown workers, Queensland first sponsored two sugar mills to fight the oligopsony of the existing major refining companies. In 1887 milling began to be consolidated under the Colonial Sugar Refining Company (CSR), a company intended to be Australian-owned. It backed labor legislation that sought to end indentured (brown) labor. Then legislation in 1893 created central mills managed by smallholders. Although under strictly economic free-trade calculations the Australians were not competitive, London leaders of the British Commonwealth decided to protect the white Australians through tariffs and bounties. Investments in modern cane species and advanced technology under the stewardship of state governments and the CSR led to a seventy-fold rise in Australia's sugar production between 1870 and 1910.[164]

The experience of sugar in Fiji, which became a British colony in 1874, contrasts with Australia's. In Fiji there was a substantial native population, but it was marginalized under colonialism. The sugar industry was run by British and Australian capital using labor from Britain's colony in India. Indeed, it has been argued that Fiji was a colony of Australia, at least insofar as it was the sugar sector that dominated exports. The same CSR that instituted policies that favored smallholders and invested domestically in Australia, controlled Fiji, where it employed poorly paid indentured Indians. Profits, instead of being reinvested in Fiji, were repatriated to Australia. Australian banks dominated in Fiji as well, but instead of aiding Fijian development as they did in Australia, they sent profits back to Australia.[165] This underlies a major difference in British colonial policy. In part this difference can be explained by the nature of the comparison—in one case, a small island dominated by one crop and few economic activities versus a vast diverse continent. Sugar islands were less able to develop than were continental spaces with sugar, like Brazil or Australia, that were not so wedded to monoculture.

But the distinction between Fiji (or Mauritius, Barbados, or Jamaica) and Australia also reflects the different policies and economic patterns of tropical and temperate colonies. Temperate-climate colonies (also thought of as settler and white when the local indigenous population was sufficiently marginalized, as in Australia, New Zealand, or earlier the United States and Canada) were awarded more local autonomy and far more European investments.[166] An enclave example of the settler colony on the southern tip of Africa was Natal, where whites displaced native Africans and then contracted Indian coolies. (Wages were too low to interest black South Africans.) As in Australia, at the end of the nineteenth century central mills were introduced, indentured labor was phased out, and plantations were replaced by smaller holdings.

A different form of sugar colonialism appeared in Formosa, which began producing sugar particularly under the supervision of Japanese colonial rulers. Although Formosa had prospered during a sugar boom in the early eighteenth century, its family-run farms and small mills had difficulty keeping up with advances in foreign production. After the Japanese occupied the island in 1895, Formosa's economy remained agricultural. Families continued to dominate farming, but sugar processing was modernized. Japanese conglomerates built large, advanced mills and acquired some of the sugar lands. As in Cuba, their mills controlled the native-owned sugar farms. Although unable to compete internationally, sugar once again became Formosa's leading export because it was sold duty-free within the protected Japanese market.[167]

US sugar colonialism in Hawai'i was similar. Cane was already being cultivated before the arrival of Captain Cook in the late eighteenth century, but it was chewed rather than made into sugar. Sugar production and exports rose only with the settling of North American missionaries, which also caused the native Hawai'ian population to dwindle, as the outsiders brought deadly diseases. To replace the natives, 46,000 Chinese, 180,000 Japanese, 126,000 Filipinos, as well as Portuguese and Puerto Ricans were brought in, often as semicoerced workers bound by "semi-military labor contracts."[168] Appropriated by the United States in 1893 and annexed five years later, Hawai'i became a significant sugar and pineapple source as large companies, such as Spreckels Sugar and Dole Pineapple, connected the islands ever closer to the United States under the umbrella of US protective tariffs.[169] These companies not only grew and processed their crops, but also branded and wholesaled them.

In the circum-Caribbean, colonies of the British, French, Dutch, Danish (until the purchase of the Virgin Islands by the United States in 1917), and Spanish (until 1898), and independent sugar-growing nations such as Brazil, found their sugar exports sharply declining and their exports diversifying into other crops, especially coffee, cacao, and bananas. With the exception of Cuba, which became one of the world's premier sugarcane producers, and to a lesser extent Puerto Rico and the Dominican Republic, New World cane growers turned inward, either to their colonial mother country or to the home market.

Independent Brazil turned after the abolition of slavery to the burgeoning domestic market for sugar as well as *cachaça* (cane spirits). The historiography of Brazil laments the collapse of its sugar industry as the Northeast failed to attract immigrants and refused to permit Africans or Asians to enter as laborers after 1888 (with the exception of Japanese, who came in large numbers to the state of São Paulo in the 1920s—but to work in coffee, not sugar). *Modernization without Change* is the subtitle of one well-known study of the purported backwardness of the sugar sector. But it looked at sugar only as an export. In fact, the construction of new railroads and central mills *(usinas)* allowed the country to remain one of the world's main sugar producers after abolition. In 1945 Brazil produced 1.2 million tons, trailing only Cuba in the Americas and Java as well as beet producers Germany and Russia in world production.[170] This feat did not receive much attention, however, because the sugar was not exported; it simply remained within the country.

Mexico followed a similar trajectory as its sugar continued to be directed to the domestic market, which was protected to benefit the local elite. Sugar producers relied on the domestic workforce from Mexico's impoverished and largely indigenous center. With labor becoming scarcer or more restive, capital in the form of mechanization and rationalization—especially in processing and transporting cane— reduced the workforce. Sugar areas in both Mexico and Brazil would become hotbeds of political agitation. In 1911 Emiliano Zapata led revolutionary peasants angered at expanding sugar plantations in their home state of Morelos just south of Mexico City. Agitation in the northeast of Brazil came only in the 1960s. Of course, the sugar-inspired revolution that would rock the world brought Fidel Castro to power in Cuba in 1959.

Peru's huge export-oriented coastal sugar plantations relied mainly on some one hundred thousand Chinese contract laborers who worked under harsh coercive conditions from the mid-nineteenth century to 1874. Almost all male, this coolie population did not expand to satisfy labor demands. Gradually, indigenous workers from the Andes were persuaded to work in sugar under the *enganche,* where indigenous laborers were literally hooked from their communities by contractors. But they were usually somewhat unreliable seasonal workers because they were ill-treated and because they continued to own small farms in the Sierra. Unlike the *colonos* of the Caribbean, they were not proletarians, though swelling population, grasping *hacendados,* and warfare had reduced peasant autonomy in the mountains. To supplement indigenous workers and the evaporated pool of coolie labor, the Peruvian government entered into a contract with a Japanese immigration company in 1898. Protected by the company and the Japanese legation, the 17,700 Japanese laborers who arrived to work in Peruvian sugar by 1923 were better treated than either the Chinese coolies or native Peruvians had been.[171]

In Argentina, the interior province of Tucumán, connected to the Buenos Aires area by a railroad in 1876 and protected by a high tariff, began to supply the national market and even export some. Instead of using workers of African, Indian, or Chinese origin, as in most other sugar economies, the Argentines mimicked the Peruvians and Mexicans by relying on debt peonage of indigenous Andean populations, a holdover from Spanish colonial labor systems but adapted to a new product. This system was sufficiently successful that Argentina began exporting sugar to neighboring countries, yet the Tucumán area remained one of the country's poorest provinces.[172] Sugar's success in Argentina's interior resulted from a national development project, in the sense that government railroad and tariff policy aided the elite of the landlocked northwest. But these measures did little for its workers.

The sugar policy of the US South came to resemble Argentina's. Sugar planters in Louisiana, for example, had originally grown for export when Louisiana had been part of the French Empire. But they had changed orientation to the US home market after the French sold their colony well before the American Civil War. The war created great destruction to life and property, and then the Emancipation

Proclamation freed the more than two hundred thousand slaves in the sugar sector, many of whom became sharecroppers. Despite the protection of import duties and bounties, southern cane production would not grow much until the 1959 Cuban Revolution and ensuing embargo.[173]

## Sugar Beets

The world sugar industry witnessed a great transformation of the trade in the nineteenth century with the development of the sugar beet, *Beta vulgaris,* which grew in temperate climates. Substitution of successful commodities, by finding new sources, new cultivars, or chemically synthesized replacements, was a common feature of the late nineteenth- and twentieth-century world economy, as we have already seen with hard fibers. In the case of sugar, the beet, a previously unimportant tuber, came to challenge cane's place as a worldwide sweetener. This was just one of the fundamental applications of German science (chemistry, agronomy, and engineering) to economic problems. Without tropical colonies or great exports, Germans had an inclination to self-reliance that would greatly affect world markets in nitrates, dyes like cochineal and indigo, rubber, and sugar. This was a result not only of German chemical prowess and sophisticated labs and universities— chemistry had been a *Lieblingswissenschaft* since the eighteenth century—but of necessity brought on by the world economy. German wool could not compete with Australian wool, German flax and hemp lost out to Mexican henequen, African sisal, and Indian jute, and their vegetable oils could not compete with petroleum jelly or margarines that used palm, soy, and peanut oil from tropical countries. The response was to improve seeds, plants, and fertilizers in agriculture and create chemical substitutes or synthetics. Their exports continued to go principally to Europe (though their imports now tended to come from the neo-Europes and tropics), but the composition of German exports changed from raw materials to finished and semifinished goods.[174] Their success at this is why the German word *ersatz* ("substitute") became part of the English vocabulary.

A German scientist, Andreas Marggraf, in 1747 became the first to extract sugar from the beet. A half century passed before research efforts led to the first sugar beet factories in Prussia, Russia, and Austria-Hungary. But it was the British blockade of Napoleonic France beginning in 1806, which drove prices for cane sugar sky-high, that encouraged the opening of more sugar beet factories. Colonial powers like the French resumed their affair with cane sugar once the blockade ended in 1815, but the Central Europeans and Russians continued to put their hopes in the beet. They bred new beet cultivars and developed processing techniques to increase sucrose content from 7 percent in the early nineteenth century to 8 percent by the 1870s, up to 11.9 percent in 1889.[175] New extraction through centrifuges beginning in the 1840s and the expanding size of mills as they became modern factories caused beet sugar production to mount.

But this is not just a story of the agronomy and technology of the beet itself. The sugar beet occupied an important place in the farm complex of the rural poor that made it economically viable. Like potatoes, the sugar beet grew in cold climates as well as warm. Densely planted, it did not require much land or many inputs. It was cultivated with a simple hoe. The beet offered side benefits because it was the highest-yielding field crop of the temperate zone in terms of volume. Its leaves as well as the pulp left over after sucrose extraction were used to feed livestock, whose manure in turn fed the beets. Beets reached maturity quickly and replenished the land with nitrogen. So rather than competing with other crops as grains did, the beet complemented them as a stage in crop rotation instead of leaving the land fallow.[176] Labor demands were not particularly time-sensitive because the ripe beet could be left in the ground until the farmer was ready to extract it. So in contrast to cane sugar—an exotic that encouraged foreign ownership, coercive labor systems, concentration of lands and profits, as well as an industrial processing plant, and imported workers—beet sugar could be more benign (though many Poles came to Saxony and many Mexicans to the US Midwest to work beet sugar in the twentieth century).

On the other hand, the advantages of beet cultivation offered few economies of scale or scope. (Sugar beets could not be used to make alcohol, for instance.) This made it socially and politically attractive in that peasants were not dislodged during the boom. On the other hand, the Prussian *Junker* landlords of Saxony combined their feudal agrarian heritage with modern industry. They retained their vast estates and turned them to the sugar beet as they invested in the most modern mills and sugar factories as well.[177] Increased output demanded more workers, who now were paid in wages rather than in kind or usufruct. By 1913 there were four hundred thousand migratory workers, mostly from Poland. The beet inverted the relationship of the state to the agricultural elite; rather than the *Junkers* dominating the state, the state subsidized the agrarian *Junkers*. To protect them, duties on imported sugar were kept high and bounties on exports, to encourage a balance-of-payments surplus, also remained high. This meant that the German consumer paid a price above the international market price for sugar while the British consumer enjoyed the treat of sugar subsidized by the German government. To protect beet growers and more importantly refiners, the German government also banished saccharin—a sugar substitute synthesized from coal tar first in 1878 by a German chemist and cheaper than beet sugar—to pharmacies as a medicine rather than a food ingredient.[178]

Beets needed government protection because they could not compete with cane on price; they were too expensive. But the governments of Prussia (and Germany after unification in 1871), Austro-Hungary, and Russia offered bounties to encourage cultivation and exports. This was not only a state-led effort to promote industrialization and positive trade balances. Protecting peasant farmers was also politically wise because German farmers had more than once shown their ability and inclination to revolt. This was a particularly sensitive issue in Germany when the expansion of cheap wheat production in Russia and in the "vacant lands," such as Argentina and the US Midwest, drove out of business some German wheat farmers working poorer fields. These were the same lands that sustained the sugar beet. By the end of the nineteenth century, government aid and peasant agriculture in France, the Netherlands, Belgium, parts of Scandinavia, and Spain were also yielding beet sugar.[179] Although beet sugar was a national crop rather than a colonial or neocolonial one like cane, it was also the product of state supervision and aid rather than a result of unadulterated market forces.

Beet sugar production was embedded in what Bukharin termed "state capitalism." As with a number of other commodities, state governments cooperated with big banks and merchant houses to create sugar-refining oligopolies and cartels. Initially beet cultivation was also concentrated in a small number of countries. Germany produced over one-third of the world's 1897 total, and together with Austria, France, and Russia fully 86 percent of the world's beet sugar. Russia and France mainly consumed their sugar while Germany and Austria exported more than half of what they produced, mostly to European neighbors.[180]

In the Midwest and West of the United States, government tariff protection encouraged beet production. But the United States, like the United Kingdom, was still one of the world's largest importers of sugar. In 1896 sugar production (and sundries) in the United States occupied about 3.6 million acres, less than 2 percent of total agricultural acreage, and yielded a similar share of agricultural production by value. Sugar remained small despite the calculation that on a returns-per-acre basis it was far more remunerative than grains, cotton, or potatoes. Only tobacco surpassed it. The reason more farmers did not embrace sugar production was that it required an ample, cheap labor force or political protection. So the United States mostly imported cane sugar, particularly from colonial or semicolonial areas such as Hawai'i, Puerto Rico, the Philippines, and Cuba. But with the dawn of the twentieth century and ample government protection, the beet industry took root, concentrating in California, Colorado, Utah, and Michigan. By 1920, after the world war and civil wars had destroyed the beet industries of Russia, damaged those of Austria and Germany, and cut world beet production in half, the United States briefly became the world's leading beet sugar producer.[181] Seeking shelter from colonial competitors, American beet growers added a loud voice to battle against American colonialism.

## The Market for Sugar

Sugar production mounted steadily, albeit haltingly, in the century after 1840 (see Table 3.5). The data implied a more homogeneous and monolithic market than was in fact the case. The difference was not only between cane and beet producers, but also between the taxation regimes of states and colonies. In Great Britain, true to its free-trade doctrine at this point, sugar cost almost half as much as in protectionist Germany, Austria, and the United States (see Table 3.6).

Given that the world sugar market was divided between colonial or neocolonial empires (cane) and national state-aided systems (beet), it should come as no surprise that the world sugar market was segmented and regulated. National governments, not individual corporations, were the players. International wars, revolutions, and civil wars shifted production. Even though the British attempted to open up the world sugar market by dropping sugar duties and reducing colonial preferences, other major consuming countries did not follow suit. Their strong state presence and contradictory interests were manifested in the numerous international sugar conferences held in the years after 1870.

TABLE 3.5

**Estimated world cane sugar and beet sugar production,**

**1841–1940 (in tons)**

|  | Cane | Beet | Total |
|---|---|---|---|
| 1841 | 829,000 | 50,929 | 879,929 |
| 1850 | 1,043,000 | 159,435 | 1,202,435 |
| 1860 | 1,376,000 | 351,602 | 1,727,602 |
| 1870 | 1,662,000 | 939,096 | 2,601,096 |
| 1880 | 1,883,000 | 1,857,210 | 3,740,210 |
| 1890 | 2,597,000 | 3,697,800 | 6,294,800 |
| 1900 | 5,252,987 | 6,005,865 | 11,258,855 |
| 1910 | 8,155,837 | 8,667,980 | 16,823,817 |
| 1913 | 9,661,165 | 9,053,561 | 18,714,726 |
| 1920 | 11,924,813 | 4,906,266 | 16,831,079 |
| 1925 | 15,140,542 | 8,617,960 | 23,758,502 |
| 1930 | 15,942,438 | 11,910,883 | 27,853,321 |
| 1935 | 16,598,262 | 10,430,394 | 27,028,656 |
| 1940 | 19,255,041 | 11,242,422 | 30,499,463 |

*Sources:* Noël Deerr, *The History of Sugar,* 2 vols. (London: Chapman and Hall, 1950), 2:490–491.

Because sugar was so central to national and colonial government policy, and world prices were falling dramatically, it seemed natural that it would be the major European producers and colonial powers—Austria-Hungary, Belgium, France, Germany, Holland, Italy, Russia, and Spain—who attempted to regulate the world sugar market. The only non-European exception was Peru, which sent a representative to three of the ten international meetings held between 1860 and 1912.[182]

They tried to hammer out differences over bounties, tariffs, and national cartels but were frustrated by failure until the 1902 Brussels Sugar Conference. The problem was that although sugar was a valuable commodity and one of the most internationally traded goods in terms of value, it was also, as historian Horacio Crespo has observed,

TABLE 3.6

**Indexed price of sugar imports, 1888**

| Britain | Germany | Austria | Sweden | Belgium | USA |
|---------|---------|---------|--------|---------|-----|
| 100 | 176 | 170 | 123 | 123 | 170 |

*Source:* Calculated from Michael G. Mulhall, *The Dictionary of Statistics,* 4th ed. (London: G. Routledge and Sons, 1899), 470.

*Note:* 100 = 17 pounds sterling, 11 pence, per ton.

one of the foods "most sensitive to strategies for national self-sufficiency" because of the high amount of calories per acre it produced. Sugar became "an article especially valued by governments in their aim to attain food autarky."[183] Domestic economies were dominated by cartels in Germany and Austria and trusts elsewhere. Other producers were offering export bounties in the attempt to enter the British market, the only free market where colonial and subsidized continental sugar competed. Even the Brussels agreement succeeded only for a few years; the Liberal Party came to power in Britain in 1905, objected to the higher prices caused by the agreement, and withdrew the United Kingdom.

World War I's destruction of European beet-growing countries drastically changed the global market. Cane growers, especially Cuba, regained their former dominance and now had to be included in conversations. But it was difficult to convince all the major sugar players to participate, even as the non-European world gained greater representation. An effort in 1931 supported by the League of Nations that included Cuba, Peru, and Java, as well as major beet growers, failed because countries that had not agreed to production quotas raised their output. A more promising agreement in London in 1937 included not only the members of the previous meetings, but also major consuming countries such as Britain and the United States, and, reflecting a true worldwide discussion, China, India, the Soviet Union, and South

Africa. The agreement, however, did not come into force before World War II broke out and suspended the pact. Sugar would remain a politically sensitive commodity in the postwar years, but its role as a major international commodity declined as mineral commodities and industrial finished products dominated.

As Table 3.5 shows, cane's share of all sugar, which had fallen from 64 percent in 1870 to 41 percent in 1890, returned to over three-quarters of all production by 1940. In part this was because war destroyed beet sugar mills and displaced farmers. Also, national policies shifted as sugar became recognized as a strategic good for wartime consumption. Both the United Kingdom and the United States responded to World War I by offering tariff protection and bounties. Other producers, battered by warfare and the Great Depression, sharply reduced sugar production. As a result, although the world sugar market stagnated between 1930 and 1942, the relative global position of the two English-speaking empires advanced. The United Kingdom, Ireland, and Commonwealth producers combined to grow 12 percent of world production in 1942. The United States, when combined with its territories or colonies of Hawai'i, Puerto Rico, and the Philippines (under US control after 1898), provided 13 to 14 percent of the world total. When Cuba is added—it alone supplied more than all the British colonies, or the United States and its territories—to the other US totals because it had privileged access to the North American market and a neocolonial relationship, the US areas produced almost a third of the world's sugar in 1930 and a quarter in 1942. Together with the United Kingdom, the two English-speaking empires supplied some 40 percent of the world's sugar at the end of our period.[184] Add the Dutch production in Java, and the three colonial powers had close to half the world's sugar output.

The boom in lower-cost, more efficient sugar production led to the creation of oligopoly in the greatest consuming countries. Sugar in the world economy was a true commodity, measured by its weight, degree of refining, and sweetness, but with little birthmark of its origins or whether it derived from cane or beet. This commodification of the final product lent itself to consolidation. A small number of large companies dominated the final processing in the largest markets. In the United States, H. O. Havemeyer oversaw the 1887 merger of eight refining companies to produce the American Sugar Refining Company. At its height in the early 1890s it controlled 90 percent of US refining. It was also politically influential, reputedly playing a large role in presidential elections and in inciting the Cuban-Spanish-American war. Other companies were created to contest its dominance, but the sector remained under oligopoly control. Although the US Sugar Company did create a brand—Domino Sugar—and Spreckels did also, as did a cooperative of Hawaiʻian producers who sold C&H sugar—the major continental European producers mostly did not. This may be because continental Europeans were slower to develop larger retail establishments or brands. There sugar was an ingredient, a sweetener, rather than an end-use product.

Even without brands, sugar did become entrenched in the daily lives of people in the most prosperous countries in North America, Western Europe, the neo-Europes and the cities of major exporting countries in Latin America. It became widespread as a sweetener in drinks (including the start of soft drinks) and as marmalade but also as a preservative and spice in processed foods. Because only the countries listed above, particularly the United States, had moved far along in the food-processing field, it was mainly in those countries that sugar became as omnipresent as it is today. Researchers included sugar as a necessity in studies of daily-life needs for artisans in England as its uses grew. Candy and treacle spread their hold on children, as we will see in our discussion of chocolate.[185] As Table 3.7 illustrates, there was a close correlation between affluent countries and high sugar consumption.[186]

TABLE 3.7

**Per capita sugar consumption, 1933 (in pounds)**

| Country | Pounds of sugar consumed |
|---|---|
| Denmark | 123 |
| Australia | 113 |
| Great Britain | 106 |
| USA | 100 |
| Cuba | 81 |
| Argentina | 63 |
| France | 55 |
| Germany | 51 |
| South Africa | 47 |
| Brazil | 46 |
| Mexico | 31 |
| Peru | 23 |
| Japan | 23 |
| India | 20 |
| China | 3 |
| World | 27 |

*Source:* Noël Deerr, *The History of Sugar,* 2 vols. (London: Chapman and Hall, 1949–1950), 2:532.

We have seen how dramatically the world sugar market changed after 1870. New species and varieties of cultivars, and innovations in agronomy, chemistry, and engineering, brought sugar production to every continent save Antarctica. Laborers varied from slaves, apprentices, and indentured workers, to plantation proletarians, smallholders, and peasants. The market for sugar, although one of the oldest, largest, and most valuable, was clearly not an open one. Colonial (or to include post-1898 Cuba, neocolonial) logics regimented the cane sugar markets while national development logics drove the beet sugar markets. In some parts of the world, cane and beet competed on price because their taste was identical. However, the largest consuming areas were caught up in what were essentially colonial or national development projects. Their criteria were much more political than economic.

## Coffee

Because tens of millions of people in the Americas, Europe, Africa, and Asia have been intimately involved in growing, trading, transporting, processing, marketing, and consuming coffee, it is more than just a case that illustrates broader trends. Coffee itself has been central to the expansion of the world economy; it was not only one of the most valuable commodities in international commerce, in much of this period exceeded only by grains and sugar, but it was the most popular legal drug. For centuries it has truly been a *global* trade good because its intolerance of frost demanded that it be grown exclusively in the tropics or semitropics, but its cost and psychoactive effects meant that since the end of the eighteenth century it has been consumed mostly in richer and colder, caffeine-craving Western Europe and North America.

Coffee embodied the diversity and contradictions of the world economy. In the cultivating countries coffee was viewed mostly as an agricultural export commodity demanding traditional manual labor and natural resources: sun, soil, rain. In the developed consuming countries it appeared as a modern labor-intensifying, sociable brain food disembodied from its agrarian past. So in the global South, coffee meant the plantation and the farm, while in the North it meant the industrial assembly line and coffeehouse as well as the domestic breakfast table. Like sugar, a taste for coffee had intensified colonialism in the early modern period. By 1870, however, the crops were grown mainly in independent countries, particularly Brazil. Coffee sales and consumption helped sustain states by providing revenue and energizing armies while coffee cultivation sparked revolts against other states and landowners.

The coffee species that became internationally popular, *Coffea arabica,* originated in what is today Ethiopia, where it grew natively in the wild. Over one hundred species of *Coffea* (and thousands of varieties) have been identified, yet only one species was widely popular in 1870. The popularity of arabica and its global diffusion were human decisions, which, as the name implies, began not in Ethiopia but across the Red Sea in Yemen.

We would not be discussing coffee had not the coffee *drink* gained popularity before 1500 in Yemen, where coffee was planted in the mountains and became a trade good.[187] Although it was also chewed, fried, and infused as a tea using *Coffea* cherry husks, the Sufi of Yemen made a drink out of the roasted cherry pit or "bean," which was much less perishable than other parts of the plant. This taste choice would prepare coffee for its precocious long-distance trade. Until the twentieth century, coffee—unlike grains and rice—was produced overwhelmingly for export.

Clearly, the coffee trade was not a European invention. Only after more than two centuries of an Arab-centered international market did British, Dutch, and French monopoly companies become involved as an extension of their spice trades.[188] By 1770 more than 80 percent of the world's production originated in the Americas. It was almost all arabica, but traders had to be aware of the differences in provenance. Because of relatively slow transport, poor packaging, and crude processing and brewing, differences in the "quality" of the beans remained at the level of visual inspection—that is, color and defects of the beans. The lore of provenance and appearance continued to dominate grading and pricing well into the twentieth century as *cupping*—actually tasting coffee brewed from a roasted sample— was slow to gain favor. This, and rudimentary international systems of credit and information, at first strengthened trade diasporas of

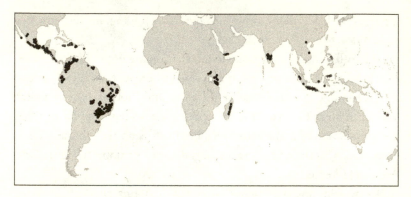

Global production of coffee, ca. 1925.

ethnic minorities and family firms, because personal reputation underlay coffee transactions.

By the second half of the nineteenth century the trade was centered in the Americas. Asia, particularly Java and Ceylon, and some
African colonies had raised their combined coffee exports to about
one-third of international trade in 1860. But the coffee disease *Hemileia
vastatrix* struck, driving their exports back to 5 percent of world trade
by 1913; they remained low (13 percent) through 1945.[189] As mentioned, these areas turned to producing sugar and rubber and, as will
be seen, tea.

The market for coffee, an urban luxury good at the beginning of the
nineteenth century, remained small until the last third of the century.
Only green arabica coffee beans were sold until technological innovations allowed the marketing of roasted, ground, and canned beans at
the end of the nineteenth century. But even just selling green beans,
coffee cultivation proliferated. Commercial competition also accelerated as traders from numerous European nationalities and the United
States began transporting and selling beans. The price spreads between
cultivators were as large as 100 percent, and because of varied taxation

policies and differing freight rates, retail prices also varied widely by nation and region.[190] Early on, green coffee was sold at auction in Europe by consignment merchants who dealt in mixed cargos. They had some idea of the amount of coffee that was reaching port but were not aware of the extent of the crop awaiting harvest. The relatively small and dispersed market was volatile. Merchants and shippers—who were often the same people—governed the trade and attempted local corners.

Merchants and planters were the main entrepreneurs in expanding the coffee trade, because unlike in sugar, European states did not play a major part in stimulating production after the middle of the nineteenth century. Even though it still was produced with coerced labor, coffee was one of the "freest" markets in the world in the sense that the colonial powers dropped out of the trade.

Dutch Java's production fell sharply after leaf rust disease attacked trees beginning in the 1870s. It returned to a position of prominence only in the late twentieth century after independence.[191] In the Americas, the Dutch preferred to serve as traders and shippers; they never developed or expanded their small colonies. The British preferred the mercantilist possibilities in exploiting the Chinese and then the Indian tea trades over protecting their colonial coffee production in Jamaica, Kenya, and Uganda. The Spanish and Portuguese colonial masters preferred cacao, so Iberian Americans had to wait until well after early nineteenth-century independence and Angolans well into the twentieth century to become significant coffee producers. Although the French were fond of coffee, they had to turn to the open world market once Haitians—the world's largest coffee exporters at the time—won their bloody fight for independence in 1804; French colonies in Africa, particularly the Côte d'Ivoire, became major coffee exporters only after World War II. The decline of colonialism in coffee production meant that when states reasserted their control over the world coffee market, they did so only in the twentieth century, and the actors were independent American nations, not European colonial regimes.

Coffee and sugar were treated differently in the nineteenth-century Age of Empire because coffee's low technological demands meant that an independent former colony, Brazil, could begin producing on an unprecedented scale. Cheap, fertile, virgin land combined with rudimentary tools and machinery and abundant and relatively inexpensive slaves (due to the proximity of Africa) allowed Brazil to cause world coffee prices to plummet after 1820. Prices remained low until the last quarter of the century. Low prices and continually expanding production stimulated demand.

Brazil's success was not because of European colonial know-how. Brazil emerged as the world's major coffee exporter only after it threw off the Portuguese yoke in 1822. In fact, colonial policy had favored sugar but hindered coffee. More important to Brazil's rise to caffeinated dominance than independence were exogenous changes in the world market: the collapse of the world leader, Haiti; desire among the swelling European and later US urban consumers for stimulants; and internationally available capital and eventually labor.

Brazilian production not only largely *satisfied* growing world demand, Brazilians *stimulated and transformed* the place of coffee in overseas cafés and homes. The dependency view of agricultural producers as servants or providers of brute labor-power, willingly serving up the fruit of their labor to thirsty European buyers who were the masters of the trade, misconstrues the nature of the relationship. Brazilians, either native-born, African, or Portuguese immigrants, developed new production techniques, discovered productive cultivars, constructed an elaborate domestic transportation network in a geographically unpromising setting, and developed market standards and financial instruments. Unlike the case in other commodities we have reviewed, such as rice and sugar, in which colonialism played a major role, for coffee, independent Brazilians out-produced all colonial growers.

To give their due to the *dependentistas* who argue that Western Europeans called the tune during the nineteenth-century export boom, Brazilians benefited in the nineteenth century because of British dominance in the form of inexpensive and reliable shipping and insurance, loans, infrastructural investments, and the protection of its sea routes. So although the tea-drinking British did not export or import much coffee from their own colonies after the middle of the nineteenth century, they exported and re-exported a lot of coffee from Brazil to the United States and continental Europe. Even so, British merchants' significant presence in the coffee trade was a minority share. Most coffee exports went to the two other fastest-industrializing countries in the world, the United States and Germany, whose merchants, along with the French, gained increasing control of the trade. The same was true with British banks, which lost their dominance of financing the coffee trade to other Europeans and native Brazilian banks by the end of the nineteenth century, as they did with railroads, many of which were nationalized by the Brazilian state or financed by local capitalists.[192]

Even with Brazil, Ceylon, and Java greatly expanding world coffee production in the first half of the nineteenth century, the essential nature of the commodity chain remained the same. All the coffee exported was still green arabica sent overseas by consignment merchants, who in turn provided planters (though not peasants) with the working capital to bring crops to port. Larger plantations set the standards for cultivation, though smaller-scale slave-worked holdings in Brazil and coerced peasant production in Java successfully competed. Unscheduled sailing ships carried coffee packed in leather pouches or cotton and jute bags to major markets, where it was often sold at auction to wholesalers. Roasting, grinding, and brewing were still done in the home or in the coffeehouse. The centuries-old frying pan and mortar and pestle remained the tools of the trade for most consumers until the twentieth century.

The creation of the liberal export economy in the Americas, which contrasted with and complemented expanding European colonialism in Africa, Asia, and Oceania, transformed the nature of the demand for coffee. At first a noble, and then a bourgeois, beverage before 1800, coffee was transformed into a mass drink in the most industrialized and prosperous countries in the last part of the nineteenth century. The slaves of Brazil (until abolition in 1888) slaked the thirst of the factory workers of the industrial countries, particularly in the United States, the German and Austrian realms, and the Netherlands.

Europeans had already changed the nature of the coffee drink in the eighteenth century when Viennese and Parisians added sugar and milk and the French and Dutch began growing it in the circum-Caribbean. These acts not only would make coffee acceptable to Christians, by Europeanizing it, but would later make coffee (and, as we will see, tea) into a popular drink for the working class. In addition to its natural psychoactive properties, which reduced the sense of hunger and sleepiness while releasing adrenalin, coffee also offered the physiological advantages of being a digestive and a diuretic, and of being safe because the water was boiled before consumption. Moreover, calories and nutrition in the form of sugar and milk were now added. Although the international trade in milk would have to wait until companies like Borden, Carnation, and Nestlé developed less-perishable condensed and evaporated milk, the vast expansion of sugar production and the dramatic drop in its price greatly stimulated coffee consumption among the less advantaged in urban Western Europe and the United States.[193]

Brazil, which produced over half the world's coffee by 1850, was responsible for about 80 percent of the unprecedented expansion of world coffee production in the nineteenth century. In the exceptional year of 1906 Brazilians *produced almost five times as much as the rest of the world combined.* And this was no marginal market. For the quarter century 1860–1887, the value of coffee trailed only grains and sugar in seaborne merchandise.[194] Coffee continued for the rest of our period to be one of the world's most valuable internationally traded commodities.

How did this happen? Brazil's remarkable expansion of the world coffee economy and the increase in the trade's breadth and complexity resulted from a unique confluence of Brazil's natural endowments; externalities such as the availability of foreign laborers in Africa—until the Atlantic slave trade was abolished in 1850—and in southern Europe after Brazilian slavery was outlawed in 1888; economies brought by revolutionary advances in transportation and communication technology; and fundamental transformations in the coffee business in the United States and Western Europe.

The explosion of coffee sales during the first three quarters of the nineteenth century had not been brought about by new production methods.[195] Only in the last quarter of the century did cultivating, harvesting, and processing transition out of the same sort of slave labor Brazilian planters had previously used for sugar. But the vastness of its plantations and industrial-scale harvesting, which lowered both the cost and the quality of coffee, were new.

Technological improvements were more evident in transportation than in cultivation. Beginning in 1854 and intensifying after the 1870s, the Brazilian coffee zones of Rio de Janeiro, Minas Gerais, and São Paulo states experienced the largest rail growth of any coffee-based economy. In 1889, when the monarchy was overthrown, the system extended about six thousand miles; at the turn of the century it was ninety-five hundred miles and had grown again by half by the beginning of World War I. Although compared to the industrialized countries of Western Europe and North America this total seemed puny, it towered over all other coffee-growing countries. In Latin America no other coffee-growing country had even one thousand miles of rail at the time. (Mexico had a larger network, but only a small share of it

Workers picking coffee berries in Brazil, ca. 1900–1923. Between 1888, when slavery was abolished in Brazil, and 1933, nearly three million immigrants from southern Europe, especially Italy and Portugal, entered Brazil, mostly to work in the coffee fields. Whole families were given the use of plots of land, and some pay, in exchange for labor in the coffee plantations. This *colono* system allowed Brazil to produce over three-quarters of the world's coffee in the period between 1880 and 1945. (Library of Congress)

served the coffee-growing areas before World War II.) Track was scarce because other coffee growers were either small islands in the Caribbean and the Indian Ocean, or poor and often politically unstable continental areas in northern South America and Central America.[196] In Africa only Ethiopia, Kenya, Uganda, and Tanganyika were connected to their ports by rail in this period. But their coffee exports were tiny. Brazil's system stood out worldwide, being larger than the entire amount of track in Africa and all of Asia outside of India.

Even though railroads did not dramatically reduce cargo costs, because rail companies in Brazil did not offer the same sort of long-distance discounts and rebates that so benefited midwestern US and Canadian wheat growers, they did help improve the quality of coffee at port. More importantly, cheaper, more fertile lands were now accessible in the interior. This was key to Brazil's astounding success, because coffee was a frontier crop—its fields were prepared by cutting down virgin forests, the coffee trees required four to six years to reach maturity and first harvest, then after twenty years of harvests the growers moved on, leaving behind pasture or unworkable lands. Instead of fertilizing, *fazendeiros* exploited the "forest rent" of rich, untilled lands and thick composted soils. Irrigation was rarely needed. Because of the land's natural fecundity, Brazilian *fazendeiros* enjoyed some of the highest-yielding coffee trees in the world. Prussian agronomist Franz Daffert called the Brazilian method *Raubbau,* or predatory agriculture.[197] Although taken aback by its nomadic destructiveness, he had to admit that it made good economic sense in the land-rich, demographically poor tropics.

With the vast interior within reach of the ports via the iron rail, ever-larger amounts of the harvest could be brought to market faster, reducing interest charges on working capital. In other words, the railroads, some of which pioneered novel engineering feats to climb the steep escarpments from the ports to the coffee fields, allowed Brazilians to take advantage of their country's vastness and *continue* their boom. They thereby escaped the geographic trap that had prevented much smaller Yemen, Java, Martinique, Dutch Guiana, and Haiti from qualitatively transforming the world market and from taking advantage of economies of scale. The railroad also temporarily intensified the use of slaves in coffee, partially explaining why Brazil was the last country in the Western Hemisphere to abolish slavery, in 1888.[198]

We should note, however, that although Brazil certainly benefited from its vastness and had some of the largest export plantations ever seen, the Italian and Portuguese immigrants who started replacing slave laborers in the late 1880s appeared to be more self-sustaining peasants than proletarians in a factory in the field, as in Cuban sugar or even in California's Central and Imperial Valleys. In Brazil their main goal was to grow corn and beans for subsistence, only secondarily paying rent for their land with the coffee trees they also tended.[199] Even coffee trees were divided up by families, which, unlike the former slave system, self-exploited women and children as well as men under the authority of the family patriarch. (In other coffee areas like Java and Chiapas, Mexico, fieldwork was done overwhelmingly by migrant men.) Over time, immigrant indentured workers in Brazil bought their own land. Unlike in sugar, the size of the average Brazilian coffee holding declined over time, even as the mills that processed the beans grew. This probably explains why rural revolts were much less common in Brazilian coffee-growing areas than in sugar fields.

Railroads were useful but not *necessary* for a coffee export economy— no other coffee producer had much track until the twentieth century (though Costa Rica's and Mexico's relatively short lines were important). But the great amount of low-priced Brazilian coffee making its way to international ports on iron tracks expanded and reconfigured the world market, because Brazil produced more than the rest of the world combined. Rail latecomers, such as Spanish American growers, then took advantage of specific niches in the larger North American and Western European markets that Brazilian rail-transported mass production had initiated. Spanish American production varied from relatively small family farms in much of Costa Rica, parts of Nicaragua, Venezuela, and parts of Colombia, to large plantations using semicoerced labor in Guatemala, southern Mexico, Nicaragua, and parts of El Salvador.[200] Growers throughout Spanish America were not able to produce as cheaply as Brazilians, but they still found buyers as North American and Western European wholesalers and roasters—particularly the Germans—blended the more expensive but higher-quality Spanish American milds with lower-cost Brazilian beans to satisfy the swelling market in the United States.[201] An important part of their formula for success, despite lacking Brazil's ample natural resources, was the use of family labor on small plots the families owned, rented, or cropped on shares. As in Brazil, they cultivated their own subsistence crops on neighboring plots and exploited the labor of the entire family. In Guatemala and southern Mexico, coffee growers also lowered costs by exploiting the coerced labor of indigenous peoples, male and female, who seasonally migrated to the fields for the harvest. As the indigenous populations grew rapidly in the twentieth century and the land they passed down and divided up became too small for subsistence, the market rather than government coercion delivered Indian workers to coffee plantations as laborers.

Coffee commodity chains grew as a side effect of transformations in the broader world economy as well as from internal dynamics. A clear case of an externality that revolutionized the relationship of Brazil's coffee (and later that of competitors) to the Atlantic world was the shipping revolution already discussed that shrank the world.[202]

Despite the fact that inexpensive and plentiful Brazilian production quenched the thirst and stimulated the wakefulness of ever more North American and European consumers, its remarkable increase in cultivation did not create a monopoly. Yes, in 1906 Brazil produced some 80 percent of the world's coffee. But the institutionalization of the market, with scheduled large steamers, railroads, warehouses, standards, futures market, and new convenience coffee products, opened North American and European ports to other Latin American producers. Rather than a zero-sum game, this was a mutual benefit for all Latin American coffee producers. In most years until the Great Depression all Latin American growers increased output. Large, inexpensive production, combined with plentiful sugar production, allowed coffee to overshadow competing caffeinated drinks such as cocoa, tea, *mate,* and substitutes such as chicory and grains. Latin America turned much of the Western world into coffee drinkers. In other words, Brazil was not just a passive bystander; it was a market maker and would become a price maker beginning in 1906 as the result of government price interventions.[203]

Coffee's heroic nineteenth century occurred not only because of Brazilian and gradually other Latin American production, but also because of burgeoning US and Western European consumption. The transportation revolution and lowered international transaction costs reduced the cost of the lengthiest section of the commodity chain; it also accelerated the commercial relationship between Brazil and the United States, which was strengthened by ever-closer diplomatic ties.[204] Coffee became truly a mass product for the first time in the United States, which was followed by wider consumption in Western Europe.

Coffee shippers benefited from the same efficient internal transportation system in the United States and Western Europe that so helped grain and other food sales. US per capita coffee consumption rose prodigiously even as the total population exploded. The same happened in Western Europe, so that coffee offloaded in Hamburg, Le Havre, Amsterdam, or Trieste could quickly and cheaply reach large and growing consumer markets in the interior.

US government policy also helped. The United States was the only major market to import coffee tax-free after 1832 (except in the Civil War period). Coffee taxes in Western Europe were all substantially higher because of their mercantilist traditions. Consequently, per cap-

A coffee seller, Tunisia, 1916. Even while the vast majority of coffee production had shifted to the Americas and consumption to the Americas and Western Europe, coffee continued to be socially important in the Middle East as it had been for almost four hundred years. This photo depicts the common sight of a street vendor serving two men. In public spaces, coffee was usually the domain of men. (National Geographic Image Collection/The Bridgeman Art Library)

ita consumption of coffee in the United States grew the fastest in the world, from one-eighteenth of a pound in 1783 to nine pounds a hundred years later. The US population's fifteen-fold explosion in that century meant that total coffee imports grew by 2,400 times. Half of the growth in world consumption in the nineteenth century was due to increased US purchases.[205] Almost all of the rest was in Western Europe, especially in the north. Coffee producers were very fortunate to find such favor in the countries whose incomes were growing the fastest in the world. (Coffee boosters argued that this relationship was not coincidental. It was not just that prosperity paid for coffee, but also that coffee as a brain food and labor stimulant brought about prosperity.) US per capita consumption would continue to grow, with some fits and starts, until the 1940s, but Western Europe would lag because of the crushing burden of two devastating world wars.

Demand in the nineteenth century, in both the United States and Europe, was initially both income- and price-elastic. The more people earned, the more likely they were to purchase coffee, and the lower the price, the more likely they were to buy it. This is because coffee initially was viewed as a luxury item, a sign of aristocratic and bourgeois distinction. As it became available to them at a relatively low price, lower-class urban inhabitants and eventually even rural populations chose real coffee over the ersatz coffees and teas they had previously drunk because coffee symbolized affluence and status. Perhaps surprisingly, as it became an accepted part of the working class's breakfast and even lunch in the factory canteen—that is, as it came to be viewed as a necessity—coffee purchases ceased growing faster than the population did. Coffee was one of the few major internationally traded commodities to enjoy a real price increase in the second half of the nineteenth century and still have a per capita consumption increase. In other words, people bought more and more of it even though its relative price continued to rise. Again the coffee chain benefited from an externality: the plunging price of many staples such as grains, due to overproduction, left the working classes of North America and Europe with more disposable income to buy occasional luxuries like coffee. Cheaper sugar made coffee more palatable and affordable.[206]

The rapid expansion and transformation of the US and Western European markets led to new institutions that gradually brought governance of the longer chain to importers and then to roasters. Merchants based in the growing countries lost leverage when a submarine telegraph cable in 1874 tied South America to New York and London. Information about prices, standards, and demand and supply were now published in newspapers and trade journals in consuming countries. Warehouses were built to hold a substantial share of the world's visible stocks, strengthening the market position of importers, who now knew where much of the coffee was and tried to control it.

Exporters ceased being consignment agents, becoming instead agents of importers abroad who dominated the trade and set the prices. Merchants such as the German Theodor Wille and Englishman Edward Johnston started their careers in Brazil, expanded their commercial business to other ports and countries, and moved up-country by opening offices in the coffee-growing interior. They invested in complementary activities such as insurance companies, banks, and warehouses, and reluctantly in plantations.[207] Rarely did they become roasters, however.

Eventually the roasters, who built large factories in the consuming countries, came to dominate the trade. Coffee had to be processed to the point of green or parchment coffee in the cultivating countries because the ripe cherries spoiled too fast to be exported in that condition. Green coffee, also known as "gold coffee" *(café oro),* was durable and transportable. Although historians often treat coffee exports as a raw material, in fact they were semifinished. Until the second half of the twentieth century, the roasting and grinding had to be done in the consuming countries because the final processed product quickly lost its flavor and aroma. Once new packaging technology permitted the exportation of roasted and even ground coffee in the twentieth century, import tariffs in consuming northern countries and the market power of the roasters in the north prevented finished coffee exports.[208] In other words, geography and climate dictated that coffee was grown within twenty-five degrees of the equator and that it be initially processed there. Roasting and distribution technology in the countries with the largest, most prosperous markets for coffee dictated that final processing and marketing be done in the United States and Western Europe; later, government tariffs protected the profits of Western

European and North American corporations. So different areas of the world coffee market had different comparative advantages and controlled different aspects of knowledge of the coffee trade. This was similar to sugar, where politics and market power prevented pure, highly refined imports in order to protect the position of oligopolistic refiners and distributors in the consuming countries. Neither of these huge international sectors operated in a truly unfettered market.

As the trade grew, so did the size and market power of the largest exporters. Most of them were Western European or North American firms (partnerships and corporations) with ample capital, access to credit, control of shipping fleets, and inside information from their branches, partners, or associates in the major overseas coffee markets. By the end of the nineteenth century the five largest exporters shipped over 40 percent of Brazil's exports, and the ten largest over 60 percent.[209] Oligopoly encouraged attempts to make speculative windfall profits by cornering the market, leading to some spectacular bubbles and busts. In response, and in imitation of grain dealers, merchants founded the New York Coffee Exchange in 1882 and then the exchange at Le Havre to attract trade to their ports and capital in the form of a futures market. They sought a frictionless transparent market where transactions were safe and capital was available. The exchanges institutionalized access to standardized information. Hamburg and London, also major coffee entrepôts, soon followed with major coffee exchanges. Already in 1880 merchants were buying an idea rather than a palpable commodity, as we saw happen in the grains futures market. In that year, sixty-one million bags were bought and sold on the Hamburg futures market, when the entire world harvest was less than seven million bags! It was this sort of speculation that caused the German government to shut down the futures market for a while.

No single port dominated coffee imports in most countries, but the huge size of the US market meant that although New York continued its dominant position as lead importer of coffee, Baltimore, New Orleans, and San Francisco all imported significant amounts to serve their hinterlands.[210] The telegraph created the possibility of an integrated international commodity market and increased the market power of importers and processors in consuming countries where they had easy access to crop and price information. Prices and grades thereby became more standardized, though this was, and still is, a fairly artisanal undertaking, reflecting personal relations and tastes.

Social practices in the largest markets, the United States and Germany, very much affected the nature of demand and the ability of roasters to respond to it and to modify it. The fact that in the United States, Germany, the Netherlands, and Scandinavia, coffee was consumed in the home much more than in coffee-houses had important implications for the organization of the trade. In the United States, coffee was overwhelmingly sold in grocery stores, so a few roasting companies such as Arbuckle and the Woolson Spice Company took advantage of the invention of industrial-scale roasters in the late nineteenth century to create brand names for their roasted coffee. The proliferation of brands meant that roasters were no longer selling a commodity—the green bean—but were selling a trademarked product such as Arbuckle's Yuban. As with other food and drug products, from crackers and flour to soft drinks and cigarettes, advertising and other marketing tactics such as colorful cans and trading cards attempted to whet the appetite for particular brands and to appeal to the expanding retail grocery sector. They provided new information that appealed to more than "quality" or price; they appealed to the aesthetics of the can, the trading cards included in it, and to fashion. Less wealthy purchasers recycled the cans and crates in which the coffee arrived by reusing them as household implements and building materials.[211]

In the second-largest coffee market, Germany, coffee was sold in specialty stores known as "Colonial Goods" stores. Even though more than 90 percent of the coffee came from Latin America, to a considerable

A Viennese coffeehouse, ca. 1900. Coffee took on a very different social role in bour-geois Vienna, the capital of the Habsburg empire, during its prosperous fin de siècle. Dapper and refined men of the middle and upper classes read newspapers and books or discussed politics and culture in elegant coffeehouses while being served by women. (© Austrian Archives / Corbis)

extent from German or German immigrant-owned plantations in Guatemala, Brazil, and Mexico, the dream of African colonies, loudly pronounced at the 1884 Berlin Conference, continued to dominate the German imagination. Some brands carried African images, often cari-catures of native black people. In fact, much of Germany's and Central Europe's coffee was actually coffee substitutes like grains or chicory root, because import taxes hindered real coffee imports.[212] So when Germans consumed coffee, often they were actually drinking locally grown tubers rather than imported tropical beans. US coffee compa-nies portrayed coffee as being inherently American by promoting brands such as "White House" with Uncle Sam as their spokesman. South America and its farmworkers were ignored. Neither the imperial German nor the republican American vision gave Latin Americans due credit.

But these appeals did sell ever more coffee. A technical breakthrough and government oversight allowed the ever-larger roasters to overtake the thousands of grocers and small roasters who sold green beans or custom roasted. Larger roasters were able to win consumer confidence in the quality of packaged beans they now could not see. The first step in winning over the suspicious buyers was vacuum sealing, which was invented in 1900. It was borrowed from a Chicago butter company, though two decades would pass before vacuum packing gained wide acceptance. By the 1920s, "convenience" started to become an important attribute of roasted coffee, just as it did in the case of other processed foods as the Jazz Age heightened the desire for speed and leisure.

But the second problem—the questionable quality of canned coffee beans—required government interventions to take command of the market away from importers, who often adulterated coffee stocks. In the United States, the Pure Food and Drug Act of 1906, based upon a British pure food law some thirty years earlier, set standards. Aimed particularly at the meat and patent medicine industries, it also decreed that imported coffee be marked according to its port of exit. Thus "Santos" became a specific type of coffee, as did "Java" or "Mocha." Germany and other Western European governments followed suit soon thereafter.

By gaining the confidence of consumers and providing mass-produced roasted coffee, large industrial roasting firms began to control the market and the chain. They lengthened the chain by industrializing and commodifying roasting and grinding, which formerly were the domain of the housewife. Brands segmented the market by selling various roasts and blends depending upon region. By 1935, 90 percent of all coffee sold in the United States was sold roasted, in branded packages. The branded coffee housewives purchased at their neighborhood grocery store was not a commodity, it was a proprietary product. In Germany, the Kaiser food chain, which began selling branded roasted coffee in 1885, had grown to 1,420 stores on the verge of World War I. Its laughing coffee pot logo spread throughout the country. The introductions of new packaging, branding, and advertising would be slower to filter to the rest of Western Europe and would take yet longer to reach Latin America and Asia, where coffee consumption was less commodified and production less industrialized.[213]

The largest roasters also integrated vertically, sending their agents into the coffee interior to purchase directly from producers and sometimes even buying plantations in growing countries. The most successful at integrating segments of the chain before World War II was the A&P chain-store empire. The company imported, roasted, canned, branded, and retailed millions of bags and cans of Eight O'Clock coffee in thousands of its own stores. With their command of "shelf space" and their increasing concentration, supermarket companies could assert ever-greater governance over the coffee commodity chain as the power of independent merchants, small-scale roasters, and shippers declined.[214] Like it was for many other transformations of processed foods commodity chains, the United States was in the forefront. Supermarkets came to most of the rest of the world only in the 1960s or later.

As a result of developments in the United States, value—in the sense of market-priced processes—was increasingly added as the housewife's unremunerated role in making coffee declined and her labors were commodified by roasters. This caused an ever-greater share of the monetary value of coffee to be added in consuming countries. A small number of US companies, such as Folgers, Maxwell House, and Hills Brothers, took advantage of marketing economies to expand regionally and finally, after World War II, nationally. They came to make the lion's share of profit in the coffee chain.

In addition to using their market power and governance of the commodity chain to gain most of the profit in the coffee trade, roasters introduced new coffee products that allowed them to add additional value. In 1901 a Japanese chemist, Katō Satori, applied to coffee a technique he had first invented for tea to create soluble (or instant) coffee. It was not very successful, commercially; "George Washington's Instant Coffee," devised in 1910 by a Belgian immigrant to the United States, fared better because of better timing. The new wonder drink arrived in time for World War I, when it was deemed by the War Department "one of the most important articles of subsistence used by the army." The Washington company's entire output was sent to US troops on the European front.[215] Once peace came, consumers reverted back to slower, but better tasting and cheaper, brewed coffee. Nonetheless, the seeds of change were planted at the end of our period when the Brazilian government, facing glutted world markets and miserable prices, appealed to the Swiss instant milk company, Nestlé, to devise a better soluble process. They introduced the world to Nescafé in 1938. It became a cherished part of soldiers' rations. Its impact would be felt after the Second World War when it gained great favor. Because instant coffee stressed convenience over taste, the cheaper, faster-growing *Coffea robusta* beans were preferred. Robusta was a different species of *Coffea* that was discovered in Central Africa in the 1860s and transported to Java and Ceylon because it resisted leaf blight better than the arabica.[216] After the end of our period, this would undercut Latin America's near monopoly on coffee cultivation as Africa and Indonesia, then much later Vietnam, rushed to plant and harvest robusta trees. Because of the large role of technology in creating instant coffee and the use of a low-quality raw material, coffee growers received an ever-smaller share of the final supermarket price for the instant coffee, just as the growers of wheat and rice, and the miners and extracters of industrial raw materials, earned a diminishing share of the final price of the finished good.

The power of the cultivating countries in the world coffee market was further undercut by the expansion of large roasting companies. Roasters' superior technology, greater efficiency, and marketing sophistication led to greater concentration of processing and distribution. By the 1950s the five largest roasters in the United States handled over one-third of all US coffee. Very large traders grew to satisfy the growing demand of roasters. According to the Federal Trade Commission, by the 1950s the top ten importers were responsible for over half of all imports.

Ten exporting houses in Brazil sent out anywhere from two-thirds to 90 percent of the exports until the 1920s and continued to control more than half after that. Because Brazil was exporting 40 to 80 percent of the world's coffee until the 1950s, and these exporting houses operated in other producing areas as well, this meant a few houses dominated world exports and information.

Government intervention had brought some governance of the chain to the producing countries in the early twentieth century. Beginning in 1906 some of Brazil's provinces held stocks off the world market to "valorize" them. Then the province of São Paulo, which single-handedly grew most of the world's coffee by the turn of the century, established in 1924 a semi-state coffee institute to oversee financing, warehousing, and sales. This led to a federal price support program in 1931. The Great Depression caused coffee demand and prices to precipitously fall and left Brazil with enormous surplus stocks on hand. The initial solution was for the Brazilian central government to burn almost ten million pounds of coffee, a year's supply for the entire world. When that did not stabilize prices, diplomacy followed.

Where an earlier effort to bring together the coffee-growing countries to defend against falling prices had failed, just as had happened with sugar and rubber, the new crisis was sufficiently dire that fourteen Latin American coffee-growing countries met to discuss their concerns. They joined together because, as one contemporary student of the sector observed: "The importance of coffee in the economic life of the American republics can hardly be exaggerated.... More than many other export commodities, the proceeds derived from its sale abroad are distributed widely among the inhabitants of the country of exports."[217] Even countries that were small exporters in the world market depended greatly on coffee for foreign exchange and government revenue. The agreement was finally consummated in 1940 because World War II blocked shipments to Europe, glutting the markets of the Americas. Washington, which had strenuously fought against Brazilian valorizations in the first decades of the century, now recognized that cooperation between the main producers and consumers was necessary. The newly created Inter-American Price Coffee Board set price controls and quotas. The 36 votes on the board were distributed between the growers (Brazil 9, Colombia 3, and others 1 each) and the main consumer (the United States—12 votes). This was the first major international agreement to include both producers and a major consumer, unless we count the sugar meetings where countries like Germany and Austria were both producers and consumers. It set a precedent for the 1962 International Coffee Agreement that would bring together the vast majority of coffee growers and consumers from all over the world.

Coffee, then, differed from other leading global commodities because of the development of extensive international coordination and the singular role played by a country from the Southern Hemisphere. Brazil's success stemmed from its natural endowments, its ability in 1822 to throw off European colonialism, and its capacity to adapt to the transformations of the world economy by taking advantage of foreign capital, technology, immigrant labor, and markets. The fact that coffee was a durable drug food that traveled well and stimulated the swelling consumer population of the urban industrializing North, combined with the power of the Brazilian postcolonial state, allowed Brazil to enjoy a position in the world economy of unprecedented strength for an agrarian exporter from the global South. Over time, however, a growing share of coffee profits would accrue to roasters and distributors in the industrialized centers.

## Tea

Tea resembled coffee in that it was a stimulant with little nutritional value, it did not spoil quickly, and it traveled well. Caffeine had important psychoactive effects on the central nervous system, so coffee and tea were treated as medicines as well as beverages and were useful in leisure, labor, and combat. The two stimulants often competed for consumers, and the same companies often sold both. In both cases, the commodities destined for an international market were grown in the South by poor workers in large part for the industrial North. However, tea's history, location, business organization, and political context were worlds apart from coffee's. Where coffee had become the product of independent national states in our period, tea—formerly the monopoly of China—became a colonial product.

For at least two thousand years tea was cultivated, processed, and consumed in China. Aside from seeds taken to Japan more than a thousand years ago by Buddhist monks, tea had been a Chinese monopoly. When the Dutch and Portuguese began importing tea in the 1600s and the English a century later, China was the sole exporter and retained its monopoly until British and Dutch colonies began sending out small amounts in the middle of the century and Japan opened up in the 1860s. Tea surpassed silk to become the most valuable product of the China trade. It came to connote great wealth: "for all the tea in China."[218]

Tea, *Camellia sinensis,* was an indigenous plant. Millions of Chinese peasants (the estimate for the 1920s was four million tea cultivators) grew the crops on their own small plots, where they processed the leaves and twigs using native technology. Drying and curing had to be done almost immediately upon picking, lest the leaves rot, so peasants were also artisanal processors. They were consumers as well as producers as the drink became entwined with Chinese and Japanese culture, religion, and identity.[219]

Tea was an expensive luxury in England because of the nature of the commodity chain. The very many peasants sold to local traders who brought it to larger markets, and weeks later it found its way from the distant interior mountains to the ports. Chinese merchants dominated the trade up to the seaside ports, such as Canton and Amboy, and took a healthy cut of the profits. Cultivation practices created no economies of scale; equally problematic for an export crop, it was expensive to bring the tea out of the interior either over land, often with human carriers, or by small boats down the rivers.

The cost of the commodity was a particular problem for Europeans because the only thing they had that the Chinese wanted in trade was silver, and that was in short supply. Much of it came from the mines of Peru and Mexico across the Pacific or around the world across the Atlantic and Indian Oceans. To create a trade good that paid for tea, in the nineteenth century the English East India Company brought from India another stimulant, opium. That drug caused devastating addiction in China and provoked wars that ultimately caused the emperor to cede to Europeans treaty ports and the right to import opium. But this still did not provide Europe with sufficient low-priced tea. Even at the height of China's tea trade, at least one-half of production was consumed by the Chinese. By the 1920s, 70 to 90 percent of Chinese production was drunk at home.[220]

The solution to the problem of trying to meet rising demand was implemented in the 1800s when the English and Dutch mercantile monopolies introduced Chinese tea seed, and new scientific techniques developed in their state-run botanical gardens, into India and Java. Using domestic indentured workers or debt peons, known as coolies in India, and European capital and new technology, they began to grow tea on a plantation scale. At first they imported Chinese tea plants, because these were the most valued by the international trade and because they did not recognize that, in quality, the little-cultivated native Indian tea plant, *Camellia sinensis var. assamica,* was for industrial purposes superior to the Chinese variety. Producers in India added a fermenting process that yielded black tea, which was less common in China and Japan than green tea. Combined with low-cost sugar, the steady supply of black tea found a swelling market among the British working class, who, unlike most original Asian consumers, liked their tea sweetened.[221] Steamships and railroads now began to bring vast amounts of black tea from Assam to Calcutta. There some of the fastest ships in the British merchant marine were waiting to take the tea to Europe to enrich British stockholders in London and the British managers in India who oversaw Indian laborers.

But though the English praised their scientific technical mastery and progressive means in the new Indian field, the plantations did not use modern capitalist labor systems. It is true that the investors were capitalists and that tea became an industrial product there. Beginning in 1872 with William Jackson's tea roller, processing became increasingly mechanized. Hot-air driers, roll breakers, and even mechanical tea sorters followed.[222]

However, as with sugar, industrial processing demanded increased manual labor in agriculture. The delicate and skilled work of planting, tending, and particularly harvesting tea was still done by hand, often female hands, under conditions that Henry Cotton, chief commissioner of Assam in 1896, called "scandalous." Imported mainly from the neighboring jurisdiction of Bengal, the coolies were, in his words, "practically bond slaves . . . the period of bondage may be interminable."[223] This was coercion on a massive scale. By 1927 Assam alone had some 420,000 acres under tea with 463,847 permanent plantation coolies and another 41,176 temporary workers brought in from outside.[224]

Colonial state power to enforce low-paying labor contracts combined with surplus population and modern transportation to ignite a veritable explosion of Indian production. Whereas in 1859 there was virtually no Indian tea trade while China exported over 70 million pounds to England, forty years later Chinese exports to London had fallen by more than three-quarters to 15 million pounds while India exported three times the earlier Chinese total, almost 220 million pounds. By 1932 Indian exports reached 385 million pounds.[225] This was a bonanza for the British colonial regime, planters, and traders and a disaster for China's balance of payments. Although ever more Indians worked in tea, relatively few of them owned tea plantations in booming Assam, where half the colony's tea was grown. However, one contemporary source notes that "in Kangra, Darjeeling, the Dooars, and the Tarai fair areas are owned by Indian companies . . . in Hill Tippera all the gardens are so controlled."[226]

So successful was the tea experiment in India that British planters in the nearby colony of Ceylon (Sri Lanka) also turned to that plant once their previously prospering coffee fields were felled by leaf rust. Again the tea system was also mainly a foreign import: British planters, using British capital, imported indentured Tamil workers from southern India to plant exotic tea bushes imported from China via India to grow a drink for British and Commonwealth consumers. The native Sinhalese would have nothing to do with tea cultivation or drinking. Tea created foreign enclaves. As Roland Wenzlhuemer has observed: "With the transition from coffee to tea cultivation in Ceylon, the immigrant labour force changed in its nature. Work in the coffee estates had been seasonal. Now tea required a permanently resident labour force. . . . Social contacts between the plantation workforce and the indigenous village communities were rare and usually confined to commercial relations."[227]

British planters in Ceylon undertook a vigorous publicity program at the end of the nineteenth century to compete with Indian tea in

Great Britain and to open new markets elsewhere, as in the United States. For the British public, advertisers deracinated the domesticated tea industry. They stressed how English, sanitary, disciplined, and modern their industry was. It worked. Ceylon became the second-largest tea exporter in the world, surpassing a politically troubled China in 1917. By 1933 Ceylon was exporting a quarter of the world's tea, more than twice China's exports. Other British colonists also tried their hand at planting tea, particularly in Africa. However, the tea plantations of Kenya, Uganda, Nyasaland (Malawi), and South Africa had little impact on the world market before 1945.[228]

Tea became a marker of British identity to the point that a meal, "tea," received its name and the military received tea rations. Britain in 1933 was still by far the world's largest tea importer, bringing in over half of all worldwide tea imports. It enjoyed the highest per capita annual consumption at almost ten pounds. Historians have persuasively argued that tea and sugar fueled the Industrial Revolution by sustaining the poorly paid, hardworking British industrial proletariat. Probably neither end of the commodity chain, Indian coolies or English proletarians, recognized the complementarity of their activities, which squeezed out surplus value through intensified labor to enrich capital over labor.

Tea became a glue of the British Empire. But elsewhere in the Commonwealth (the United Kingdom plus Australia, Canada, New Zealand, and South Africa), tea fueled colonialism rather than industrialism. Commonwealth members consumed over 70 percent of the international trade and averaged almost seven pounds per person in the white settler areas. The indigenous Indian population had drunk tea only in the areas where it naturally occurred, like Assam, before the British popularized it across the colony. Though it began as a white person's habit, its popularity spread. By the 1950s India had become the world's second-largest tea consumer.

We find a peculiar variation on British tea influence in the most prosperous neocolony of the United Kingdom, Argentina, which also

Workers moving Lipton tea sacks in Ceylon (now Sri Lanka), early twentieth century. In order to supplant China's tea monopoly in the second half of the nineteenth century, Britain brought more than two million Tamils from the southern part of India to Ceylon to work in tea either seasonally or permanently. Nearly three-quarters of internationally traded tea was sold inside the British Commonwealth, especially the United Kingdom. Companies such as the British leader, Lipton, grew, cured, transported, branded, and sold tea wholesale and retail. (© Hulton-Deutsch Collection / Corbis)

showed a preference for tea over coffee. However, there, as in the south of Brazil, it was local *erva mate* tea rather than the Indian import. And instead of serving as a sign of cosmopolitanism, tea drinking in Argentina was an indigenous habit tied to Argentine rural identity. *Mate* found almost no market outside the Southern Cone.[229]

The other major tea drinker was a former British colony, the United States. Its 13 percent of world tea commerce made it the world's second-largest market, even though this translated to less than a pound per capita because Americans were as enamored of coffee as the British were of tea.[230]

The only major tea consumer outside of China and Japan not related to the British experience was China's neighbor Russia. Tea was of course important to Russian culture, with the samovar as iconic as an Orthodox icon or a bottle of vodka. Russian firms established some eighteen tea factories in China, in Hangzhou and Fujian, when the Suez Canal provided a sea route from China to the populated core of Russia via the Black Sea. Robert Gardella, studying this trade, finds that the trade in brick tea, "rightly considered as a 'manufactured' commodity, rather than simply a cash crop," led to "an impressive degree of commercialization." Nonetheless, Gardella concludes that "the premodern Chinese economy was organized to accommodate cycles of extensive commercial expansion and contraction *without* the need for structural transformation."[231] In fact, Russian imports of brick tea from China fell sharply in the wake of political troubles in both countries after the turn of the twentieth century, and because by the last quarter of the nineteenth century tea was also produced for the Russian market in neighboring Georgia.

The other major tea producers and exporters were the first Europeans to engage in the trade, the Dutch. Importing tea seeds from China and then from India, they were able to have some success in Java and later in Sumatra. Earlier efforts were stepped up, like the British in Ceylon, when leaf rust devastated their thriving coffee plantations beginning in the 1870s. In coffee's place, Dutch planters, using coerced Javanese peasants, forced tea exports to jump tenfold between 1900 and 1927. By 1933 the colony was the world's third-largest tea exporter, providing a fifth of the international trade. The cruel methods led to nationalist outcries in the Dutch East Indies (today Indonesia) and humanitarian campaigns in the Netherlands.[232]

The Japanese increased tea cultivation in their newly won colony of Formosa at the end of the century, turning it into a major exporter of oolong tea, particularly to Japan itself and to the United States. Production grew some 50 percent between the last decade of the nineteenth century and the period 1931–1940. But the system differed sharply from those used in the British and Dutch colonies. In both Japan itself and Formosa, tea was grown on small hillside plots by peasant family labor. It complemented other agriculture, such as rice growing. Improvements in yield allowed the Japanese and Formosan farmers to reduce the size of their tea fields while increasing production and devoting more land to other crops. Even though much of Japan's exports were marketed by US exporting firms, tea in Japan obeyed domestic farm logic, not an export logic as elsewhere in colonial Asia.[233]

In England, tea, which had begun in coffeehouses, became a domesticated drink served at home and drunk by men and women alike. Seen as a temperance drink, just like coffee, tea was considered by Victorians to be a civilizing beverage. Purveyors began branding different sorts of tea and retailing through grocers. Some companies, such as Lipton, purchased plantations in Ceylon, where the tea was grown and cured, and sold the tea in its chain of grocery stores in the United Kingdom and the United States, "direct from the tea garden to the tea pot." The same was done in the United States by the Great Atlantic and Pacific Tea Company (the A&P), which by the 1920s had some twenty-four hundred outlets. Americans changed the nature of tea consumption by developing a product that distressed Britons, who were more concerned with flavor, but appealed to Americans who wanted speed and convenience: tea bags. Created in 1908 by Thomas Sullivan as tiny samples for marketing purposes, tea in pouches of silk, and then cotton gauze, vastly increased the number of US tea drinkers. As Roy Moxham observed, tea bags "turned tea from being a drink of ceremony into a drink of convenience."[234] Although they took decades to follow suit, by the end of our period even Tetley, Lipton, and Twinings were producing tea bags for an ever less reluctant English

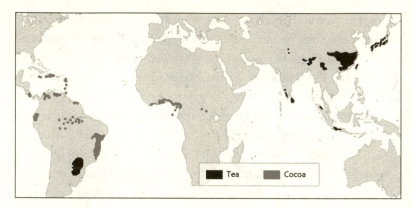

Global production of tea and cocoa, ca. 1925.

public. That dramatic change in consumption practice had a similarly huge effect on production, because tea bags were filled with broken leaf or even leaf dust. The lowered common denominator put an end to finely graded teas on most tea plantations.[235] Another similar American innovation was iced tea. Drunk mainly in hot climates, it required the advent of refrigeration machines to make ice. Heavily sweetened, iced tea used low-quality leaf. The Chinese and Japanese spiritual cultural custom had become fully commodified, adapted, secularized, internationalized, and modernized.

## Chocolate

The last of the major stimulants that we discuss, chocolate, was native to the Americas and initially was spread overseas by the Spanish. Another tree crop with the alkaloid caffeine and to a greater extent a cousin of caffeine, theobromine, cacao traveled and stored well once harvested and processed. Domesticated by the Olmecs of southern Mexico before 1000 BCE, cacao became much later an important symbol of Aztec culture and status as the *xocoatl* trade spread long distances through Mesoamerica. It was paired with processed seeds of another indigenous Mexican plant, the orchid vanilla, which was first domesticated by the Totonac Indians of Veracruz but joined in chocolate by the Aztecs. The Spanish became fond of the drinking cacao with vanilla hot or cold, calling it "chocolate," but it was seldom eaten. Indigenous cultivation methods and indigenous farmers continued to produce the fine *criollo* beans after the Conquest in Mesoamerica. In Venezuela, the hardier and more prolific *forastero* variety found a market abroad once sugar was added.[236]

Chocolate as a drink found some favor in Western Europe, particularly in the south among the aristocracy and the wealthy, but it was unable to compete well in the north with coffee and tea, which were usually served in the same cafés or meted out by the same apothecaries. Like its competitors, cacao was thought of as a temperance beverage. Perhaps unfairly, it was branded a Catholic and a feminine drink in northern Europe; it languished until the nineteenth century when new industrial methods and new chocolate products made the *forastero* more appealing and its production spread and grew.[237]

Two of the most important inventions in transforming the world of chocolate were undertaken by Dutch and Swiss entrepreneurs. The Dutchman C. J. Van Houten in 1829 devised a means to remove the cocoa butter from the bean to create an easily soluble cocoa powder. That it was a Dutchman is not surprising, because Amsterdam was the world's main chocolate market as the Dutch Caribbean colony of Curaçao became a gateway for Venezuelan cocoa. Van Houten's process opened the door for producers of drinkable chocolate. The falling price of sugar helped increase the market for the beverage, though it was not able to compete with tea and coffee. Chocolate purveyors such as the Swiss Phillip Suchard and the Englishman John Cadbury, who began branding their drinking product in the 1820s and 1830s, adopted Van Houten's process to create a more soluble powder that was still somewhat coarse and bitter. Now coca powder became a cooking ingredient as well as a drink mix. But their dark chocolate became widely popular, and a treat for children as well as adults, only when in 1875 the Swiss Daniel Peter joined his chocolate with his neighbor Henri Nestlé's powdered milk to produce milk chocolate. Other chocolatiers, such as the Swiss Lindt and Tobler companies, spread the new product as it became increasingly a mass treat and sometimes a military provision. The American Milton Hershey was able to mass-produce inexpensive confections like "Kisses" and "Mr. Good-bar," creating in 1894 the world's largest integrated factory in Pennsylvania, where he joined milk from his local dairies and sugar from his plantation in Cuba with imported chocolate. Other manufacturers were finding reliable, inexpensive milk ever more available as legislation, refrigeration, and new hygienic practices allowed milk to be sold at a distance from dairies. Combination candy bars, often with caramel and nuts covered by chocolate, like the Clark Bar, Baby Ruth, and the Mars Company's Snickers and Milky Way bars, as well as M&Ms, spread the chocolate candy snack habit widely after the First World War.[238] Chocolate had become an input in the processed food industry.

Vanilla continued to accompany chocolate as a drink and as a food. A demanding parasite that was difficult to sustain because it was ecologically sensitive and required a specific bee, butterfly, ant, or hummingbird to pollinate, vanilla did not lend itself to industrial-scale production or international travel. Fortunately for consumers, small amounts could flavor a substantial amount of chocolate. Indigenous people in Veracruz, growing the orchids as a subsidiary crop, had a world monopoly until French immigrants to the state in the mid-eighteenth century discovered a way to manually pollinate the orchids. This permitted other Frenchmen to move vanilla plants to French colonies in the Indian Ocean, such as Réunion and Madagascar.[239] Its taste was spread even more after German chemists synthesized vanilla in 1874, bringing its production from the forest to the lab.

A young girl discovering candy in a songbird's nest: an advertisement for Nestlé chocolate, ca. 1910. By the beginning of the twentieth century, the popularity of chocolate,
which originated in Mexico and South America, had spread to Europe in the form of
candy, once sugar and milk were added and cocoa butter was removed. Still grown
mainly in Latin America in 1900, the majority of production would move to African
colonies by 1914. Nestlé's advertisement, however, did not betray its chocolate's origins to consumers. Once the drink of Aztec warriors and later of European nobles, it
had become feminized as the food for the young and the romantic. (Getty Images)

Low-priced milk chocolate created booming demand for cacao (and vanilla) just as an increasing supply of cacao permitted the rapid expansion of the low-priced confection. First, the variety of cacao employed changed because the addition of milk and sugar neutralized the bitterness of the rugged and productive *forastero* bean. The early leaders in *criollo* cacao—Mexico, Central America, and Venezuela—gradually lost their grip on the world market as they could not expand to satisfy the explosion of demand. Ecuador and some Caribbean islands, particularly Trinidad, began to send out cacao. In 1890 the international trade supplied less than 60,000 metric tons of cacao; by 1914 the trade more than quadrupled to some 280,000 metric tons. World commerce in cacao surpassed 600,000 metric tons in the 1940s. Although small in comparison to coffee's 1.5 million metric tons in the 1940s, cacao did experience an unprecedented burst of expanded cultivation. Its rate of expansion—growing tenfold in a half century—far outpaced coffee's tripling and tea's decline in those same years. The secret of this unprecedented jump in world cacao production was the colonial transplanting to Africa of *forastero* trees and a variety developed in Trinidad, *trinitario*. Begun by the Portuguese on their islands of São Tomé and Principe, cacao moved onshore to the British colony of Gold Coast (Ghana) followed by Nigeria and the French in Côte d'Ivoire. By 1914 Africa was producing most of the world's cacao, much of it on small indigenous farms. This had risen to two-thirds of the international total by the end of our period.[240] As a result, cacao was, along with palm oil, one of Africa's most important agricultural exports prior to 1945.

The nature of labor and land systems in cacao production during our period was probably even more diverse than in any other of the commodities we have studied. This is because cacao production was divided among many independent countries and colonies and, as with coffee, the scale of production actually declined, so there were more growers. William Clarence-Smith observed: "As the volume of cocoa production increased prodigiously, techniques of cultivation actually became less intensive."[241] Estates were not an efficient way to grow cacao. Nonetheless, because of uneven power and land-owning relations, estates continued to exist and even dominate in some places. But even when they did, they were not capital intensive and labor was mostly not coerced. For example, in the domestically owned estates in Ecuador, entire families of Ecuadorians were contracted for five- or six-year periods. Labor contracting was also used in the British colony of Trinidad, where the workers were often from other British Caribbean colonies as well as some indentured South Asians. The same was true in Dutch Surinam. Venezuela and Costa Rica did not have access to Asian British colonial migrants, but tapped the crowded Caribbean islands whose former sugar workers now sought other employ. The Dominican Republic and Bahia, Brazil, had sufficient local small-scale growers and workers that they did not import either capital or workers. Instead, native migrants came as wage workers, sharecroppers, or smallholders. In Chiapas, Mexico, and Guatemala, however, the indigenous Maya were subjected on some cacao plantations to the same slavelike conditions they faced on some coffee fields.

Africa displayed the most variation. Colonial regimes differed on their acceptance of slavery and coercion, though all favored colonial landowners. The British in Nigeria and the very successful Gold Coast gradually ended the slave trade and then slavery itself. Their problem was convincing the chiefs, who "used a medley of pawns, slaves and corvée labour to create their coca farms," to end coercion.[242] Still, the great majority of the colony's production was undertaken by African smallholders. The Germans in Cameroon and Togo were more permissive of labor coercion of Africans in cacao farming, as were the Spanish in Spanish Guinea and the French in Congo and Madagascar. Actual legal slavery, however, was phased out. The Portuguese may have been the most severe in ignoring the worldwide abolition movement. After abolishing slavery in 1875 in Angola, they reinstated it in the

1880s. Until 1908 thousands of slaves and contract workers were sent to São Tomé and Principe cacao farms from the Portuguese colonies of Cape Verde, Angola, and Mozambique.[243]

In the seven decades after 1870 chocolate grew as a romantic gift, a leisure drink, and a child's treat. The sweet-consuming experience clashed with the sometimes bitter reality of its global production. Over time, however, even in growing countries the scale and extent of foreign ownership of landowning tended to decline. But as with coffee and tea, the chocolate commodity chain bridged continents, straddled colonial systems, brought disproportionate profits to processors in the developed world, and became characterized by heterodox labor systems that moved in the direction of freer labor while maintaining considerable coercion in many growing areas. Science, in the form of chemistry, agronomy, and engineering, played an important role in cultivation, processing, transporting, industrializing, marketing, and distributing the stimulants.

## Outlaws

A final note on our commodity chains: We have pointed to the importance of nature, technology, international politics, and social customs in creating and attending to demand. The legal apparatus of patents, copyrights, and trademarks underlay property rights and value. What we have not much discussed is the legal boundary that protected and celebrated some commodities, creating great wealth and status for their producers, while denouncing other products as outlaws. Sugar, coffee, tea, and chocolate were considered respectable and modern by most people and all governments, even when their cultivation and processing were done under troubling conditions. But other goods that had equally long histories and that were often first considered miracle medicines became marginalized. Opium, heroin—synthesized by the former dye-producing Bayer Chemical Company—cocaine, and marijuana were condemned for their addictive properties despite their valuable medicinal effects as painkillers, anesthetics, and sleep aids. Revealing the whims of regulatory agencies, at the same time as it abandoned heroin Bayer became one of the world's largest pharmaceutical corporations largely on the merits of another painkiller, aspirin. International conventions led by the United States, and gradually and reluctantly accepted by the colonial powers through the League of Nations and then the United Nations, began to successfully forbid narcotics just as other legal pharmaceuticals became enormously profitable.[244] Only in the last decades of the twentieth century would government agencies lose their control over narcotics production and imports, as cultivators in areas rather on the periphery of the world economy, such as Bolivia, Colombia, Afghanistan, and Turkey, smuggled them into the most prosperous countries. A similar effort to close down and outlaw the most popular social drug, alcohol, had already failed in our period as the US Volstead Act of 1919 was repealed in 1933. Prohibiting legal drinking had spurred bootleg production and the rise of gangsters. More importantly, too many people wanted a drink and too many government agencies wanted the revenue. Nonetheless, we still live with the porous and sometimes arbitrary international legal boundary first systematically instituted in the years before 1945.

Clearly, commodity chains were not governed just by the forces of supply and demand. They did not entirely operate in an ethical vacuum where profit and loss overshadowed concerns of justice and equity, and they could not entirely transcend cultural values. Just as it is difficult to account for taste, so it was hard to forecast the line between the legally permitted and the prohibited as new products came on the market.

# Conclusions

The seventy-five years that followed 1870 witnessed an unprecedented explosion of production leading to heightened market transactions, many of which crossed national borders and spanned continents. Industrialization, agricultural innovation, and marketing revolutions touched most people on Earth by the 1940s. Electricity and oil joined with steam to power the world in wholly new ways, shrinking distance and abolishing the night in cities.

This could fairly be called the first era of intensified globalization. But global spread did *not* create homogeneous actors, nor was everything commodified or predictable. Our use of the commodity chains approach and our emphasis on agriculture has allowed us to outline the broader contours of these frenzied changes while at the same time highlighting the extent of variation in production systems, processing, transporting, marketing, and consumption, even for the same product, such as wheat or sugar. We have seen that commodities such as cotton, grains, and stimulants interacted in different ways with the natural environments, social systems, value regimes, market institutions, and state or colonial agencies they encountered and shaped.

These contexts of economic transactions changed over time and by geographic location. As a result, the forward and backward linkages of the commodities to other economic activities, and their consequences for providing employment and tax revenues, also varied by place and time. The heterogeneity of the world economy meant that simultaneously with the "Great Acceleration" that brought people together through intensified international economic relations made possible by accelerated transport and communications there also grew a "Great Divergence" that distributed the benefits of economic and technological advance unequally. The gulf between, on the one side, Western Europe, North America, and the "neo-Europes," and, on the other side, the rest of the world tended to widen. By using a commodity chains approach we are able to palpably connect growers, processors, shippers, and marketers on different continents even though they did not know each other at the time and did not necessarily realize that they were participating in a complex international chain.

Technological advances in communications, transportation, processing, preserving, and packaging caused an enormous expansion of the volume, speed, and content of world trade. Space was rearranged by the steamship, canals, and railroad as well as the telegraph and finally the telephone. Geography was also modified by the transoceanic transplanting of various agricultural cultivars and massive migrations of people, as humans increasingly dominated and transformed nature. In some sectors, particularly food, people began questioning what was meant by "natural" and the extent to which that was pure and wholesome or unrestrained and dangerous. Some things that were unknown or rare in 1870 became necessities for many peoples by 1945, enriching the material lives of some participants in the world economy but making them more dependent on monetized market transactions. In the most prosperous countries there arose a whole new class of market-oriented consumers and new sites for purchases, such as chain stores and department stores.

The expansion of consumption of goods was directly related to the intensification of labor. Stimulants, machines, and new agricultural techniques squeezed more labor power out of workers. Leisure increasingly became a valued commodity. Managers, investors, and workers came to think that time was money for ever more people, as clocks and electrical lighting regimented and even replaced individual biorhythms and seasonal cycles in industrialized areas. This intensification and global spread of what Jan de Vries has called the Industrious Revolution (1650–1850) was mitigated and abetted some by leaps in food and medicine production. Just as, during this era, matter and energy were shown by Einstein to be interchangeable when enough force is brought to bear, so did labor and things appear to become fungible. Traditional labor and land conventions succumbed, if unevenly, to market forces. Markets for important commodities like wheat, coffee, tea, and hard fibers tended to regional and even worldwide price convergence while futures trading sold things that did not yet exist.

This period was not an uninterrupted monolith, a steadily rising curve of prosperity. It was pervaded by cycles, booms, and crashes, by fads and backlashes. Whereas the years up to 1914 were generally marked by the rapid rise and spread of liberalism, reduced customs duties, diminished state interference, and increasing reliance on foreign trade—particularly in the British Empire—the three decades after the eruption of world war at Sarajevo witnessed mainly a "retreat from a short brush with liberalism."[1] However, because ours is a world history not solely concentrated on the economies of the North Atlantic, we cannot fully agree with O'Rourke and Williamson that "the world economy had lost all its globalization achievement in the three decades between 1914 and 1945."[2] Although the previous price convergence dissipated and overall global trade slowed, the organizational structures—the sinews—for trade and new technologies remained.

Figuring the balance sheet for the global spread of commodity chains is tricky, because it is ambiguous. On the one hand, the changes we have examined brought the world closer together through trade, technological diffusion, and formal and informal imperialism. On the other hand, most of the benefits of the commercial revolution were concentrated in just a few places. Between 1870 and 1945 there was an unprecedented international concentration of power and wealth. The concentration centered in certain nations, mostly Western European and North American; within them was also a great class divide and continuing regional divide (think of the US South versus the US Northeast). But it would be simplistic and wrong to think the world was divided into the West versus the rest, between colonizers and colonized, or between industrialists and agriculturalists. There was ample variety and growth in the "non-West," tied to a considerable extent to their connections to the world economy. There was also significant interregional trade, as in China, that did not register in global trade statistics. There was certainly more wealth and advanced technology in global cities like Buenos Aires, Rio de Janeiro, and Shanghai than in, not only their own hinterlands, but, say, Wales, Andalusia, or New Mexico. With the rise of agro-industry in some crops like sugar and wheat, as well as large-scale processing of the harvests, the divide between industry and agriculture/extraction often became fuzzy.

People not incorporated into the world market did not necessarily consider themselves "losers." There was notable resistance by colonial peasants and ethnic minorities such as the Maya, the Zulu, the Apache, and the Tamils who were conquered or subjugated. These people did not submit meekly. Our period witnessed a double movement of resistance leading to internal warfare and civil wars as well as more benign reforms. At the same time, many religious movements rejected the primacy of materialist market values over spiritual values, and more secular anarchists, socialists, and social democrats fought to reform or overthrow capitalism's bourgeois individualist property regimes. Ideological hegemony was contested all over the globe even though a small number of people exercised unprecedented power in this era.

The growing concentration of power derived not only from a small group of people controlling most of the capital and know-how, but also from the industrialization of destruction. Modern new weapons (machine guns, railroads, gunboats, bomber planes, and, at the end, missiles) and means of delivering them over long distances reinforced the advantages of the rich and created gigantic new markets and fortunes. Apparent economic decisions, such as the shift of ships from coal to oil or connecting colonies by telegraph, were as likely based on strategic considerations as they were motivated by the desire to maximize profit. Indeed, many of the imperial or defensive decisions to build infrastructure did not make much short-run economic sense. The celebration of the "economically rational man" was challenged by irrational and racist destruction.

Although stores and markets found their shelves and stalls filled with more and different things, growing choice did not greatly affect the lives of most people. In fact, coercion was as much a central theme of the period as was opportunity. Semi-free trade and bountiful markets resplendent with new modern goods lived in a world also marred by peonage and authoritarianism. True, this was the era of growing rights through the abolition of slavery and the first women's suffrage. Democracy was spread by liberals and social democrats. But it was also the age of pogroms in Russia and Turkey; internal wars against indigenous peoples in such areas as Argentina, northern Mexico, the US Prairie, and the Australian Outback; and more institutionalized and deadlier "racial cleansing" by German Nazis.

This period saw at its beginning the high tide of British imperialism but then witnessed London's power subsiding in the twentieth century as the United States, Germany, France, the Soviet Union/Russia, and Japan challenged its dominance. British rule had never been monolithic anyway, because its treatment of white settler colonies, such as Australia and Canada, was far different from its treatment of the brown colonies of Africa, Asia (with the partial exception of India), and the Caribbean. Independent areas such as Argentina, Uruguay, and southeastern Brazil received more British capital, trade, and technology than did most formal colonies.

Great advances in transportation and communications joined with international empires, corporations, institutions, and nongovernmental organizations to standardize weights, measures, international laws, and property rights. These in turn strengthened the private sector.

Transaction costs of doing business fell dramatically in some places because of the widespread acceptance of the gold standard and large international banking syndicates, conventions, and cartels facilitated by the advent of the telegraph and then the telephone.

But even in the heyday of economic liberalism, states were fundamental to ensuring that conditions of the market prevailed. Without government interventions such as trust busting and treaties, monopoly would have triumphed over competition, stymieing innovation. Governments did not merely interfere and tax, as their loudest critics complained. Public officials also coordinated and financed the construction of infrastructure, fomented scientific advances, and tried to prevent actors from unfairly restraining trade. They also attempted to pacify and control workers. States defined and protected newly invented commodity rights by overseeing trademarks, patents, copyrights, stocks, bonds, monetary conventions, and the value of currency as well as land titles. Through their courts and jails, states were fundamental to protecting and inventing property rights, facilitating great accumulations of wealth. In some fortunate lands they also oversaw the reproduction of the labor force by beginning to enforce new health regulations, funding medical advances, and expanding educational systems.

As populations grew, migrated, and urbanized, societies moved away from natural economies and face-to-face transactions toward market commodification. The growth of anonymous and impersonal relations mediated by local markets and long-distance trade called for greater third-party—usually state—oversight. In numerous commodities, such as coffee, rubber, sugar, and tea, states attempted to join together to regulate or corner the market. The public sphere that arose in this period transformed the divide between the private and the public. In the relatively few places where there began to appear laws protecting workers—women and children as well as men—and protecting the integrity of products such as food and medicines, states helped ensure the long-run health of the economy and the society they served. In the

most prosperous countries and in the Soviet Union, they also sometimes responded to labor unions by increasing regulation of the work-
place. Sometimes, as in Brazilian coffee and North American wheat,
farmers banded together to demand government intervention.

Moreover, for many commodities, tariffs, treaties, and imperial preferences shaped markets. State officials were as likely to be as motivated
by concerns about national defense and integration, and about state
building and social peace, as about maximizing the profits of the private
sector or enriching specific capitalists. Religious values also impinged on
secular public actions. Markets and the struggle for profit did not in-
dependently rule human actions.

The birth of the modern world showered wealth, power, unimag-
ined products, and lifestyle possibilities on the fortunate. For many
people, life expectancies and life choices improved. Urbanization, the
popularization of the press, and ease of movement gave voice to many
who had formerly been muted. This was the high point not only of
monopolies and multinational companies but also of labor unions and
international socialist movements.

We even see the beginning of concern about the treatment of the
environment. But people continued to think of "nature" as natural resources meant for human use. The world's flora, fauna, and minerals
seemed limitless, and human ingenuity and appetite unbounded.

At the dawn of the twentieth century, many observers enthusiasti-
cally predicted worldwide peace and prosperity because of the alleged
dominance of reason and science. The Prometheus of global trade and
industry promised a bright future. Then the last thirty-one years of
our period were darkened by crushing war and debilitating economic
depression. Tens of millions of deaths and economic stagnation brought
widespread disillusionment and revolutionary fervor.

Peering back at the world of more than sixty years ago, we need to
consider which are its most important legacies. This was both the triumphant era of the railroad, airplane, and radio, of mass production

and mass consumption, *and* the era of wealth concentration, two world wars, the Russian Revolution, and the atomic bomb. Accelerated economic interactions led to cultural diffusion and syncretic amalgamation. Greater communication only sometimes yielded greater understanding. It was an era of sharp contrasts. The telegraph, steamship, and global markets led some people to think of One World, shorn of divisive differences. They launched the League of Nations, the International Court, Esperanto, and NGOs like the Red Cross and the Boy Scouts to traverse national borders. World fairs and the Olympics brought people together from many corners of the Earth. But the urge to compete was probably stronger than the desire to cooperate. Intensified international transactions also intensified nationalism and imperialism.

The fleshing-out of the international commodity chains of some key illustrative goods shows that the concept of "*the* market" is simplistic, that markets were more fragmented, unstable, and heterodox as new products became more valuable for different reasons. Certainly people in places geographically remote from each other began to affect each other in unexpected and unforeseen ways. Whether chaining farmers together in networks of commodity exchanges was positive or detrimental depended upon specific historical circumstances. Outcomes were not uniform, foreordained, consistent, or constant. The genie released by new energy forms, new mechanical and chemical techniques, new means of transport and communication, and new products was not necessarily benevolent or malignant. Human history and the environment in which people lived shaped the consequences of this first modern age of globalization as commodity chains linked areas and peoples that historically had limited interactions. The global forces unleashed in that period still reverberate today. As William Faulkner warned us: "The past is never dead, it is not even past."

# Notes

INTRODUCTION

1 Lance Davis and Robert Huttenback, *Mammon and the Pursuit of Empire: The Political Economy of British Imperialism, 1860–1912* (New York: Cambridge University Press, 1987); C. A. Bayly, *The Birth of the Modern World, 1780–1914: Global Connections and Comparisons* (Malden, MA: Blackwell, 2004), 472; Karl Polanyi, *The Great Transformation: The Political and Economic Origins of Our Time* (1944; Boston: Beacon Press, 2001).

2 Kevin H. O'Rourke and Jeffrey G. Williamson, *Globalization and History: The Evolution of a Nineteenth-Century Atlantic Economy* (Cambridge, MA: MIT Press, 1999), 2. The word *globalization* entered into use in the 1960s and became popular in the 1970s and 1980s. Nayan Chanda, *Bound Together: How Traders, Preachers, Adventurers, and Warriors Shaped Globalization* (New Haven, CT: Yale University Press, 2007), 245–251; Jürgen Osterhammel and Niels P. Peterson, *Globalization: A Short History,* trans. Dona Geyer (Princeton, NJ: Princeton University Press, 2005).

3 Jürgen Osterhammel, *Die Verwandlung der Welt: Eine Geschichte des 19. Jahrhunderts* (Munich: C. H. Beck, 2009), 1029–1030.

4 Frank Trentmann, "Before Free Trade: Empire, Free Trade and the Moral Economies of Food in the Modern World," in *Food and Globalization: Consumption, Markets and Politics in the Modern World,* ed. Alexander Nützenadl and Frank Trentmann (Oxford: Berg, 2008), 254.

5 Michael Adas, *Machines as the Measure of Men* (Ithaca, NY: Cornell University Press, 1989). For first-rate works of economic history that accentuate the Eurocentric stress on technology, see David Landes, *The Unbound Prometheus: Technological Change and Industrial Development in Western Europe from 1750 to the Present* (Cambridge: Cambridge University Press, 1969); Landes, *The Wealth and Poverty of Nations* (New York: W. W. Norton, 1999); and Joel Mokyr, *The Lever of Riches* (New York: Oxford University Press, 1990).

6 Eric Hobsbawm, *The Age of Extremes: The Short Twentieth Century, 1914–1991* (London: Abacus, 1995), 112–141; José Ortega y Gasset, *La rebelión de las*

*masas* (Madrid: Revista de Occidente, 1930); Jackson Lears, *Rebirth of a Nation: The Making of Modern America, 1877–1920* (New York: HarperCollins, 2009), 92–132.

7 Eric Hobsbawm, *The Age of Empire, 1875–1914* (New York: Pantheon, 1987); Rudolf Hilferding, *Das Finanzkapital: Eine Studie über die jüngste Entwicklung des Kapitalismus* (1910; Berlin: Dietz, 1955).

8 Kaoru Sugihara, "An Introduction," Man-houng Lin, "China's 'Dual Economy' in International Trade Relations, 1842–1949," and Hajime Kose, "Foreign Trade, International Trade, and Industrialization: A Statistical Analysis of Regional Commodity Flows in China, 1914–1931," all in *Japan, China, and the Growth of the Asian International Economy, 1850–1949*, vol. 1, ed. Kaoru Sugihara (Oxford: Oxford University Press, 2005), 5, 179–197, 198–213; John Gallagher and Ronald Robinson, "The Imperialism of Free Trade," *Economic History Review* 6, no. 1 (1953): 1–15. For a perceptive overview of colonialism that emphasizes the role of "indirect rule," see Jürgen Osterhammel, *Colonialism: A Theoretical Overview,* trans. Shelley Fritsch (Princeton, NJ: Marcus Wiener, 2005). See also James Belich, *Replenishing the Earth: The Settler Revolution and the Rise of the Anglo-World, 1783–1939* (Oxford: Oxford University Press, 2009), 554–559. For examples of neo-imperialist approaches, see Andre Gunder Frank, *Capitalism and Underdevelopment in Latin America: Historical Studies of Chile and Brazil* (New York: Monthly Review Press, 1967); Fernando Henrique Cardoso and Enzo Faletto, *Dependency and Development in Latin America,* trans. Marjorie Mattingly Urquidi (Berkeley: University of California Press, 1979); and Immanuel Wallerstein, *The Modern World-System,* 3 vols. (New York: Academic Press, 1974, 1980, 1989).

9 Osterhammel, *Die Verwandlung der Welt,* 20. Thanks to Bob Moeller for help with the translation.

10 J. F. de Barros Pimental, *A política do café* (São Paulo: Empreza Graphica da Revista dos Tribunais, 1930), 4.

11 Victoria de Grazia, *Irresistible Empire: America's Advance through Twentieth-Century Europe* (Cambridge, MA: Belknap Press of Harvard University Press, 2005), 75–129; Kristin L. Hoganson, *Consumers' Imperium: The Global Production of American Domesticity, 1865–1920* (Chapel Hill: University of North Carolina Press, 2007).

12 Gary Gereffi, G. J. Humphrey, and T. Sturgeon, "The Governance of Global Value Chains," *Review of International Political Economy* 12, no. 1 (2005): 78–104. Also see Jennifer Bair, ed., *Frontiers of Commodity Chain Research* (Stan-

ford, CA: Stanford University Press, 2009); Arjun Appadurai, *The Social Life of Things: Commodities in Cultural Perspective* (New York: Cambridge University Press, 1986); Victoria de Grazia and Ellen Furlough, eds., *The Sex of Things: Gender and Consumption in Historical Perspective* (Berkeley: University of California Press, 1996); Jan de Vries, *The Industrious Revolution: Consumer Behavior and the Household Economy, 1650 to the Present* (Cambridge: Cambridge University Press, 2008), 270.

## 1. TRANSFORMATIONS

1  Walt W. Rostow, *The British Economy of the Nineteenth Century* (Oxford: Clarendon Press, 1948); Rostow, *The World Economy: History and Prospect* (Austin: University of Texas Press, 1978), 81–88; Giovanni Arrighi, *The Long Twentieth Century* (London: Verso, 1994), 85–238; Eric Hobsbawm, *Industry and Empire: An Economic History of Britain since 1750* (London: Weidenfeld and Nicolson, 1968), 101; 231; W. David Landes, *The Unbound Prometheus: Technological Change and Industrial Development in Western Europe from 1750 to the Present* (Cambridge: Cambridge University Press, 1969), 231; W. Arthur Lewis, *Growth and Fluctuations, 1870–1913* (London: George Allen and Unwin, 1978), 15–32.

2  Eric Hobsbawm, *The Age of Empire, 1875–1914* (New York: Pantheon, 1987), 44. One could argue that the neoliberalism of our day surpasses the pre-1945 period in its worship of free markets and capital efficiency. But the era after 1870 was nonetheless a striking departure. Before 1870 the world had never experienced such international flows of goods, people, and capital. See Rudolf Hilferding, *Das Finanzkapital: Eine Studie über die jüngste Entwicklung des Kapitalismus* (1910; Berlin: Dietz, 1955).

3  Alfred D. Chandler Jr., *Scale and Scope: The Dynamics of Industrial Capitalism* (Cambridge, MA: Belknap Press of Harvard University Press, 1990).

4  Paul Boyer, ed., *The Oxford Companion to United States History* (New York: Oxford University Press, 2001); James C. Riley, *Rising Life Expectancy: A Global History* (New York: Cambridge University Press, 2001). Nonwhites experienced markedly lower life expectancies in the United States, graphic evidence of racism and inequality. For a visual graphing of changing world life expectancies and per capita incomes, see www.gapminder.org.

5  Joseph Schumpeter, *Capitalism, Socialism and Democracy* (New York: Harper, 1947), which borrowed the concept from Werner Sombart, *Krieg und Kapitalismus* (Leipzig: Duncker und Humblot, 1913), 207.

6   Diarmuid Jeffreys, *Hell's Cartel: IG Farben and the Making of Hitler's War Machine* (New York: Metropolitan Books, 2008).

7   Chandler, *Scale and Scope*. Liebig's was a molasses-like black spread of reduced meat stock used as a supplement for the malnourished, and in cooking, more generally.

8   Daniel Yergin, *The Prize: The Epic Quest for Oil, Money, and Power* (New York: Free Press, 1991), 59, 63; Chandler, *Scale and Scope,* 270–273; Kenne Fant, *Alfred Nobel: A Biography* (New York: Arcade, 2006).

9   Kenneth Pomeranz, *The Great Divergence: China, Europe, and the Making of the Modern World Economy* (Princeton, NJ: Princeton University Press, 2000); Jeffrey Williamson, "Globalization and the Great Divergence: Terms of Trade Booms, Volatility and the Poor Periphery, 1782–1913," *European Review of Economic History* 12 (2008): 355–391.

10  Hobsbawm, *The Age of Empire,* 15. See also François Bourguignon and Christian Morrisson, "Inequality among World Citizens: 1820–1992," *American Economic Review* 92, no. 4 (September 2002): 728, 737, 739. For a thoughtful discussion of studies on the Great Divergence after 1800, see M. Shahid Alam, "Global Disparities since 1800: Trends and Regional Patterns," *Journal of World-Systems Research* 12, no. 2 (July 2006): 37–59.

11  Alam, in "Global Disparities since 1800," 52, defines "periphery" as East Asia minus Japan, West Asia, Africa, and Latin America.

12  Bourguignon and Morrisson, "Inequality among World Citizens," 734. Mark Twain meant "the Gilded Age" ironically in his 1873 novel to underline corruption rather than plenty. Twain, *The Gilded Age* (Hartford: Hartford American, 1874).

13  David Landes, in his *The Wealth and Poverty of Nations* (New York: W. W. Norton, 1999), 32, awards the West the prize of having invented the notion of development, whereas Andre Gunder Frank, in *Capitalism and Underdevelopment in Latin America: Historical Studies of Chile and Brazil* (New York: Monthly Review Press, 1967), contends that it had fostered underdevelopment. Even though Kevin O'Rourke and Jeffrey G. Williamson, in *Globalization and History: The Evolution of a Nineteenth-Century Atlantic Economy* (Cambridge, MA: MIT Press, 1999), find *convergence* in our period, they concentrate on the Northern Atlantic. They note that "true, much of the unconditional convergence since 1870 disappears when the net is widened to include Eastern Europe and . . . if it were widened still further to the Third World, unconditional convergence would totally evaporate" (9). Our book considers the entire world.

14  Warren Dean, *With Broadsword and Firebrand: The Destruction of the Brazilian Atlantic Forest* (Berkeley: University of California Press, 1995); Gary Okihiro, *Pineapple Culture: A History of the Tropical and Temperate Zones* (Berkeley: University of California Press, 2009); Alfred Crosby, *Ecological Imperialism: The Biological Expansion of Europe, 900–1900* (New York: Cambridge University Press, 1986).

15  See, for example, Patricia Seed, *Ceremonies of Possession in Europe's Conquest of the New World, 1492–1640* (New York: Cambridge University Press, 1995); and Seed, *American Pentimento: The Invention of Indians and the Pursuit of Riches* (Minneapolis: University of Minnesota Press, 2001).

16  Stephen Yaffa, *Cotton: The Biography of a Revolutionary Fiber* (New York: Penguin Books, 2005), 130; Sven Beckert, "Emancipation and Empire: Reconstructing the Worldwide Web of Cotton Production in the Age of the American Civil War," *American Historical Review* 109, no. 5 (December 2004): 1405–1438.

17  Michael Mulhall, *The Dictionary of Statistics* (London: G. Routledge, 1899), 130; Susan B. Carter et al., eds., *Historical Statistics of the United States, from Colonial Times to the Present* (New York: Cambridge University Press), 546, online at http://www.cambridge.org; A. G. Kenwood and A. L. Lougheed, *The Growth of the International Economy, 1820–1990: An Introductory Text* (London: Routledge, 1999), 215–219.

18  Raymond Vernon, *Storm over the Multinationals: The Real Issues* (Cambridge, MA: Harvard University Press, 1977).

19  Jean-Yves Grenier, *L' économie d'Ancien Régime: Un monde de l' échange et de l'incertitude* (Paris: Albin Michel, 1996); Edmund Whittaker, *Schools and Streams of Economic Thought* (Chicago: Rand McNally, 1960); Frank Trentmann, *Free Trade Nation: Commerce, Consumption and Civil Society in Modern Britain* (Oxford: Oxford University Press, 2008).

20  Paul Gootenberg, *Between Silver and Guano: Commercial Policy and the State in Postindependence Peru* (Princeton, NJ: Princeton University Press, 1989); Gootenberg, *Imagining Development: Economic Ideas in Peru's Fictitious Prosperity of Guano, 1840–1880* (Berkeley: University of California Press, 1993). On the relative advantages of backwardness, see Alexander Gerschenkron, *Economic Backwardness in Historical Perspective: A Book of Essays* (Cambridge, MA: Belknap Press of Harvard University Press, 1962). See also Thomas Smith, *Native Sources of Japanese Industrialization, 1750–1920* (Berkeley: University of California Press, 1988).

21 John Coatsworth and Jeffrey G. Williamson, "Always Protectionist? Latin American Tariffs from Independence to the Great Depression," *Journal of Latin American Studies* 36, no. 2 (2004): 205–232; Carlos Marichal and Steven Topik, "The State and Economic Growth in Latin America: Brazil and Mexico, Nineteenth and Early Twentieth Centuries," in *Nation, State, and the Economy in History,* ed. Alice Teichova and Herbert Matis (Cambridge: Cambridge University Press, 2003).

22 See, for example, E. Bradford Burns, *The Poverty of Progress: Latin America in the Nineteenth Century* (Berkeley: University of California Press, 1980); Nícea Vilela Luz, *A luta pela industrialização do Brasil* (1967; São Paulo: Alfa-Omega, 1975); and Domingo Sarmiento, *Life in the Argentine Republic in the Days of the Tyrant,* trans. Mrs. Horace Mann (1868; New York: Collier Books, 1961).

23 For a discussion of these debates, see Steven C. Topik, *Trade and Gunboats: The United States and Brazil in the Age of Empire* (Stanford, CA: Stanford University Press, 1996); Edward Stanwood, *American Tariff Controversies in the Nineteenth Century* (Boston: Houghton and Mifflin, 1903); Frank Taussig, *The Tariff History of the United States,* 8th ed. (New York: G. P. Putnam's Sons, 1931); Edward Crapol, *America for Americans: Anglophobia in the Late Nineteenth Century* (Westport, CT: Greenwood, 1973).

24 Donald Denoon, *Settler Capitalism: The Dynamics of Dependent Development in the Southern Hemisphere* (New York: Oxford University Press, 1983), 50; James Belich, *Replenishing the Earth: The Settler Revolution and the Rise of the Anglo-World, 1783–1939* (Oxford: Oxford University Press, 2009), 456–501; P. J. Cain and A. G. Hopkins, *British Imperialism: Innovation and Expansion, 1688–1914* (London: Longmans, 1993), 272.

25 Steven Topik, *The Political Economy of the Brazilian State, 1889–1930* (Austin: University of Texas Press, 1987); Gunnar Myrdal, *Development and Underdevelopment: A Note on the Mechanism of National and International Economic Inequality* (Cairo: National Bank of Egypt, 1956).

26 Charles Bergquist, *Labor in Latin America: Comparative Essays on Chile, Argentina, Venezuela, and Colombia* (Stanford, CA: Stanford University Press, 1986); Thomas O'Brien, *The Revolutionary Mission: American Enterprise in Latin America, 1900–1945* (New York: Cambridge University Press, 1996); John Hart, *Empire and Revolution: The Americans in Mexico since the Civil War* (Berkeley: University of California Press, 2002).

27 Victoria de Grazia, *Irresistible Empire: America's Advance through Twentieth-Century Europe* (Cambridge, MA: Belknap Press of Harvard University Press, 2005).

28  Kenwood and Lougheed, *Growth*, 10, 83, 86. Peter Stearns, *The Industrial Revolution in World History*, 3rd ed. (Boulder, CO: Westview Press, 2007), 1, 2; Landes, *The Unbound Prometheus;* Cain and Hopkins, *British Imperialism: Innovation and Expansion*, 44.

29  Niall Ferguson, *Empire: How Britain Made the Modern World* (London: Penguin Books, 2004), xxii; Cain and Hopkins, *British Imperialism: Innovation and Expansion*, 170.

30  For useful case studies of states' roles in Latin American export economies, see Joseph Love and Nils Jacobsen, *Guiding the Invisible Hand: Economic Liberalism and the State in Latin America* (New York: Praeger, 1988); and Steven C. Topik and Allen Wells, eds., *The Second Conquest of Latin America: Coffee, Henequen and Oil during the Export Boom, 1850–1930* (Austin: University of Texas Press, 1998).

31  Thanks to William Clarence-Smith for reminding us of these crucial actors. See Philip D. Curtin, *Cross-Cultural Trade in World History* (Cambridge: Cambridge University Press, 1984), for an overview of trade diasporas before the Age of Empire.

32  Hobsbawm, *The Age of Empire*, 43, 44; Frank B. Tipton, "Government and the Economy in the Nineteenth Century," and Volker Wellhöner and Harald Wixforth, "Finance and Industry," both in *Germany since 1800: A New Social and Economic History*, ed. Sheilagh Ogilvie and Richard Overy (London: Arnold, 2003), 118, 122, 161–164.

33  Chandler, *The Visible Hand: The Managerial Revolution in American Business* (Cambridge, MA: Harvard University Press, 1977), 311–312.

34  Ibid., 89.

35  Allison Frank, "The Petroleum War of 1910: Standard Oil, Austria, and the Limits of the Multinational Corporation," *American Historical Review* 114, no. 1 (February 2009): 16–41, esp. 17; Rondo Cameron and V. I. Bovykin, eds., *International Banking, 1870–1914* (New York: Oxford University Press, 1991); Niall Ferguson, *The House of Rothschild*, vol. 2, *The World's Banker, 1849–1999* (New York: Penguin, 1999); and Barbara Stallings, *Banker to the World: U.S. Portfolio Investment in Latin America, 1900–1986* (Berkeley: University of California Press, 1987).

36  Akira Iriye, *Global Community: The Role of International Organizations in the Making of the Contemporary World* (Berkeley: University of California Press, 2002), 9–36.

37  Jon Savage, *Teenage: The Prehistory of Youth Culture, 1875–1945* (New York: Viking Penguin, 2007), 38.

38  Landes, *Wealth and Poverty of Nations*, 274.

39  Leon Trotsky, *The History of the Russian Revolution*, trans. Max Eastman (1932; London: Pluto Press, 1977), 26–27; Stephen Haber, *Industry and Underdevelopment: The Industrialization of Mexico, 1890–1940* (Stanford, CA: Stanford University Press, 1989); Steven C. Topik, "The Emergence of Finance Capital in Mexico," in *Five Centuries of Mexican History/Mexico en el medio milenio*, ed. Virginia Guedea and Jaime Rodríguez (Mexico City: Instituto de Investigaciones Doctor José Maria Mora, 1992), 227–242; Mario Cerutti and Carlos Marichal, eds., *La banca regional en México, 1870–1930* (Mexico City: El Colegio de México, Fondo de Cultura Económica, 2003); Jeffrey Bortz and Stephen Haber, *The Mexican Economy, 1870–1910: Essays on the Economic History of Institutions, Revolution and Growth* (Stanford, CA: Stanford University Press, 2002); Vladimir Lenin, *Imperialism, the Highest Stage of Capitalism: A Popular Outline* (New York: International, 1939); and William E. Lockwood, *The Economic Development of Japan*, 2nd ed. (Princeton, NJ: Princeton University Press, 1968).

40  Jang-Sup Shin, *The Economics of the Latecomers: Catching-up, Technology Transfer and Institutions in Germany, Japan and South Korea* (London: Routledge, 1996); Hidemasa Morikawa, "Japan's Unstable Course during Its Remarkable Economic Development," in Teichova and Matis, *Nation, State, and the Economy*, 332–345; Lockwood, *Economic Development of Japan*, 214–232; Carl Mosk, "Japanese Industrialization and Economic Growth," EH.Net, http://eh.net/encyclopedia/article/mosk.japan.final.

41  The Chinese Empire, of course, had preceded the imperialist era by millennia.

42  D. C. M. Platt, *Britain's Investment Overseas on the Eve of the First World War: The Use and Abuse of Numbers* (Basingstoke, UK: Macmillan, 1986). We include some estimates on capital flows, but these numbers are only approximations. Students of foreign investment acknowledge that the nationality of investment and the amount repatriated cannot always be identified, because global investors put capital into markets and corporations in many areas.

43  Kenwood and Lougheed, *Growth*, 86, 215; P. J. Cain and A. G. Hopkins, *British Imperialism: Crisis and Deconstruction, 1914–1990* (London: Longman, 1993), 37, 123.

44  Cain and Hopkins, *British Imperialism: Crisis and Deconstruction*, 45, 231.

45  League of Nations, *Statistical Year-Book of the League of Nations, 1926* (Geneva: League of Nations, Economic and Financial Section, 1927–1945), 77, 78, http://digital.library.northwestern.edu/league/stat.html.

46  We thank Ken Pomeranz for this observation.

47 "Vacant areas" is a term used by Oswaldo Sunkel, *Development from Within: Toward a Neostructuralist Approach for Latin America* (Boulder, CO: L. Rienner, 1993); "Neo-Europe" is taken from Crosby's *Ecological Imperialism;* "settler colonies" is adopted from Denoon, *Settler Capitalism;* and "Western offshoot" is preferred by Angus Maddison, *The World Economy* (Paris: Development Centre of the Organization for Economic Cooperation and Development, 2006).

48 Stephen Haber, *How Latin America Fell Behind: Essays on the Economic History of Brazil and Mexico, 1800–1914* (Stanford, CA: Stanford University Press, 1997).

## 2. THE SINEWS OF TRADE

1 Emily Rosenberg, *Financial Missionaries to the World: The Politics and Culture of Dollar Diplomacy, 1900–1930* (Durham, NC: Duke University Press, 2003); Paul Drake, *Money Doctors: Foreign Debts and Economic Reforms in Latin America from the 1890s to the Present* (Wilmington, DE: Scholarly Resources, 1994); J. P. Wileman, *Brazilian Exchange: The Study of an Inconvertible Currency* (1896; New York: Greenwood, 1969); Carlos Marichal and Steven Topik, "The State and Economic Growth in Latin America: Brazil and Mexico, Nineteenth and Early Twentieth Centuries," in *Nation, State, and the Economy in History,* ed. Alice Teichova and Herbert Maris (Cambridge: Cambridge University Press, 2003); Thomas G. Rawski, *Economic Growth in Prewar China* (Berkeley: University of California Press, 1989), 155–164.

2 For a trenchant contemporary discussion of the gold standard and the ideology behind it, see Karl Polanyi, *The Great Transformation: The Political and Economic Origins of Our Time* (1944; Boston: Beacon Press, 2001). For the most recent overview of the international debate and system, see Barry Eichengreen, *Globalizing Capital: A History of the International Monetary System* (Princeton, NJ: Princeton University Press, 2008).

3 Niall Ferguson, *Paper and Iron: Hamburg Business and German Politics in the Era of Inflation, 1897–1927* (Cambridge: Cambridge University Press, 1995).

4 There was an interruption in the decline between 1852 and 1873. Douglass North, "Ocean Freight Rates and Economic Development, 1750–1913," *Journal of Economic History* 18, no. 4 (December 1958): 537–555, esp. 542.

5 Eric Hobsbawm, *The Age of Empire, 1875–1914* (New York: Pantheon, 1987), 28, 350; Daniel Headrick, *The Tentacles of Progress: Technology Transfer in the Age of Imperialism, 1850–1940* (New York: Oxford University Press, 1988), 23–25;

Peter J. Hugill, *World Trade since 1431: Geography, Technology, and Capitalism* (Baltimore: Johns Hopkins University Press, 1993), 125–158.

6 There was a reciprocal relationship between the rapid expansion of faster, cheaper freight carriers and the growth of world commerce. Ship technology continued to improve with the invention of the steam turbine in 1894 and the introduction of the diesel engine in the 1920s. The fourfold growth in ship size brought with it further economies because fuel consumed per pound of freight declined proportionately, as did the size of the crew. Headrick, *The Tentacles of Progress*, 27–31; Walt W. Rostow, *The World Economy: History and Prospect* (Austin: University of Texas Press, 1978), 669. The change in fuel would have enormous consequences after World War I, though in 1914 only 2 percent of world shipping was fueled by oil. A. G. Kenwood and A. L. Lougheed, *The Growth of the International Economy, 1820–1990: An Introductory Text* (London: Routledge, 1999), 15.

7 John Soluri, *Banana Cultures: Agriculture, Consumption, and Environmental Change in Honduras and the United States* (Austin: University of Texas Press, 2005). The world would have to wait until 1956 for the next giant step in the shipping revolution, the shipping container. Marc Levinson, *The Box: How the Shipping Container Made the World Smaller and the World Economy Bigger* (Princeton, NJ: Princeton University Press, 2006).

8 North, "Ocean Freight Rates," 543.

9 Gary Okihiro, *Pineapple Culture: A History of the Tropical and Temperate Zones* (Berkeley: University of California Press, 2009); and Lawrence Clayton, *Grace: W. R. Grace and Company, the Formative Years, 1850–1930* (Ottawa, IL: Jameson Books, 1985).

10 Robert Greenhill, "Shipping," in *Business Imperialism*, ed. D. C. M. Platt (Oxford: Clarendon Press, 1977).

11 Jeffrey G. Williamson, "Winners and Losers over Two Centuries of Globalization," National Bureau of Economic Research Working Paper Series, Working Paper No. 9161, September 2002.

12 Michael G. Mulhall, *The Dictionary of Statistics*, 4th ed. (London: G. Routledge, 1899), 520.

13 Hobsbawm, *The Age of Empire*, 51.

14 US Bureau of the Census, *Historical Statistics of the United States from Colonial Times to 1957* (Washington, DC: US Government Printing Office, 1960), 450.

15 Quoted in Daniel Yergin, *The Prize: The Epic Quest for Oil, Money, and Power* (New York: Free Press, 1991), 12, 154. Alfred Thayer Mahan, *The Influence of Sea Power upon History, 1660–1783* (1892; New York: Hill and Wang, 1957); Harold

Sprout and Margaret Sprout, *The Rise of American Naval Power, 1776–1918* (Princeton, NJ: Princeton University Press, 1939).

16 Charles Flint, *Memories of an Active Life* (New York: G. P. Putnam's Sons, 1923); Steven C. Topik, *Trade and Gunboats: The United States and Brazil in the Age of Empire* (Stanford, CA: Stanford University Press, 1996): V. G. Kiernan, *Marxism and Imperialism* (London: Edward Arnold, 1974), 105.

17 Greenhill, "Shipping," 141.

18 E. Sydney Crawcour, "Industrialization and Technological Change, 1885–1920," in *The Economic Emergence of Modern Japan*, ed. Kozo Yamamura (Cambridge: Cambridge University Press, 1997), 97–99; William E. Lockwood, *The Economic Development of Japan*, 2nd ed. (Princeton, NJ: Princeton University Press, 1968), 348–351, 544–549; Peter N. Davies, "Japanese Shipping and Shipbuilding: An Introduction to the Motives behind Its Early Expansion," and Kunio Katayama, "Japanese Economic Development Strategy and the Shipping Industries, 1881–1894," both in Discussion Paper No. JS/99/376, November 1999, The Suntory Centre, Suntory and Toyota International Centres for Economic and Related Disciplines, London School of Economics and Political Science.

19 Headrick, *The Tentacles of Progress*, 20.

20 Mira Wilkins, *The Emergence of Multinational Enterprise* (Cambridge, MA: Harvard University Press, 1970), 35.

21 Hugill, *World Trade since 1431*, 159–166; David Landes, *The Wealth and Poverty of Nations* (New York: W. W. Norton, 1999), 215–216; Kenneth Pomeranz, *The Great Divergence: China, Europe, and the Making of the Modern World Economy* (Princeton, NJ: Princeton University Press, 2000), 183–185.

22 Kenneth Pomeranz, *The Making of a Hinterland: State, Society, and Economy in Inland North China, 1853–1937* (Berkeley: University of California Press, 1993), 153–211.

23 Headrick, *The Tentacles of Progress*, 28. In the days of the pharaohs, the canal linked the Red Sea to the Nile and from there to the Mediterranean.

24 Had Senator John McCain won the US presidential election in 2008, he could have taken office because the Panama Canal Zone, where he was born, was considered US soil.

25 Julie Greene, *The Canal Builders: Making America's Empire at the Panama Canal* (New York: Penguin, 2009), 367, 2, 132, 133, 396–399, quotation at 367; Michael Conniff, *Black Labor on the White Canal: Panama, 1904–1908* (Pittsburgh: University of Pittsburgh Press, 1985), 30–31.

26 Quoted in Greene, *The Canal Builders*, 351.

27  Headrick, *Power over Peoples: Technology, Environments, and Western Imperialism, 1400 to the Present* (Princeton, NJ: Princeton University Press, 2010), 226–251; Paul Janosz, "Dr. Gorgas and Yellow Fever: Destiny through Disease" (unpublished manuscript, University of California, Irvine, February 2011).

28  Paul Cottrell, *Industrial Finance, 1830–1914: The Finance and Organization of English Manufacturing Industry* (London: Methuen, 1983), 40–55; Geoffrey Jones, *British Multinational Banking, 1830–1990* (New York: Oxford University Press, 1993).

29  Headrick, *The Tentacles of Progress,* 36–38.

30  Hobsbawm, *The Age of Empire,* 27, 52.

31  Robert Fogel, *Railroads and American Economic Growth: Essays in Econometric History* (Baltimore: Johns Hopkins University Press, 1964); Alfred D. Chandler Jr., *The Visible Hand: The Managerial Revolution in American Business* (Cambridge, MA: Harvard University Press, 1977); Michael J. Twomey, *A Century of Foreign Investment in the Third World* (London: Routledge, 2000), 44.

32  Kenwood and Lougheed, *Growth,* 36. Admittedly, miles of track do not necessarily reflect the intensity of use, because the smaller lines tended to pass through more heavily used areas. For example, in 1887–1888 the United States had 20 percent more track than all of Europe but carried only one-fourth the number of passengers and 80 percent as much freight. Mulhall, *The Dictionary of Statistics,* 496.

33  Headrick, *The Tentacles of Progress,* 55.

34  Kenwood and Lougheed, *Growth,* 13.

35  Pomeranz, *Making of a Hinterland,* 146–152; B. R. Mitchell, *International Historical Statistics: Africa, Asia and Oceania, 1750–2005,* 5th ed. (London: Palgrave, 2007), 723, 724.

36  Mulhall, *The Dictionary of Statistics,* 523 for world port capacities.

37  John H. Coatsworth, *Growth against Development: The Economic Impact of Railroads in Porfirian Mexico* (De Kalb: Northern Illinois University, 1981).

38  Sandra Kuntz Ficker, *Empresa extranjera y mercado interno: El Ferrocarril Central Mexicano, 1850–1950* (Mexico City: El Colegio de México, 1995); Kuntz Ficker and Paolo Riguzzi, eds., *Ferrocarriles y vida económica en México, 1850–1950* (Mexico City: El Colegio Mexiquense-Universidad Autónomo Metropolitana, Xochimilco, 1996); Mario Cerruti and José Reséndiz Balderas, eds., *Monterrey, Nuevo León, el Noreste: Siete estudios históricos* (Monterrey: Universidad Autónoma de Nueva León, 1987).

39  James Scobie, *Argentina: A City and a Nation* (New York: Oxford University Press, 1964); Carlos Díaz Alejandro, *Essays on the Economic History of the Argentine Republic* (New Haven, CT: Yale University Press, 1970); Roberto Cortés Conde, *Argentina since Independence* (New York: Cambridge University Press, 1993).

40  Steven C. Topik, *The Political Economy of the Brazilian State, 1889–1930* (Austin: University of Texas Press, 1987), 93–128; and Julian Duncan, *Public and Private Ownership of Railroads in Brazil* (New York: Faculty of Political Science, Columbia University, 1932).

41  Quoted in H. A. Mwanzi, "African Initiatives and Resistance in East Africa, 1880–1914," in *General History of Africa*, vol. 7: *Africa under Colonial Domination, 1880–1935*, ed. A. Adu Boahen (Berkeley: University of California Press, 1985), 163.

42  Colin Leys, *The Political Economy of Neo-Colonialism, 1964–1971* (Berkeley: University of California Press, 1975), 28–35,

43  Mwanzi, "African Initiatives," 164, 165; Brad Weiss, *Sacred Trees, Bitter Harvests: Globalizing Coffee in Northwest Tanzania* (Portsmouth, NH: Heinemann, 2003), 14–21.

44  Calculated from Mitchell, *International Historical Statistics: Africa, Asia and Oceania, 1750–2005*, 715–718.

45  Ibid.; Donald Denoon, *Settler Capitalism: The Dynamics of Dependent Development in the Southern Hemisphere* (New York: Oxford University Press, 1983), 51.

46  Headrick, *The Tentacles of Progress*, 55–91.

47  Quoted in ibid., 73.

48  Ibid., 87.

49  Rawski, *Economic Growth in Prewar China*, 181–189.

50  Wolfgang Schivelbusch, *Geschichte der Eisenbahnreise*, translated as *The Railway Journey: The Industrialization of Time and Space in the Nineteenth Century* (Berkeley: University of California Press, 1986).

51  Headrick, *The Tentacles of Progress*, 277.

52  Rostow, *The World Economy*, 199; calculated from the *Statistical Year-Book of the League of Nations, 1926*, 87; calculated from the *Statistical Year-Book of the League of Nations, 1942–44*, 159; Lockwood, *Economic Development of Japan*, 106.

53  Headrick, *The Tentacles of Progress*, 293–295.

54  *Statistical Year-Book of the League of Nations, 1942–44*, 85.

55 Brasil, Presidente, *Mensagem dirigida ao Congresso Nacional, 1926* (Rio de Janeiro: Imprensa Nacional, 1926), 152.

56 On early Mexico estimate, see Coatsworth, *Growth against Development.* For revised estimates, see Kuntz Ficker, *Empresa extranjera;* and Kuntz Ficker and Riguzzi, eds., *Ferrocarriles y vida económica.* For Brazil, see Topik, *The Political Economy.* On different periods showing the domestic multiplier effects of railroads, see William Summerhill, *Order against Progress: Government, Foreign Investment, and Railroads in Brazil* (Stanford, CA: Stanford University Press, 2003).

57 John Coatsworth and Jeffrey G. Williamson, "Always Protectionist? Latin American Tariffs from Independence to the Great Depression," *Journal of Latin American Studies* 36, no. 2 (2004).

58 Topik, *The Political Economy,* 93–129.

59 See Greg Grandin, *Fordlandia: The Rise and Fall of Henry Ford's Forgotten Jungle City* (New York: Metropolitan Books, 2009), for the positive and repressive sides of Fordism in the United States.

60 Ibid., 80, 194, 208; and US Bureau of the Census, *Historical Statistics of the United States,* 462; Hugill, *World Trade since 1431,* 218; and Lockwood, *Economic Development of Japan,* 107.

61 US Bureau of the Census, *Historical Statistics of the United States,* 546.

62 James M. Laux, *The European Automobile Industry* (New York: Twayne, 1992), 104, 115; Joel Wolff, *Autos and Progress: The Brazilian Search for Modernity* (New York: Oxford University Press, 2010), 38.

63 Calculated from Laux, *The European Automobile Industry,* 74; Rostow, *The World Economy,* 196–197; Hugill, *World Trade since 1431,* 238, 241–244; Jürgen Osterhammel, *Die Verwandlung der Welt: Eine Geschichte des 19. Jahrhunderts* (Munich: C. H. Beck, 2009), 318.

64 James E. Vance Jr., *Capturing the Horizon: The Historical Geography of Transportation since the Transportation Revolution of the Sixteenth Century* (New York: Harper and Row, 1986), 530–539; Daniel Yergin, *The Prize: The Epic Quest for Oil, Money, and Power* (New York: Free Press, 1991), 172.

65 Charles Quilter, "In Any Weather" (PhD diss., University of California, Irvine, 2010).

66 R. E. G. Davies, *Airlines of Latin America since 1919* (Washington, DC: Smithsonian Institution Press, 1984).

67 Ibid., 2; Hugill, *World Trade since 1431,* 249–283; R. E. G. Davies, *Airlines of Asia since 1920* (McLean, VA.: Paladwr Press, 1997), 340–349; Vance, *Capturing the Horizon,* 545–576.

68  Vance, *Capturing the Horizon;* Davies, *Airlines of Latin America,* 336–344.

69  Davies, *Airlines of Asia,* 1, 231–233.

70  Ibid., 6–14.

71  Headrick, *Power over Peoples,* 306–328.

72  Tom Standage, *The Victorian Internet: The Remarkable Story of the Telegraph and the Nineteenth Century's On-line Pioneers* (New York: Walker and Co., 1998).

73  Dwayne R. Winseck and Robert M. Pike, *Communication and Empire: Media, Markets, and Globalization, 1860–1939* (Durham, NC: Duke University Press, 2007), 90.

74  This is a controversial point. Some scholars, like Rondo Cameron (in Cameron and V. I. Bovykin, eds., *International Banking, 1870–1914* [New York: Oxford University Press, 1991], 4), argue that banks were the first multinational companies, dating back to medieval Italy. Others point to the Dutch East India Company's charter in 1602. Wilkins, in *The Emergence of Multinational Enterprise,* 35, puts it around 1865 for the United States.

75  Standage, *The Victorian Internet;* Rudolf Stöber, *Deutsche Pressgeschichte: Von den Anfängen bis zum Gegenwart* (Constance: UVK Verlagsgesellschaft, 2005), 131–136; and Winseck and Pike, *Communication and Empire,* 5, 149, 203, 258.

76  B. R. Mitchell, *International Historical Statistics: Europe, 1750–2000,* 6th ed. (Basingstoke, UK: Palgrave Macmillan, 2007), 52–760; and US Bureau of the Census, *Historical Statistics of the United States,* 485.

77  Rawski, *Economic Growth,* 217; Henry Brunton, *Building Japan, 1868–1876* (1877; London: Routledge, 1991), 27–29.

78  Quoted in Headrick, *The Tentacles of Progress,* 121.

79  Mitchell, *International Historical Statistics: Africa, Asia and Oceania, 1750–2005,* 830–835.

80  Winseck and Pike, *Communication and Empire,* 105, 147.

81  Brunton, *Building Japan,* 28.

82  Quoted in Winseck and Pike, *Communication and Empire,* 36.

83  F. Leslie Smith, John Wright II, and David H. Ostroff, *Perspectives on Radio and Television: Telecommunication in the United States,* 4th ed. (Mahwah, NJ: Erlbaum, 1998), 37.

84  Carole E. Scott, "The Technological Development of Radio: From Thales to Marconi," http:// eh.net/encyclopedia/article/scott.radio.industry.history.

85  Calculated from Mitchell, *International Historical Statistics: Africa, Asia and Oceania, 1750–2005,* and Mitchell, *International Historical Statistics: Europe, 1750–2005;* US Bureau of the Census, *Historical Statistics of the United States;*

Winseck and Pike, *Communication and Empire*, 315; Hugill, *World Trade since 1431*, 321–322.

86  Hans-Ulrich Wehler, *Deutsche Gesellschaftsgeschichte: Von der "Deutschen Doppelrevolution" bis zum Beginn des Ersten Weltkriges, 1849–1914* (Munich: C. H. Beck, 1995), 612, 613.

87  Volker Wellhöner and Harald Wixforth, "Finance and Industry," in *Germany since 1800: A New Social and Economic History*, ed. Sheilagh Ogilvie and Richard Overy (London: Arnold, 2003), 161–164; William J. Hausman, Peter Hertner, and Mira Wilkins, *Global Electrification: Multinational Enterprise and International Finance in the History of Light and Power, 1878–2007* (New York: Cambridge University Press, 2008), 75–124.

88  Steven C. Topik, "Economic Nationalism and the State in an Underdeveloped Country: Brazil, 1889–1930" (PhD diss., University of Texas, Austin, 1978); Hausman et al., *Global Electrification*, 75–124.

89  Hausman et al., 102–103.

90  Lockwood, *Economic Development of Japan*, 49, 224–225.

91  Hausman et al., 94, 95, 253, 254.

92  Ibid., 201, 234.

93  Wolfgang Schivelbusch, *Lichtblicke: Zur Geschichte der Kunstlichen Helligkeiten im 19 Jahrhundert* (Munich: C. Hauser, 1983).

94  Calculated from Mulhall, *The Dictionary of Statistics*, 156; *Statistical Year-Book of the League of Nations, 1939–40*, 146; *Statistical Year-Book of the League of Nations, 1926*, 88.

95  *Statistical Year-Book of the League of Nations, 1939–40*, 146.

96  Chandler, *Scale and Scope*, 125; Wilkins, *Emergence of Multinational Enterprise*, 80–82, 116–118, 178–184.

97  Robert Franz, "The Statistical History of the German Banking System," *Miscellaneous Articles on German Banking*, US Senate Document 508 (Washington, DC: US Government Printing Office, 1910), 29–33; Albert Broder, "Banking and the Electrotechnical Industry in Western Europe," in Cameron and Bovykin, *International Banking, 1870–1914*, 474–480; and Hans-Ulrich Wehler, *Von der "Deutschen Doppelrevolution" bis zum Beginn des Ersten Weltkrieges, 1849–1914*, vol. 3 of *Deutsche Gesellschaftsgeschichte* (Munich: C. H. Beck, 1995).

98  Rosemary Thorp and Geoffrey Bertram, *Peru, 1890–1977: Growth and Policy in an Open Economy* (New York: Columbia University Press, 1978), 72–95; Wilkins, *Emergence of Multinational Enterprise*, 80–82, 116–118, 178–184.

99 Charles Bergquist, *Labor in Latin America: Comparative Essays on Chile, Argentina, Venezuela, and Colombia* (Stanford, CA: Stanford University Press, 1986); Thomas O'Brien, *The Revolutionary Mission: American Enterprise in Latin America, 1900–1945* (New York: Cambridge University Press, 1996); Thomas Klubock, *Contested Communities: Class, Gender, and Politics in Chile's El Teniente Copper Mine, 1904–1951* (Durham, NC: Duke University Press, 1998); John Hart, *Revolutionary Mexico: The Coming and Process of the Mexican Revolution* (Berkeley: University of California Press, 1987); Alan Knight, *The Mexican Revolution*, 2 vols. (New York: Cambridge University Press, 1986).

100 Dennis Kortheuer, "Santa Rosalía and Compagnie du Boleó: The Making of a Town and Company in the Porfirian Frontier, 1885–1900" (PhD diss., University of California, Irvine, 2001).

101 Alfred D. Chandler Jr., with Takashi Hikino, *Scale and Scope: The Dynamics of Industrial Capitalism* (Cambridge, MA: Belknap Press of Harvard University Press, 1990), 70, 122–124.

102 Yergin, *The Prize*, 55.

103 Ibid., 100, 113; Naomi Lamoreaux, *The Great Merger Movement in American Business, 1895–1904* (New York: Cambridge University Press, 1985).

104 Quoted in Yergin, *The Prize*, 14–56, 110.

105 Ibid., 79, 80, 112.

106 Quoted in ibid., 154.

107 Nuno Luís Madureira, "Oil in the Age of Steam," *Journal of Global History* 5, no. 1 (2010): 75–94.

108 Jonathan Brown, *Oil and Revolution* (Berkeley: University of California Press, 1992); Sandra Kuntz Ficker, *Las exportaciones mexicanas durante la primera globalizacion, 1870–1929* (Mexico City: El Colegio de México, 2010); Miguel Tinker Salas, *The Enduring Legacy: Oil, Culture, and Society in Venezuela* (Durham, NC: Duke University Press, 2009).

109 Calculated from Susan B. Carter et al., *Historical Statistics of the United States: Millennial Edition Online* (Cambridge: Cambridge University Press, 2006), tables 184–186, 208–217, online at http://www.cambridge.org; Grandin, *Fordlandia;* Hugill, *World Trade since 1431,* 208–212.

110 US Bureau of the Census, *Historical Statistics of the U.S. 1960,* 548; Brasil, Diretoria Geral da Estatística (DGE), *Anuário Estatístico, 1930/1940* (Rio de Janeiro: Imprensa Nacional, 1940), 1380; Zephyr Frank and Aldo Mussachio, "Brazil in the International Rubber Trade, 1870–1930," in Steven Topik, Carlos Marichal, and Zephyr Frank, eds., *From Silver to Cocaine: Latin American Commodity*

Chains and the Building of the World Economy, *1500–2000* (Durham, NC: Duke University Press, 2006), 275.

111 Michael Stanfield, *Red Rubber, Bleeding Trees: Violence, Slavery and Empire in Northwest Amazonia, 1850–1933* (Albuquerque: University of New Mexico Press, 1998); Barbara Weinstein, *The Amazon Rubber Boom, 1850–1920* (Stanford, CA: Stanford University Press, 1983); Burns, *The Unwritten Alliance: Rio Branco and Brazilian-American Relations* (New York: Columbia University Press, 1966).

112 Mark R. Finlay, *Growing American Rubber: Strategic Plants and the Politics of National Security* (New Brunswick, NJ: Rutgers University Press, 2009).

113 Joe Jackson, *The Thief at the End of the World: Rubber, Power and the Seeds of Empire* (New York: Penguin, 2009).

114 Ann Stoler, *Capitalism and Confrontation in Sumatra's Plantation Belt, 1870– 1979* (New Haven, CT: Yale University Press, 1985), 209; T. A. Tengwall, "History of Rubber Cultivation and Research in the Netherlands Indies," in *Science and Scientists in the Netherlands Indies,* ed. Pieter Honig and Frans Verdoom (New York: Board for the Netherlands Indies, Surinam and Curaçao, 1945); and *Statistical Year-Book of the League of Nations, 1926,* 80.

115 Adam Hochschild, *King Leopold's Ghost: A Story of Greed, Terror, and Heroism in Colonial Africa* (Boston: Houghton Mifflin, 1998).

116 Finlay, *Growing American Rubber,* 152–157; Kuntz Ficker, *Las exportaciones mexicanas,* 394–405.

## 3. COMMODITY CHAINS

1 Victor Bulmer-Thomas, *The Economic History of Latin America since Independence* (Cambridge: Cambridge University Press, 1994), 15.

2 For a discussion of international regimes, see Stephen Krasner, *The Structural Conflict: The Third World against Global Liberalism* (Berkeley: University of California Press, 1985); and David Smith, Dorothy Solinger, and Steven C. Topik, eds., *States and Sovereignty in the Global Economy* (London: Routledge, 1999).

3 For cocaine chains, see Gootenberg, *Andean Cocaine: The Making of a Global Drug* (Chapel Hill: University of North Carolina Press, 2008); Gootenberg, "Cocaine in Chains: The Rise and Demise of a Global Commodity, 1860– 1950," in *From Silver to Cocaine: Latin American Commodity Chains and the Building of the World Economy, 1500–2000,* ed. Steven Topik, Carlos Marichal, and Zephyr Frank (Durham, NC: Duke University Press, 2006), 321–351.

4 This is less true in studies of US agriculture in our period because of the early rise of agro-industry, but that is an exceptional case.

5 This is in response to David Landes's concentration on the industrial side of the story in *The Unbound Prometheus: Technological Change and Industrial Development in Western Europe from 1750 to the Present* (Cambridge: Cambridge University Press, 1969).

6 Sidney W. Mintz, *Sweetness and Power: The Place of Sugar in Modern History* (New York: Penguin, 1986); Eric Hobsbawm, *The Age of Empire, 1875–1914* (New York: Pantheon, 1987), 50.

7 According to Mulhall's 1889 estimate, already in that year Australia had the highest per capita income in the world, with Canada not far behind France and the Low Countries. *The Dictionary of Statistics* (London: G. Routledge, 1899), 589.

8 David S. Jacks, "Intra- and International Commodity Market Integration in the Atlantic Economy, 1800–1913," *Explorations in Economic History* 42 (2005): 381–413, esp. 399.

9 C. Knick Harley, "Transportation, the World Wheat Trade and the Kuznets Cycle, 1850–1913," *Explorations in Economic History* 17 (1980): 218–250, esp. 218; Patricia Herlihy, *Odessa: A History, 1794–1914* (Cambridge, MA: Harvard University Press, 1986).

10 *World Agriculture: An International Survey* (London: Oxford University Press, 1932), 138.

11 Quoted in Edgars Dunsdorfs, *The Australian Wheat-Growing Industry, 1788–1948* (Melbourne: University Press, 1956), 167.

12 Quoted in Dan Morgan, *Merchants of Grain* (New York: Viking, 1979), 36–37.

13 Harley, "Transportation, the World Wheat Trade," 218, 233; Carl Solberg, *The Prairies and the Pampas: Agrarian Policy in Canada and Argentina, 1880–1930* (Stanford, CA: Stanford University Press, 1987), 39; Peter Dondlinger, *The Book of Wheat: An Economic History and Practical Manual of the Wheat Industry* (New York: Orange, Judd Co., 1912), 238.

14 Alan Olmstead and Paul Rhode, "Biological Globalization: The Other Grain Invasion," in *The New Comparative Economic History: Essays in Honor of Jeffrey G. Williamson,* ed. Timothy Hatton, Kevin H. O'Rourke, and Alan Taylor (Cambridge, MA: MIT Press, 2007): 115–140, quotation at 122; Dunsdorfs, *Australian Wheat-Growing Industry,* 190.

15 William P. Rutter, *Wheat-Growing in Canada, the United States and the Argentine: Including Comparisons with Other Areas* (London: Adam and Charles Black, 1911), 118.

16  Dondlinger, *The Book of Wheat,* 106.

17  *World Agriculture,* 38ff.

18  Dondlinger, *The Book of Wheat,* 237.

19  Kevin O'Rourke and Jeffrey G. Williamson, in *Globalization and History: The Evolution of a Nineteenth-Century Atlantic Economy* (Cambridge, MA: MIT Press, 1999), 220.

20  Dondlinger, *The Book of Wheat,* 241.

21  *World Agriculture,* 209.

22  Kevin H. O'Rourke, "The European Grain Invasion," *Journal of Economic History* 57, no. 4 (December 1977): 775–781, esp. 781. Compare a recent econometric analysis of the wheat market that questions price convergence: Giovanni Federico and Karl Gunnar Perrson, "Market Integration and Convergence in the World Wheat Market," in Hatton et al., *New Comparative Economic History,* 87–113. Rory Miller and Robert Greenhill, "The Fertilizer Commodity Chains: Guano and Nitrate, 1840–1930," in Topik et al., *From Silver to Cocaine,* 228–270.

23  Paul Gootenberg, *Between Silver and Guano: Commercial Policy and the State in Postindependence Peru* (Princeton, NJ: Princeton University Press, 1989); Rosemary Thorp and Geoffrey Bertram, *Peru, 1890–1977: Growth and Policy in an Open Economy* (New York: Columbia University Press, 1978); Heraclio Bonilla, *Guano y burguesia* (Lima: Instituto de Estudios Peruanos, 1973); Shane A. Hunt, "Distribution, Growth, and Government Economic Behavior in Peru," in *Government and Economic Development,* ed. G. Ranis (New Haven, CT: Yale University Press, 1971); Jonathan Levin, *The Export Economies: Their Patterns of Development in Historical Perspective* (Cambridge, MA: Harvard University Press, 1960); Thomas F. O'Brien, *The Nitrate Industry and Chile's Crucial Transition, 1870–1891* (New York: New York University Press, 1982); Michael Monteon, *Chile in the Nitrate Era: The Evolution of Economic Dependence, 1880–1930* (Madison: University of Wisconsin Press, 1982).

24  A. J. H. Latham and Larry Neal, "The International Market in Rice and Wheat, 1868–1914," *Economic History Review* 36, no. 2 (May 1983): 260–280, esp. 270–272; Frank Surface, *The Grain Trade during the World War: Being a History of the Food Administration and the United States Grain Corporation* (New York: Macmillan, 1928), 212.

25  Mintz, *Tasting Food, Tasting Freedom: Excursions into Eating, Culture and the Past* (Boston: Beacon Press, 1996), 24.

26  *World Agriculture,* 31; Morgan, *Merchants of Grain,* 77.

27  Rutter, *Wheat-Growing*, 7; Vernon Wickizer and M. K. Bennett, *The Rice Economy of Monsoon Asia* (Palo Alto, CA: Stanford University Food Research Institute, 1941), 2.

28  N. Jasny, *Competition among Grains* (Palo Alto, CA: Stanford University Food Research Institute, 1940), 7.

29  William Cronon, *Nature's Metropolis: Chicago and the Great West* (New York: W. W. Norton, 1991), 99–100; Donald Denoon, *Settler Capitalism: The Dynamics of Dependent Development in the Southern Hemisphere* (New York: Oxford University Press, 1983), 46; Jasny, *Competition among Grains*, 24–25, 84.

30  Wheat is or has been grown in highland areas on or near the equator, in such disparate climatic zones as Ecuador, Colombia, Nigeria, Saudi Arabia, and Brazil. Wilfred Malenbaum, *The World Wheat Economy, 1885–1939* (Cambridge, MA: Harvard University Press, 1953), 52, 62–63.

31  M. K. Bennett, "World Wheat Crops, 1885–1932: New Series, with Areas and Yields by Countries," *Wheat Studies* 9 (1933): 239–266, esp. 241.

32  Ibid., 258.

33  C. Knick Harley, "Western Settlement and the Price of Wheat, 1872–1913," *Journal of Economic History* 38, no. 4 (December 1978): 865–878, esp. 878; Wickizer and Bennett, *Rice Economy of Monsoon Asia*, 2; Morgan, *Merchants of Grain*, 78–80.

34  Sally Clarke, *Regulation and the Revolution in United States Farm Productivity* (New York: Cambridge University Press, 1994), 249.

35  Ibid., 47.

36  George Pavlovsky, *Agricultural Russia on the Eve of the Revolution* (London: Routledge, 1930), quotation at 254; Alexis Antsiferov et al., *Russian Agriculture during the War* (New Haven, CT: Yale University Press, 1930), chaps. 1–2.

37  Cronon, *Nature's Metropolis*, chap. 3; Jonathan Dekel-Chan, *Farming the Red Land: Jewish Agricultural Colonization and Local Soviet Power, 1924–1941* (New Haven, CT: Yale University Press, 2005).

38  *World Agriculture*, 152–154.

39  Solberg, *Prairies and the Pampas*, 35; *World Agriculture*, 78ff.

40  US Bureau of the Census, *Historical Statistics of the United States*, 14; Solberg, *Prairies and the Pampas*, 35.

41  Surface, *The Grain Trade*, 273, 289; Morgan, *Merchants of Grain*, 45; Dunsdorfs, *Australian Wheat-Growing Industry*, 169–170.

42  *World Agriculture*, 81.

43  Rutter, *Wheat-Growing*, 134–135.

44 Ibid., 188; Dondlinger, *The Book of Wheat,* 191.

45 Cronon, *Nature's Metropolis,* 83–84, quotation at 80.

46 Ibid., 109; and Solberg, *Prairies and the Pampas,* 114. Although Argentine governments were laissez-faire prior to the Great Depression, populist governments during the 1930s and 1940s would become more protective of their farmers after grain prices collapsed.

47 Cronon, *Nature's Metropolis,* 111–112. Elsewhere, the transition to bulk storage and transport of grain was more gradual. Australia, for instance, did not make the change from sacks to bulk shipments until the 1920s. Dunsdorfs, *Australian Wheat-Growing Industry,* 260.

48 Dondlinger, *The Book of Wheat,* 203–208, quotation at 207.

49 Harley, "Transportation, the World Wheat Trade," 227–233.

50 The classic formulation of the US frontier is Frederick Jackson Turner, "The Significance of the Frontier in American History," in *The Frontier in American History* (New York: H. H. Holt, 1920). For a critique, see Paul Gates, *Landlords and Tenants on the Prairie Frontier: Studies in American Land Policy* (Ithaca, NY: Cornell University Press, 1973); and Allan Bogue, *From Prairie to Corn Belt: Farming on the Illinois and Iowa Prairies in the Nineteenth Century* (Chicago: University of Chicago Press, 1963). On Canada, see Harold Innis, *Problems of Staple Production in Canada* (Toronto: Ryerson Press, 1933); Melville Watkins, "A Staple Theory of Economic Growth," *Canadian Journal of Economics and Political Science* 29 (May 1963): 141–158; and John Richards, "The Staples Debates," in *Explorations in Canadian Economic History: Essays in Honor of Irene Spry,* ed. Cameron Duncan (Ottawa: University of Ottawa Press, 1985). On Argentina, see James Scobie, *Revolution on the Pampas: A Social History of Argentine Wheat* (Austin: University of Texas Press, 1964); Jonathan Brown, *A Socio-Economic History of Argentina, 1776–1860* (New York: Cambridge University Press, 1979); David Rock, *Argentina, 1516–1982: From Spanish Colonization to Alfonsín* (Berkeley: University of California Press, 1987); and Aldo Ferrer, *La economía argentina: Las etapas de su desarrollo y problemas actuales* (Mexico City: Fondo de Cultura Económica, 1963). On Chile, see Carl Solberg, *Immigration and Nationalism, Argentina and Chile, 1890–1914* (Austin: University of Texas Press, 1970); and Arnold Bauer, *Chilean Rural Society from the Spanish Conquest to 1930* (New York: Cambridge University Press, 1975).

51 Peter Smith, *Politics and Beef in Argentina: Patterns of Conflict and Change* (New York: Columbia University Press, 1969); Charles Bergquist, *Labor in*

*Latin America: Comparative Essays on Chile, Argentina, Venezuela, and Colombia* (Stanford, CA: Stanford University Press, 1986); Hilda Sabato, *Agrarian Capitalism and the World Market: Buenos Aires in the Pastoral Age, 1840–1890* (Albuquerque: University of New Mexico Press, 1990), 29–52.

52  Jeremy Adelman, *Frontier Development: Land, Labour, and Capital on the Wheatlands of Argentina and Canada, 1890–1914* (Oxford: Clarendon Press, 1994), 80; Solberg, *Prairies and the Pampas,* 63.

53  Adelman, *Frontier Development,* 94.

54  Solberg, *Prairies and the Pampas,* 28; Malenbaum, *The World Wheat Economy,* 138–139.

55  Denoon, *Settler Capitalism,* 100.

56  Adelman, *Frontier Development,* 117–118.

57  Malenbaum, *The World Wheat Economy,* 139–140.

58  Solberg, *Prairies and the Pampas,* 106–108; Malenbaum, *The World Wheat Economy,* 139–140.

59  Quoted in Solberg, *Prairies and the Pampas,* 107.

60  Dondlinger, *The Book of Wheat,* 231–232.

61  Solberg, *Prairies and the Pampas,* 3–4.

62  Ibid., 40. Only Canada, Australia, and Argentina exported more than half of their wheat crop. The same held true for the rice market. Siam and Indochina, where rice constituted 60 to 70 percent of exports during this period, exported only a quarter of all the rice they produced. *World Agriculture,* 7.

63  The following discussion of Canadian wheat farming draws largely on Adelman, *Frontier Development,* and Solberg, *Prairies and the Pampas.*

64  Adelman, *Frontier Development,* 53.

65  Ibid., 61.

66  Quoted in ibid., 61.

67  Dondlinger, *The Book of Wheat,* 228–231, quotation at 230.

68  Morgan, *Merchants of Grain,* 36.

69  Rutter, *Wheat-Growing,* 187–188.

70  The ensuing discussion on futures markets draws on Cronon, *Nature's Metropolis;* A. J. H. Latham and Larry Neal, "The International Market in Rice and Wheat, 1868–1914," *Economic History Review* 36, no. 3 (May 1983): 260–280; Rutter, *Wheat-Growing;* Paul Allen, "The Past and Future of the Commodity Exchanges," *Agricultural History* 56, no. 1 (January 1982): 287–305; Jeffrey Williams, "The Origin of Futures Markets," *Agricultural History* 56, no. 1 (January 1982): 306–316; Williams, *The Economic Function of Futures Markets* (New

York: Cambridge University Press, 1986); and Owen Gregory, "Futures Markets: Comment," *Agricultural History* 56, no. 1 (January 1982): 317–325.

71 Rutter, *Wheat-Growing*, 210; Cronon, *Nature's Metropolis*, 115–116.

72 Cronon, *Nature's Metropolis*, 116, quotation at 126.

73 Quoted in ibid., 210–211.

74 Morgan, *Merchants of Grain*, 59; Cronon, *Nature's Metropolis*, 127.

75 Rutter, *Wheat-Growing*, 194–198.

76 Ibid., 199–200; Dondlinger, *The Book of Wheat*, 219–222.

77 Rutter, *Wheat-Growing*, 203.

78 Arturo Warman, *Corn and Capitalism: How a Botanical Bastard Grew to Global Dominance*, trans. Nancy Westrate (Chapel Hill: University of North Carolina Press, 2003).

79 Ibid., 223.

80 Hungarian millers were the first to adopt iron and porcelain rollers to process local hard-wheat varieties. In 1839 the Budapest Walzmuhle flour mill opened and soon gained a well-deserved reputation for producing "flours of such fineness" by employing rollers and sifters in addition to the traditional millstones. French innovation focused on the purifier, which helped recoup the middlings. G. R. Stevens, *Ogilvie in Canada: Pioneer Millers, 1801–1951* (Toronto: Ashton-Potter, 1951), 23–24, 28.

81 Charles Kuhlmann, *The Development of the Flour-Milling Industry in the United States with Special Reference to the Industry in Minneapolis* (Boston: Houghton Mifflin, 1929), 113–115.

82 John Storck and Walter D. Teague, *Flour for Man's Bread: A History of Milling* (Minneapolis: University of Minnesota Press, 1952), 241.

83 Stephen George, *Enterprising Minnesotans: 150 Years of Business Pioneers* (Minneapolis: University of Minnesota Press, 2003), 23–24.

84 Harry Bullis, *Buffalo: Its Flour Milling Heritage* (New York: Newcomen Society of England, 1948), 10.

85 Hungarian exports to England were hard hit by this surge in US exports. Storck and Teague, *Flour for Man's Bread*, 269; Kuhlmann, *Flour-Milling Industry*, 295–296.

86 George, *Enterprising Minnesotans*, 23–30.

87 Storck and Teague, *Flour for Man's Bread*, 128, 240.

88 Kuhlmann, *Flour-Milling Industry*, 134, 240; Storck and Teague, *Flour for Man's Bread*, 308–309.

89 General Mills, "History of Innovation: Our Milling Roots and Beyond," http://www.generalmills.com/Company/History.aspx.

90 Alfred D. Chandler Jr., *The Visible Hand: The Managerial Revolution in American Business* (Cambridge, MA: Harvard University Press, 1977); Chandler, *Scale and Scope: The Dynamics of Industrial Capitalism* (Cambridge, MA: Belknap Press of Harvard University Press, 1990).

91 The farm implement industry went through a similar trajectory. See Allen Wells and Gilbert M. Joseph, *Summer of Discontent, Seasons of Upheaval: Elite Politics and Rural Insurgency in Yucatán, 1876–1915* (Stanford, CA: Stanford University Press, 1996), chap. 4.

92 Storck and Teague, *Flour for Man's Bread*, 269.

93 Ibid., 272; Kuhlmann, *Flour-Milling Industry*, 295–296.

94 Kuhlmann, *Flour-Milling Industry*, 274–275, 295–296, 310; Stevens, *Ogilvie in Canada*, 50–51; George, *Enterprising Minnesotans*, 29.

95 Kuhlmann, *Flour-Milling Industry*, 232.

96 Stevens, *Ogilvie in Canada*, 50.

97 A number of states went farther, passing laws to ban artificially bleached flour, but the US Supreme Court, siding with the flour companies, ruled the statutes unconstitutional. Ibid., 232–239.

98 Storck and Teague, *Flour for Man's Bread*, 327.

99 Ibid., 231.

100 *Washington Post*, September 4, 2005, http://www.washingtonpost.com/wp-dyn/content/article/2005/09/02/AR2005090200846.html.

101 Storck and Teague, *Flour for Man's Bread*, 219–220.

102 Ibid; George, *Enterprising Minnesotans*, 25–26.

103 Bullis, *Buffalo*, 12–15; Kuhlmann, *Flour-Milling Industry*, 176–177, 218, 221.

104 This discussion of consumption relies principally on Harvey Levenstein, *Revolution at the Table: The Transformation of the American Diet* (New York: Oxford University Press, 1988), esp. chap. 3.

105 Quoted in Jackson Lears, *Fables of Abundance: A Cultural History of Advertising in America* (New York: Basic Books, 1994), 225.

106 Ibid., 139.

107 Quoted in ibid., 158.

108 Levenstein, *Revolution at the Table*, 33.

109 Quoted in ibid., 153. For a comic view of the Kellogg sanitarium, read T. Coraghessan Boyle, *The Road to Wellville* (New York: Viking, 1993), or see the movie.

110 Thomas Hine, *The Total Package: The Evolution and Secret Meanings of Boxes, Bottles, Cans, and Tubes* (Boston: Little, Brown, 1995), 61–62.

111 Storck and Teague, *Flour for Man's Bread*, 275.

112 Quoted in Levenstein, *Revolution at the Table*, 155.

113  Stevens, *Ogilvie in Canada,* 54.

114  James Gray, *Business without Boundary: The Story of General Mills* (Minneapolis: University of Minnesota Press, 1954), 60.

115  Lears, *Fables of Abundance,* 138.

116  Scanlon, *Inarticulate Longings,* 172, 197–198.

117  Lears, *Fables of Abundance,* 384.

118  Roland Marchand, *Advertising the American Dream: Making Way for Modernity, 1920–1940* (Berkeley: University of California Press, 1985), 353–354.

119  Gray, *Business without Boundary,* 173, quotation at 182; General Mills, "History of Innovation."

120  Gray, *Business without Boundary,* chap. 11.

121  Ibid.

122  Levenstein, *Revolution at the Table,* 35; William G. Panschar, *Baking in America,* 2 vols. (Evanston, IL: Northwestern University Press, 1956), 1:83. British bakers had been putting crackers in tins for quite some time. What was different was Nabisco's massive advertising, which was so ubiquitous that "Uneeda is widely thought to be the first packaged product." Hine, *The Total Package,* 82.

123  Gray, *Business without Boundary,* 88.

124  Ibid., 102.

125  This section on rice relies on Randolph Barker and Robert Herdt with Beth Rose, *The Rice Economy of Asia* (Washington, DC: Resources for the Future, 1985); Francesca Bray, *The Rice Economies: Technology and Development in Asian Societies* (Oxford: Basil Blackwell, 1986); Latham and Neal, "The International Market in Rice"; Wickizer and Bennett, *Rice Economy of Monsoon Asia;* Michael Adas, *The Burma Rice Delta: Economic Development and Social Change on an Asian Rice Frontier, 1852–1941* (Madison: University of Wisconsin Press, 1974); and Cheng Siok-Hwa, *The Rice Industry of Burma, 1852–1940* (Kuala Lumpur: University of Malaya Press, 1968).

126  Rice can grow in temperate or more arid zones as well, but only with the aid of irrigation.

127  Adas suggests that disease was a formidable obstacle in the Lower Burma rice delta, however. Adas, *The Burma Rice Delta,* 62.

128  Bray, *The Rice Economies,* 15.

129  Ibid., 26.

130  Wickizer and Bennett, *Rice Economy of Monsoon Asia,* 56–57.

131  Ibid., 70.

132  Ibid., 74, 79.

133  Ibid., 100.

134  Adas, *The Burma Rice Delta,* 33.

135  Ibid., 141.

136  This section draws on Allen Wells, "Reports of Its Demise Are Not Exaggerated: The Life and Times of Yucatecan Henequen," in Topik et al., *From Silver to Cocaine,* 300–320; Sterling Evans, *Bound in Twine: The History and Ecology of the Henequen-Wheat Complex for Mexico and the American and Canadian Plains, 1880–1950* (College Station: Texas A&M Press, 2007); Rakibuddin Ahmed, *The Progress of the Jute Industry and Trade, 1855–1966* (Dacca: Pakistan Central Jute Committee, 1966); Samita Sen, *Women and Labour in Late Colonial India: The Bengal Jute Industry* (New York: Cambridge University Press, 1999); Dipesh Chakrabarty, *Rethinking Working-Class History: Bengal, 1890–1940* (Princeton, NJ: Princeton University Press, 1999); Gordon Stewart, *Jute and Empire: The Calcutta Jute Wallahs and the Landscapes of Empire* (Manchester: Manchester University Press, 1998); Omkar Goswami, *Industry, Trade and Peasant Society: The Jute Economy of Eastern India, 1900–1947* (New York: Oxford University Press, 1991); Norman Owen, *Prosperity without Progress: Manila Hemp and Material Life in the Colonial Philippines* (Berkeley: University of California Press, 1984).

137  Quoted in Stewart, *Jute and Empire,* 44.

138  Ibid., quotation at 2.

139  Ibid., 3.

140  Goswami, *Industry, Trade,* 4–5, 54.

141  Ibid., 240.

142  Warman, *Corn and Capitalism.*

143  Landes, "The 'Great Drain' and Industrialisation: Commodity Flows from Periphery to Centre in Historical Perspective," in *Economic Growth and Resources,* vol. 2: *Trends and Factors,* ed. R. C. O. Matthews (London: Macmillan, 1980), 294, 297, 303.

144  Useful overviews of stimulants include: David R. Courtwright, *Forces of Habit: Drugs and the Making of the Modern World* (Cambridge, MA: Harvard University Press, 2001); Jordan Goodman, Paul Lovejoy, and Andrew Sherratt, eds., *Consuming Habits: Drugs in History and Anthropology* (London: Routledge, 1995); R. Rudgley, *Essential Substances: A Cultural History of Intoxicants in Society* (New York: Kodassha International, 1993); Wolfgang Schivelbusch, *Tastes of Paradise: A Social History of Spices, Stimulants, and Intoxicants,* trans. David Jacobsen (New York: Vintage Books, 1993).

145  W. Arthur Lewis, ed., *Tropical Development, 1880–1913* (Evanston, IL: Northwestern University Press, 1970).

146  J. H. Galloway, "Sugar," in *The Cambridge History of Food,* vol. 1, ed. K. F. Kiple and K. C. Ornelas (Cambridge: Cambridge University Press, 2000), 437–449.

147  For an overview of sugar's journey to the modern world, see Stuart Schwartz, *Sugar Plantations in the Formation of Brazilian Society: Bahia, 1550–1835* (New York: Cambridge University Press, 1985).

148  Courtwright, *Forces of Habit,* 28.

149  Noël Deerr, *The History of Sugar,* 2 vols. (London: Chapman and Hall, 1949–1950), 2:467.

150  Ibid., 490–491; Mintz, *Sweetness and Power,* 197.

151  Manuel Moreno Fraginals, *The Sugarmill: The Socio-Economic Complex of Sugar in Cuba,* trans. Cedric Belfrage (New York: Monthly Review Press, 1976). Also see Rebecca Scott, *Slave Emancipation in Cuba: The Transition to Free Labor, 1860–1899* (Princeton, NJ: Princeton University Press, 1985).

152  For nineteenth- and twentieth-century technical advances, see Alan Dye, *Cuban Sugar in the Age of Mass Production: Technology and the Economics of the Sugar Central, 1899–1929* (Stanford, CA: Stanford University Press, 1998).

153  William Albert and Adrian Graves, eds., *Crisis and Change in the International Sugar Economy, 1860–1914* (Norwich, England: ISC Press, 1984), 3.

154  Dye, *Cuban Sugar,* 1.

155  Mintz, *Sweetness and Power,* 143.

156  Scott, *Slave Emancipation.*

157  Fernando Ortiz, *Cuban Counterpoint: Tobacco and Sugar,* trans. Harriett de Onís (New York: Knopf, 1947), 53–54.

158  Rebecca J. Scott, "The Transformation of Sugar Production in Cuba after Emancipation," in Albert and Graves, *Crisis and Change,* 112–117; Mulhall, *The Dictionary of Statistics,* 633; Victor Bulmer-Thomas, *The Economic History of Latin America since Independence* (New York: Cambridge University Press, 1994), 74; Ramiro Guerra y Sánchez, *Sugar and Society in the Caribbean: An Economic History of Cuban Agriculture,* trans. Marjory M. Urquidi (1927; New Haven, CT: Yale University Press, 1964), 77–79.

159  Deerr, *The History of Sugar,* 2:530–531.

160  Guerra y Sánchez's *Sugar and Society in the Caribbean* was published in 1927. Other, later good examples of this literature are Ortiz, *Cuban Counterpoint* (1947); Eric Williams, *Capitalism and Slavery* (New York: Capricorn Books, 1944); and Andre Gunder Frank, *Capitalism and Underdevelopment in Latin America: Historical Studies of Chile and Brazil* (New York: Monthly Review Press, 1967).

161 Deerr, *The History of Sugar,* 1:131; Christian Schnakenbourg, "From the Sugar Estate to the Central Factory," in Albert and Graves, *Crisis and Change,* 93.

162 Geertz, *Agricultural Involution: The Processes of Ecological Change in Indonesia* (Berkeley: University of California Press, 1971), 69–79; Horacio Crespo, "Trade Regimes and the International Sugar Market, 1850–1980: Protectionism, Subsidies, and Regulation," in Topik et al., *From Silver to Cocaine,* 150.

163 Geertz, *Agricultural Involution,* 61–62.

164 Denoon, *Settler Capitalism,* 102, 103; Robert F. McKillop, "Australia's Sugar Industry," Light Railway Research Society of Australia, http://www.lrrsa.org .au/LRR_SGRa.htm#EarlyHistory.

165 Waden Narsey, "Fiji's Economic History, 1874–1939," *The Contemporary Pacific* (Spring 1990): 208–213.

166 One could say "British," but D. C. M. Platt has shown, in *Britain's Investment Overseas on the Eve of the First World War: The Use and Abuse of Numbers* (Basingstoke, UK: Macmillan 1986), that a considerable amount of the funds invested in London actually derived from small-scale continental investors, mostly from northwest Europe. Also, Denoon, *Settler Capitalism,* 121.

167 Kelly Olds, "The Economic History of Taiwan," EH Network, http://eh.net/ encyclopedia/ article/olds.taiwan.economic.history.

168 University of Hawai'i–West O'ahu, Center for Labor Education and Research, "Hawai'i Labor History: A Brief Overview," http://homepages.uhwo.hawaii. edu/clear/Lhistory.html.

169 Okihiro, *Pineapple Culture.*

170 Deerr, *The History of Sugar,* 1:113; and Peter Eisenberg, *The Sugar Industry in Pernambuco: Modernization without Change, 1840–1910* (Berkeley: University of California Press, 1974).

171 Michael Gonzales, "Economic Crisis: Chinese Workers and Peruvian Sugar Planters, 1875–1900," and William Albert, "The Labour Force on Peru's Sugar Plantations 1820–1930," both in Albert and Graves, *Crisis and Change,* 181–195, 198–215.

172 Scobie, *Argentina,* 144; Denoon, *Settler Capitalism,* 99; Donna Guy, *Argentine Sugar Politics: Tucumán and the Generation of 80* (Tempe: Arizona State University, 1980).

173 Deerr, *The History of Sugar,* 1:248–249; Rebecca Scott, *Degrees of Freedom: Louisiana and Cuba after Slavery* (Cambridge MA: Belknap Press of Harvard University Press, 2005), 72, 73, 258; Gail M. Hollander, *Raising Cane in the*

*'Glades: The Global Sugar Trade and the Transformation of Florida* (Chicago: University of Chicago Press, 2008).

174 Karl Hufbauer, *The Formation of the German Chemical Community (1720–1795)* (Berkeley: University of California Press, 1982), 145; Martin Kitchen, *The Political Economy of Germany, 1815–1914* (London: Croom Helm, 1978), 200–206; Cornelius Torp, *Die Herausforderung der Globalisierung: Wirtschaft und Politik in Deutschland, 1860–1914* (Göttingen: Vandenhoeck und Ruprecht, 2005), 77, 81.

175 Mulhall, *The Dictionary of Statistics*, 550.

176 John Perkins, "The Political Economy of Sugar Beet in Imperial Germany," in Albert and Graves, *Crisis and Change*, 39; Galloway, "Sugar."

177 Perkins, "Political Economy of Sugar Beet," 31–46.

178 Ibid., 41. Perkins points out that the inventor Constantin Fahlberg was working in the United States at the time. One should add that although saccharin was cheaper than sugar, it did not provide calories so it was an empty sweetener.

179 Galloway, "Sugar."

180 Nikolai Bukharin, *Imperialism and World Economy* (Moscow: International, 1929), chap. 8; Mulhall, *The Dictionary of Statistics*, 809.

181 Calculated from Deerr, *The History of Sugar*, 2:490–498; Mulhall, *The Dictionary of Statistics*, 626.

182 Ph. G. Chalmin, "The Important Trends in Sugary Diplomacy before 1914," in Albert and Graves, *Crisis and Change*, 17.

183 Horacio Crespo, "Trade Regimes and the International Sugar Market," in Topik et al., *From Silver to Cocaine*, 148.

184 Calculated from Deerr, vols. 1 and 2.

185 Mintz, *Sweetness and Power*, 125–150.

186 The numbers may be skewed toward the more affluent countries, where it was sold in markets. In the lands where it was grown, probably a good deal of sugar was consumed as cane or juice and not tabulated.

187 Michel Tuchscherer, "Coffee in the Red Sea Areas from the Sixteenth Century to the Nineteenth Century," in *The Global Coffee Economy in Africa, Asia and Latin America, 1500–1989*, ed. William G. Clarence-Smith and Steven Topik (New York: Cambridge University Press, 2003).

188 Kristof Glamann, *Dutch-Asiatic Trade, 1620–1740* (Copenhagen: Danish Science Press, 1958); Brian Cowan, *The Social Life of Coffee: The Emergence of the British Coffeehouse* (New Haven, CT: Yale University Press, 2005).

189 William Clarence-Smith, "The Coffee Crisis in Asia, Africa, and the Pacific, 1870–1914," in Clarence-Smith and Topik, *Global Coffee Economy*, 100.

190 Steven Topik and Michelle Craig McDonald, "Culture and Consumption: National Drinks and National Identity in the Atlantic World," in *Food and Globalization: Consumption, Markets and Politics in the Modern World,* ed. Alexander Nützenadel and Frank Trentmann (Oxford: Berg, 2008); N. Posthumus, *Inquiry into the History of Prices in Holland,* vol. 1 (Amsterdam: Brill, 1946), 75–79.

191 M. R. Fernando, "Coffee Cultivation in Java, 1830–1917," in Clarence-Smith and Topik, *Global Coffee Economy,* 161, 162.

192 P. J. Cain and A. G. Hopkins, *British Imperialism, 1688–2000,* 2nd ed. (London: Longman, 2001), 298–306; Richard Graham, *Britain and the Onset of Modernization in Brazil* (Cambridge: Cambridge University Press, 1968); D. C. M. Platt, ed., *Business Imperialism* (Oxford: Clarendon Press, 1977); and Rory Miller, *Britain and Latin America in the Nineteenth and Twentieth Centuries* (London: Longman, 1993).

193 Anne Hanley, *Native Capital: Financial Institutions and Economic Development in São Paulo, Brazil, 1850–1920* (Stanford, CA: Stanford University Press, 2005); Gail Triner, *Banking and Economic Development: Brazil, 1889–1930* (New York: Palgrave, 2000); Miller, *Britain and Latin America;* and Steven C. Topik, *The Political Economy of the Brazilian State, 1889–1930* (Austin: University of Texas Press, 1987). On the history of milk consumption in the United States, see E. Melanie DuPuis, *Nature's Perfect Food: How Milk Became America's Drink* (New York: New York University Press, 2002); and Chandler, *Scale and Scope,* 156.

194 Calculated from Robert Greenhill, "E. Johnston: 150 Anos em Café," in *150 Anos de Café,* ed. Marcellino Martins and E. Johnston (Rio: Marcellino Martins, 1993), 307; José Antonio Ocampo, *Colombia y la economía mundial, 1830–1910* (Bogotá: Siglo Veintiuno Ocampo, 1984), 303; and Brazil, IGBE *Séries Estatísticas Retrospectivas,* vol. 1 (Rio: IBGE, 1986), 84; Mulhall, *The Dictionary of Statistics,* 130. Admittedly, this datum privileges coffee, because other important internationally traded goods such as sugar and grains often traveled more by land than by sea.

195 Vernon Wickizer, *Coffee, Tea, and Cocoa* (Palo Alto, CA: Stanford University Food Research Institute, 1951), 36.

196 Frederick Stirton Weaver, *Latin America in the World Economy: Mercantile Colonialism to Global Capitalism* (Boulder, CO: Westview Press, 2000), 69; William Summerhill, *Order against Progress: Government, Foreign Investment, and Railroads in Brazil* (Stanford, CA: Stanford University Press, 2003), 54.

197  Franz Daffert, *Über die gegenwärtige Lage des Kaffeebaus in Brasilien* (Amsterdam: J. H. de Bussy, 1898).

198  Almir Chaiban El-Kareh, *Filha branca de mae preta: A Companhia de Estrada de Ferro Dom Pedro II* (Petrópolis, R.J. Brazil: Editora Vozes, 1980); Steven Topik, "Coffee," in *The Second Conquest of Latin America: Coffee, Henequen, and Oil during the Export Boom, 1850–1930,* ed. Steven C. Topik and Allen Wells (Austin: University of Texas Press, 1998).

199  Topik, "La hacienda brasileña: Fabrica en el campo o pueblo campesino?" *Revista de Historia* (San José, Costa Rica), no. 36 (July–December 1997); Cary McWilliams, *Factories in the Field: The Story of Migratory Farm Labor in California* (Boston: Little, Brown, 1939).

200  We are referring to the predominant scale of production in different countries. There were some very large, medium, and small coffee fields in every country. For excellent studies of the Nicaraguan system, see Elizabeth Dore, *Myths of Modernity: Peonage and Patriarchy in Nicaragua* (Durham, NC: Duke University Press, 2006), and Julie Charlip, *Cultivating Coffee: The Farmers of Carazo, Nicaragua, 1880–1930* (Athens: Ohio University Press, 2003); for Guatemala, see David McCreery, *Rural Guatemala, 1760–1940* (Stanford, CA: Stanford University Press, 1994); for El Salvador, see Jeffrey L. Gould and Aldo A. Lauria-Santiago, *To Rise in Darkness: Revolution, Repression, and Memory in El Salvador, 1920–1932* (Durham N.C.: Duke University Press, 2008); and for Costa Rica, see Mario Samper, *Generations of Settlers: Rural Households and Markets on the Costa Rican Frontier, 1850–1935* (Boulder, CO: West-view Press, 1990).

201  It is worth noting that "quality" was in the palate of the drinker. There was no chemical scale, such as those used to determine purity or sucrose content in sugar. Probably most of the difference between Central American/Colombian coffee and its Brazilian competitor stemmed from the greater care the former took during harvest.

202  Robert Greenhill, "Shipping," in *Business Imperialism,* ed. Platt, 119–155; Paul Bairoch, "Geographical Structure and Trade from 1800 to 1970," *Journal of European Economic History* 3, no. 3 (Winter 1974): 606; Douglass North, "Ocean Freight Rates and Economic Development, 1750–1913," *Journal of Economic History* 18, no. 4 (December 1958).

203  Marcelo de P. Abreu and Afonso S. Bevilaqua, "Brazil as an Export Economy, 1880–1930," in *An Economic History of Twentieth-Century Latin America,* 2 vols., ed. Enrique Cárdenas, José Antonio Ocampo, and Rosemary Thorp (New York: Palgrave, 2000), 1:32–54.

204 Steven C. Topik, *Trade and Gunboats: The United States and Brazil in the Age of Empire* (Stanford, CA: Stanford University Press, 1996).

205 Calculated from Greenhill, "Shipping," 119–155, and Greenhill, "E. Johnston," 330–331; A. Wakeman, "Reminiscences of Lower Wall Street," *Spice Mill*, March 1911, 193; Joseph Walsh, *Coffee: Its History, Classification and Description* (Philadelphia: Henry T. Coates and Co., 1902); Mario Samper and Radin Fernando, "Historical Statistics of Coffee Production and Trade from 1700 to 1960," in Clarence-Smith and Topik, *Global Coffee Economy*, 443, 446–447.

206 The US Federal Trade Commission estimated income elasticity in 1954 at only 0.2 percent. US Federal Trade Commission, *Investigation of Coffee Prices* (Washington, DC: US Government Printing Office, 1954), 39–40. Edmar Bacha, "Política brasileira de café," in Martins and Johnston, *150 Anos de Café*, 20; José Antonio Ocampo, *Colombia y la economia mundial, 1830–1910* (Bogotá: Siglo Veintiuno, 1984), 302–303; Mintz, *Sweetness and Power*.

207 Greenhill, "E. Johnston"; Greenhill, "Investment Group, Free-Standing Company or Multinational: Brazilian Warrant 1909–1952," *Business History* 37 (1995): 86–111; Siegfried Zimmerman, *Theodor Wille* (Hamburg: n.p., 1969). Also see Steven Topik and Mario Samper, "The Latin American Coffee Commodity Chain: Brazil and Costa Rica," in Topik et al., *From Silver to Cocaine*.

208 John Talbot, "The Struggle for the Control of a Commodity Chain: Instant Coffee from Latin America," *Latin American Research Review* 32 (1997); Talbot, *Grounds for Agreement: The Political Economy of the Coffee Commodity Chain* (Lanham, MD: Rowman and Littlefield, 2004), 140–156.

209 Martins and Johnston, *150 Anos de Café*, 371.

210 Richard P. Tucker, *Insatiable Appetite: The United States and the Ecological Degradation of the Tropical World* (Berkeley: University of California Press, 2000), 190–191.

211 Francis L. Fugate, *Arbuckles: The Coffee That Won the West* (El Paso: Texas Western Press, 1994).

212 Julia Laura Rieschbieter, "Kaffee im Kaiserreich: Eine Geschichte der Globalisierung" (PhD diss., Europea-Universität Viadrina Frankfurt, Oder, 2009).

213 *Spice Mill*, January 1912, 28. Little has been done on the history of consumption outside of North America and Western Europe, but one breakthrough study on Costa Rica is Patricia Vega Jiménez's *Con sabor a tertulia: Historia del consumo del café en Costa Rica (1840–1940)* (San José: Editorial de la Universidad de Costa Rica, 2004). For a collection on European coffee drinking, see Daniela

U. Ball, ed., *Kaffee im Speigel euopäischer Trinksitten* (Zurich: Johann Jacobs Museum, 1991).

214  M. E. Goetzinger, *History of the House of Arbuckle* (n.p.: The Percolator, 1921), 3; Zimmerman, *Theodor Wille,* 123; Morris Adelman, *A&P: A Study in Price-Cost Behavior and Public Policy* (Cambridge, MA: Harvard University Press, 1959). Richard S. Tedlow, *New and Improved: The Story of Mass Marketing in America* (New York: Basic Books, 1990); Levenstein, *Revolution at the Table.*

215  Quoted in William Ukers, *All about Coffee* (New York: Tea and Coffee Trade Journal, 1935), 466.

216  Stuart McCook, "Global Rust Belt: *Hemileia vastatrix* and the Ecological Integration of World Coffee Production since 1850," *Journal of Global History* 1, no. 2 (2006): 177–195.

217  Paul C. Daniels, "The Inter-American Coffee Agreement," *Law and Contemporary Problems* 8, no. 4 (Autumn, 1941): 708.

218  A new account of the British planting of tea in India by Sarah Rose has that name: *For All the Tea in China: How England Stole the World's Favorite Drink and Changed History* (New York: Viking, 2010).

219  William H. Ukers, *All about Tea* (New York: Tea and Coffee Trade Journal Co., 1935), 2:333.

220  *Statistical Year-Book of the League of Nations, 1925,* 58.

221  Ranajit das Gupta, "Plantation Labor in Colonial India," *Journal of Peasant Studies* 19, nos. 3–4 (1992): 173–198; Kavita Philip, *Civilizing Nature: Race, Resources, and Modernity in Colonial India* (New Brunswick, NJ: Rutgers University Press, 2004); Erika Rappaport, "Tea Parties: Britain, Empire and the Making of a Global Consumer Culture" (unpublished manuscript), chaps. 4 and 5; Mintz, *Sweetness and Power.*

222  Alan Macfarlane and Iris Macfarlane, *The Empire of Tea: The Remarkable History of the Plant That Took Over the World* (Woodstock, NY: Overlook, 2004), 195–197.

223  Ibid., quotation at 206. Also see Roy Moxham, *Tea: Addiction, Exploitation and Empire* (New York: Carroll and Graf, 2003), 127–155.

224  MacFarlane and MacFarlane, *The Empire of Tea,* 214.

225  Ibid., 199; Ukers, *All about Tea,* 2:334.

226  Ukers, *All about Tea,* 1:407.

227  Roland Wenzlhuemer, *From Coffee to Tea Cultivation in Ceylon, 1880–1900: An Economic and Social History* (Leiden: Brill, 2008), 316–317.

228  Erica Rappaport, "Packaging China: Foreign Articles and Dangerous Tastes in the Mid-Victorian Tea Party," in *The Making of the Consumer: Knowledge,*

*Power and Identity in the Modern World,* ed. Frank Trentmann (Oxford: Berg, 2006), 125–146; Ukers, *All about Tea,* 2:334, 345.

229 Fernando Rocchi, "From Consumption to Consumer Society: The Evolution of Demand in Argentina, 1920s–1940s" (paper presented at Institute of Latin American Studies, University of London, workshop, November 14–15, 2002); Rocchi, *Chimneys in the Desert: Industrialization in Argentina during the Export Boom Years, 1870–1930* (Stanford, CA: Stanford University Press, 2006).

230 Calculated from Ukers, *All about Tea,* 2:349, 350.

231 Robert Gardella, *Harvesting Mountains: Fujian and the China Tea Trade, 1757–1937* (Berkeley: University of California Press, 1994), 171, emphasis in the original.

232 Ukers, *All about Tea,* 2:334; Macfarlane and Macfarlane, *The Empire of Tea,* 99–165.

233 Lockwood, *Economic Development of Japan,* 357–358; Ukers, *All about Tea,* 2:328, 334.

234 Moxham, *Tea,* 202.

235 Ibid.

236 Sophie D. Coe, *America's First Cuisines* (Austin: University of Texas Press, 1994), 101–104; Murdo Macleod, "Cacao," in *Cambridge World History of Food,* vol. 1, ed. K. Kipler (Cambridge: Cambridge University Press, 2000), 635–640.

237 Mary Ann Mahoney, "The Local and the Global: Internal and External Factors in the Development of Bahia's Cacao Sector," in Topik et al., *From Silver to Cocaine,* 184–190; Courtwright, *Forces of Habit,* 23–25; Schivelbusch, *Tastes of Paradise.*

238 DuPuis, *Nature's Perfect Food;* Andrew F. Smith, *Eating History: Turning Points in the Making of American Cuisine* (New York: Columbia University Press, 2009), 127, 128.

239 *Cambridge World History of Food,* vol. 2, ed. Kiple and Ornelas, 1874–1875; Sandra Kuntz Ficker, *Las exportaciones mexicanas durante la primera globalization, 1870–1929* (Mexico City: El Colegio de México, 2010), 350–357.

240 William Clarence-Smith, *Cocoa and Chocolate, 1765–1914* (London: Routledge, 2000), 238–239; Robin Dand, *The International Cocoa Trade* (New York: Wiley, for Woodhead Publishing, 1997), 15, 54; calculated from Dand, *International Cocoa Trade;* Mario Samper and Radin Fernando, "Appendix: Historical Statistics of Coffee Production and Trade from 1700 to 1960," in Clarence-Smith and Topik, *Global Coffee Economy,* 418; Ukers, *All about Tea,* 2:234.

241 Clarence-Smith, *Cocoa and Chocolate,* 7.

242 Ibid.

243 Ibid., 195–225.

244 Martin Booth, *Opium: A History* (New York: St. Martin's Griffin, 1996), 175–190; Gootenberg, *Andean Cocaine.*

### CONCLUSIONS

1 O'Rourke and Williamson, *Globalization and History: The Evolution of a Nineteenth-Century Atlantic Economy* (Cambridge, MA: MIT Press, 1999), 3.

2 Ibid., 2.

# Selected Bibliography

Adas, Michael. *The Burma Delta: Economic Development and Social Change on an Asian Rice Frontier, 1852–1941.* Madison: University of Wisconsin Press, 1974.

Adelman, Jeremy. *Frontier Development: Land, Labour, and Capital on the Wheatlands of Argentina and Canada, 1890–1914.* Oxford: Clarendon Press, 1994.

Albert, Bill, and Adrian Graves, eds. *Crisis and Change in the International Sugar Economy, 1860–1914.* Norwich, UK: ISC Press, 1984.

Appadurai, Arjun, ed. *The Social Life of Things: Commodities in Cultural Perspective.* New York: Cambridge University Press, 1986.

Arrighi, Giovanni. *The Long Twentieth Century: Money, Power, and the Origins of Our Times.* London: Verso, 1994.

Bair, Jennifer, ed. *Frontiers of Commodity Chain Research.* Stanford, CA: Stanford University Press, 2009.

Bairoch, Paul, and Bouda Etemad. *Structure par produits des exportations du Tiersmonde.* Geneva: Droz, 1985.

Ball, Daniel U., ed. *Kaffee im Spiegel europäischer Trinksitten.* Zurich: Johann Jacobs Museum, 1991.

Baranowski, Shelley. *Nazi Empire: German Colonialism and Imperialism from Bismarck to Hitler.* New York: Cambridge University Press, 2011.

Barker, Randolph, and Robert W. Herdt, with Beth Rose. *The Rice Economy of Asia.* Washington, DC: Resources for the Future, 1985.

Bayly, C. A. *The Birth of the Modern World, 1780–1914: Global Connections and Comparisons.* Malden, MA: Blackwell, 2004.

Belich, James. *Replenishing the Earth: The Settler Revolution and the Rise of the Anglo World, 1783–1939.* New York: Oxford University Press, 2009.

Boahen, A. Adu, ed. *Africa under Colonial Domination, 1880–1935,* vol. 7 of *General History of Africa.* Berkeley: University of California Press, 1985.

Bott, Sandra, ed. *The Global Gold Market and the International Monetary System from the Late Nineteenth Century to the Present: Actions, Networks, Power.* London: Palgrave Macmillan, 2013.

Brasil, Diretoria Geral da Estatística (DGE). *Anuário Estatístico, 1930/1940.* Rio de Janeiro: Imprensa Nacional, 1940.

Bray, Francesca. *The Rice Economies: Technology and Development in Asian Societies.* Oxford: Blackwell, 1986.

Brown, Jonathan C. *Oil and Revolution in Mexico.* Berkeley: University of California Press, 1992.

Bulmer-Thomas, Victor. *The Economic History of Latin America since Independence.* New York: Cambridge University Press, 1994.

Burke, Edmund, III, and Kenneth Pomeranz, eds. *The Environment and World History.* Berkeley: University of California Press, 2009.

Cain, P. J., and A. G. Hopkins. *British Imperialism: Innovation and Expansion, 1688–1914.* London: Longman, 1993.

Cameron, Rondo, and V. I. Bovykin, eds. *International Banking, 1870–1914.* New York: Oxford University Press, 1991.

Cárdenas, Enrique, José Antonio Ocampo, and Rosemary Thorp, eds. *An Economic History of Twentieth-Century Latin America.* 3 vols. New York: Palgrave, 2000.

Carter, Susan B., et al., eds. *Historical Statistics of the United States: Millennial Edition Online.* Cambridge: Cambridge University Press, 2006–. http://www.cambridge.org.

Chakrabarty, Dipesh. *Rethinking Working-Class History: Bengal, 1890–1940.* Princeton, NJ: Princeton University Press, 1989.

Chandler, Alfred D., Jr. *The Visible Hand: The Managerial Revolution in American Business.* Cambridge, MA: Belknap Press of Harvard University Press, 1977.

Chandler, Alfred D., Jr., with Takashi Hikino. *Scale and Scope: The Dynamics of Industrial Capitalism.* Cambridge, MA: Belknap Press of Harvard University Press, 1990.

Cheng, Siok-Hwa. *The Rice Industry of Burma, 1852–1940.* Kuala Lumpur: University of Malaya Press, 1968.

Clarence-Smith, William Gervase. *Cocoa and Chocolate, 1765–1914.* London: Routledge, 2000.

Clarence-Smith, William Gervase, and Steven Topik, eds. *The Global Coffee Economy in Africa, Asia and Latin America, 1500–1989.* New York: Cambridge University Press, 2003.

Coatsworth, John H., and Alan M. Taylor, eds. *Latin America and the World Economy since 1800.* Cambridge, MA: Harvard University Press/David Rockefeller Center for Latin American Studies, 1998.

Conrad, Sebastian. *German Colonialism: A Short History.* New York: Cambridge University Press, 2012.

———. *Globalization and the Nation in Imperial Germany.* Translated by Sorcha O'Hagan. Cambridge: Cambridge University Press, 2012.

Coppolaro, Lucia, and Francine McKenzie, eds. *A Global History of Trade and Conflict since 1500*. London: Palgrave, 2013.

Cronon, William. *Nature's Metropolis: Chicago and the Great West*. New York: W. W. Norton, 1991.

Crosby, Alfred W. *Ecological Imperialism: The Biological Expansion of Europe, 900–1200*. New York: Cambridge University Press, 1986.

Dand, Robin. *The International Cocoa Trade*. New York: J. Wiley, 1997.

Darwin, John. *Unfinished Empire: The Global Expansion of Britain*. New York: Bloomsbury Press, 2012.

Davis, Lance E., and Robert A. Huttenback, with Susan Gray Davis. *Mammon and the Pursuit of Empire: The Political Economy of British Imperialism, 1860–1912*. New York: Cambridge University Press, 1986.

Davis, Lance E., Robert A. Huttenback, and Douglass North. *Institutional Change and American Economic Growth*. Cambridge: Cambridge University Press, 1971.

Dean, Warren. *With Broadax and Firebrand: The Destruction of the Brazilian Atlantic Forest*. Berkeley: University of California Press, 1995.

Deerr, Noël. *The History of Sugar*. 2 vols. London: Chapman and Hall, 1949–1950.

De Grazia, Victoria. *Irresistible Empire: America's Advance through Twentieth-Century Europe*. Cambridge, MA: Belknap Press of Harvard University Press, 2005.

De Vries, Jan. *The Industrious Revolution: Consumer Behavior and the Household Economy, 1650 to the Present*. Cambridge: Cambridge University Press, 2008.

Dore, Elizabeth. *Myths of Modernity: Peonage and Patriarchy in Nicaragua*. Durham, NC: Duke University Press, 2006.

Drinot, Paulo, and Alan Knight. *The Great Depression in the Americas*. Durham, NC: Duke University Press, 2013.

Dunsdorfs, Egards. *The Australian Wheat-Growing Industry, 1788–1948*. Melbourne: University Press, 1956.

Dye, Alan. *Cuban Sugar in the Age of Mass Production: Technology and the Economics of the Sugar Central, 1899–1929*. Stanford, CA: Stanford University Press, 1998.

Eichengreen, Barry J. *Globalizing Capital: A History of the International Monetary System*. 2nd ed. Princeton, NJ: Princeton University Press, 2008.

Evans, Sterling. *Bound in Twine: The History and Ecology of the Henequen-Wheat Complex for Mexico and the American and Canadian Plains, 1880–1950*. College Station: Texas A&M University Press, 2007.

Ferguson, Niall. *Empire: How Britain Made the Modern World*. London: Penguin Books, 2004.

Findlay, Ronald, and Kevin H. O'Rourke. *Power and Plenty: Trade, War, and the World Economy in the Second Millennium.* Princeton, NJ: Princeton University Press, 2007.

Finlay, Mark R. *Growing American Rubber: Strategic Plants and the Politics of National Security.* New Brunswick, NJ: Rutgers University Press, 2009.

Fishlow, Albert. *American Railroads and the Transformation of the Antebellum Economy.* Cambridge, MA: Harvard University Press, 1965.

Fogel, Robert William. *Railroads and American Economic Growth: Essays in Econometric History.* Baltimore: Johns Hopkins University Press, 1964.

Gallagher, John, and Ronald Robinson. "The Imperialism of Free Trade." *Economic History Review* 6 (1953): 1–15.

Gardella, Robert. *Harvesting Mountains: Fujian and the China Tea Trade, 1757–1937.* Berkeley: University of California Press, 1994.

Gereffi, Gary, John Humphrey, and Timothy Sturgeon. "The Governance of Global Value Chains." *Review of International Political Economy* 12 (2005): 78–104.

Gootenberg, Paul. *Andean Cocaine: The Making of a Global Drug.* Chapel Hill: University of North Carolina Press, 2008.

Goswami, Omkar. *Industry, Trade, and Peasant Society: The Jute Economy of Eastern India, 1900–1947.* New York: Oxford University Press, 1991.

Gould, Jeffrey L., and Aldo A. Lauria-Santiago. *To Rise in Darkness: Revolution, Repression, and Memory in El Salvador, 1920–1932.* Durham, NC: Duke University Press, 2008.

Haber, Stephen, ed. *How Latin America Fell Behind: Essays on the Economic Histories of Brazil and Mexico, 1800–1914.* Stanford, CA: Stanford University Press, 1997.

Headrick, Daniel R. *Power over Peoples: Technology, Environments, and Western Imperialism, 1400 to the Present.* Princeton, NJ: Princeton University Press, 2010.

———. *The Tentacles of Progress: Technology Transfer in the Age of Imperialism, 1850–1940.* New York: Oxford University Press, 1988.

Hine, Thomas. *The Total Package: The Evolution and Secret Meanings of Boxes, Bottles, Cans, and Tubes.* Boston: Little, Brown, 1995.

Hobsbawm, Eric. *The Age of Empire, 1875–1914.* New York: Pantheon, 1987.

———. *The Age of Extremes: The Short Twentieth Century, 1914–1991.* London: Michael Joseph, 1994.

Hochschild, Adam. *King Leopold's Ghost: A Story of Greed, Terror, and Heroism in Colonial Africa.* Boston: Houghton Mifflin, 1998.

Hoganson, Kristin L. *Consumers' Imperium: The Global Production of American Domesticity, 1865–1920.* Chapel Hill: University of North Carolina Press, 2007.

Hugill, Peter J. *World Trade since 1431: Geography, Technology, and Capitalism.* Baltimore: Johns Hopkins University Press, 1993.

Innis, Harold A. *Problems of Staple Production in Canada.* Toronto: Ryerson, 1933.

Jackson, Joe. *The Thief at the End of the World: Rubber, Power, and the Seeds of Empire.* New York: Viking, 2008.

Jones, Geoffrey. *British Multinational Banking, 1830–1930.* Oxford: Clarendon Press, 1993.

Kenwood, A. G., and A. L. Lougheed. *The Growth of the International Economy, 1820–2000: An Introductory Text.* 4th ed. London: Routledge, 1999.

Kuntz Ficker, Sandra. *Las exportaciones mexicanas durante la primera globalización, 1870–1929.* Mexico City: El Colegio de México, Centro de Estudios Históricos, 2010.

Landes, David S. "The 'Great Drain' and Industrialisation: Commodity Flows from Periphery to Centre in Historical Perspective." In *Economic Growth and Resources,* vol. 2: *Trends and Factors,* ed. R. C. O. Matthews. London: Macmillan, 1980.

———. *The Wealth and Poverty of Nations: Why Some Are So Rich and Some So Poor.* New York: W. W. Norton, 1998.

Laux, James M. *The European Automobile Industry.* New York: Twayne, 1992.

League of Nations. *Statistical Year-Book of the League of Nations.* Geneva: League of Nations, Economic and Financial Section, 1927–1945. http://digital.library .northwestern.edu/league/stat.html.

Lears, T. J. Jackson. *Fables of Abundance: A Cultural History of Advertising in America.* New York: Basic Books, 1994.

Levenstein, Harvey A. *Revolution at the Table: The Transformation of the American Diet.* New York: Oxford University Press, 1988.

Levin, Jonathan V. *The Export Economies: Their Pattern of Development in Historical Perspective.* Cambridge, MA: Harvard University Press, 1960.

Lewis, W. Arthur. *Growth and Fluctuations, 1870–1913.* London: Allen and Unwin, 1978.

Macfarlane, Alan, and Iris Macfarlane. *The Empire of Tea: The Remarkable History of the Plant That Took Over the World.* Woodstock, NY: Overlook, 2004.

Maddison, Angus. *The World Economy.* Paris: Development Centre of the Organisation for Economic Co-operation and Development, 2006.

McCreery, David. *Rural Guatemala, 1760–1940.* Stanford, CA: Stanford University Press, 1994.

McNeill, J. R. *Something New under the Sun: An Environmental History of the Twentieth-Century World.* New York: W. W. Norton, 2000.

Miller, Michael B. *The Bon Marché: Bourgeois Culture and the Department Store.* Princeton, NJ: Princeton University Press, 1981.

———. *Europe and the Maritime World: A Twentieth-Century History.* Cambridge: Cambridge University Press, 2012.

Miller, Rory. *Britain and Latin America in the Nineteenth and Twentieth Centuries.* London: Longman, 1993.

Mintz, Sidney W. *Sweetness and Power: The Place of Sugar in Modern History.* New York: Penguin, 1986.

Mitchell, B. R. *International Historical Statistics: Africa, Asia and Oceania, 1750–2005.* 5th ed. Basingstoke, UK: Palgrave Macmillan, 2007.

———. *International Historical Statistics: The Americas, 1750–2005.* 6th ed. Basingstoke, UK: Palgrave Macmillan, 2007.

———. *International Historical Statistics: Europe, 1750–2005.* 6th ed. Basingstoke, UK: Palgrave Macmillan, 2007.

Mokyr, Joel. *The Lever of Riches: Technological Creativity and Economic Progress.* New York: Oxford University Press, 1990.

Moreno Fraginals, Manuel. *The Sugarmill: The Socioeconomic Complex of Sugar in Cuba, 1760–1860.* Translated by Cedric Belfrage. New York: Monthly Review Press, 1976.

Morgan, Dan. *Merchants of Grain.* New York: Viking, 1979.

Moxham, Roy. *Tea: Addiction, Exploitation and Empire.* New York: Carroll and Graf, 2003.

Mulhall, Michael G. *The Dictionary of Statistics.* 4th ed. London: G. Routledge, 1899.

Nord, Philip. *France's New Deal: From the Thirties to the Postwar Era.* Princeton, NJ: Princeton University Press, 2010.

Nützenadel, Alexander, and Frank Trentmann, eds. *Food and Globalization: Consumption, Markets and Politics in the Modern World.* Oxford: Berg, 2008.

O'Brien, Patrick. *The New Economic History of the Railways.* New York: St. Martin's Press, 1977.

O'Brien, Thomas F. *The Revolutionary Mission: American Enterprise in Latin America, 1900–1945.* New York: Cambridge University Press, 1996.

Ocampo, José Antonio. *Colombia y la economía mundial, 1830–1910.* Mexico City: Siglo Veintiuno, 1984.

Ogilvie, Sheilagh, and Richard Overy, eds. *Germany since 1800.* Vol. 3 of *Germany: A New Social and Economic History.* London: Arnold, 2003.

Okihiro, Gary Y. *Pineapple Culture: A History of the Tropical and Temperate Zones.* Berkeley: University of California Press, 2009.

O'Rouke, Kevin H., and Jeffrey G. Williamson. *Globalization and History: The Evolution of a Nineteenth-Century Atlantic Economy*. Cambridge, MA: MIT Press, 1999.

Osterhammel, Jürgen. *Die Verwandlung der Welt: Eine Geschichte des 19. Jahrhunderts*. Munich: C. H. Beck, 2009.

Owen, Norman G. *Prosperity without Progress: Manila Hemp and Material Life in the Colonial Philippines*. Berkeley: University of California Press, 1984.

Platt, D. C. M., ed. *Business Imperialism, 1840–1930: An Inquiry Based on British Experience in Latin America*. Oxford: Clarendon Press, 1977.

Polanyi, Karl. *The Great Transformation: The Political and Economic Origins of Our Time*. 2nd paperback ed. Boston: Beacon Press, 2001.

Pomeranz, Kenneth. *The Great Divergence: China, Europe, and the Making of the Modern World Economy*. Princeton, NJ: Princeton University Press, 2000.

Rappaport, Erika. "Packaging China: Foreign Articles and Dangerous Tastes in the Mid-Victorian Tea Party." In *The Making of the Consumer: Knowledge, Power and Identity in the Modern World*, edited by Frank Trentmann. Oxford: Berg, 2006.

Rawski, Thomas G. *Economic Growth in Prewar China*. Berkeley: University of California Press, 1989.

Richards, John. "The Staples Debates." In *Explorations in Canadian Economic History: Essays in Honour of Irene M. Spry*, edited by Duncan Cameron. Ottawa: University of Ottawa Press, 1985.

Rieschbieter, Julia Laura. "Kaffee im Kaiserreich: Eine Geschichte der Globalisierung." PhD diss., Europea-Universität Viadrina Frankfurt, 2009.

Rosenberg, Emily S. *Financial Missionaries to the World: The Politics and Culture of Dollar Diplomacy, 1900–1930*. Durham, NC: Duke University Press, 2003.

———, ed. *A World Connecting: 1870–1945*. Cambridge, MA: Harvard University Press, 2012.

Rostow, W. W. *The World Economy: History and Prospect*. Austin: University of Texas Press, 1978.

Rothermund, Dietmar. *The Global Impact of the Great Depression, 1929–1939*. New York: Routledge, 1996.

Sen, Samita. *Women and Labour in Late Colonial India: The Bengal Jute Industry*. New York: Cambridge University Press, 1999.

Shin, Jang-Sup. *The Economics of the Latecomers: Catching-Up, Technology Transfer, and Institutions in Germany, Japan, and South Korea*. London: Routledge, 1996.

Smith, Andrew F. *Eating History: Thirty Turning Points in the Making of American Cuisine*. New York: Columbia University Press, 2009.

Smith, F. Leslie, John W. Wright II, and David H. Ostroff, eds. *Perspectives on Radio and Television: Telecommunication in the United States.* 4th ed. Mahwah, NJ: Erlbaum, 1998.

Soluri, John. *Banana Cultures: Agriculture, Consumption, and Environmental Change in Honduras and the United States.* Austin: University of Texas Press, 2005.

Stanfield, Michael Edward. *Red Rubber, Bleeding Trees: Violence, Slavery, and Empire in Northwest Amazonia, 1850–1933.* Albuquerque: University of New Mexico Press, 1998.

Stewart, Gordon T. *Jute and Empire: The Calcutta Jute Wallahs and the Landscapes of Empire.* Manchester: Manchester University Press, 1998.

Stoler, Ann Laura. *Capitalism and Confrontation in Sumatra's Plantation Belt, 1870–1979.* New Haven, CT: Yale University Press, 1985.

Sugihara, Kaoru, ed. *Japan, China, and the Growth of the Asian International Economy, 1850–1949.* Oxford: Oxford University Press, 2005.

Tedlow, Richard S. *New and Improved: The Story of Mass Marketing in America.* New York: Basic Books, 1990.

Tinker Salas, Miguel. *The Enduring Legacy: Oil, Culture, and Society in Venezuela.* Durham, NC: Duke University Press, 2009.

Topik, Steven, Carlos Marichal, and Zephyr Frank, eds. *From Silver to Cocaine: Latin American Commodity Chains and the Building of the World Economy, 1500–2000.* Durham, NC: Duke University Press, 2006.

Topik, Steven, and Allen Wells, eds. *The Second Conquest of Latin America: Coffee, Henequen, and Oil during the Export Boom, 1850–1930.* Austin: University of Texas Press, 1998.

Torp, Cornelius. *Die Herausforderung der Globalisierung: Wirtschaft und Politik in Deutschland, 1860–1914.* Göttingen: Vandenhoeck und Ruprecht, 2005.

Trentmann, Frank. *Free Trade Nation: Commerce, Consumption, and Civil Society in Modern Britain.* Oxford: Oxford University Press, 2008.

Tucker, Richard P. *Insatiable Appetite: The United States and the Ecological Degradation of the Tropical World.* Berkeley: University of California Press, 2000.

Twomey, Michael J. *A Century of Foreign Investment in the Third World.* London: Routledge, 2000.

Ukers, William H. *All about Coffee.* 2nd ed. New York: Tea and Coffee Trade Journal Co., 1935.

———. *All about Tea.* 2 vols. New York: The Tea and Coffee Trade Journal Co., 1935.

Vance, James E., Jr. *Capturing the Horizon: The Historical Geography of Transportation since the Transportation Revolution of the Sixteenth Century.* New York: Harper and Row, 1986.

Wallerstein, Immanuel. *The Modern World-System.* 4 vols. to date. New York: Academic Press, 1974–2011.

Weaver, Frederick Stirton. *Latin America in the World Economy: Mercantile Colonialism to Global Capitalism.* Boulder, CO: Westview Press, 2000.

Wehler, Hans-Ulrich. *Von der "Deutschen Doppelrevolution" bis zum Beginn des Ersten Weltkrieges, 1849–1914.* Vol. 3 of *Deutsche Gesellschaftsgeschichte.* Munich: C. H. Beck, 1995.

Wells, Allen. "Reports of Its Demise Are Not Exaggerated: The Life and Times of Yucatecan Henequen." In *From Silver to Cocaine: Latin American Commodity Chains and the Building of the World Economy, 1500–200,* edited by Steven Topik, Carlos Marichal, and Zephyr Frank. Durham, NC: Duke University Press, 2006.

Wells, Allen, and Gilbert M. Joseph. *Summer of Discontent, Seasons of Upheaval: Elite Politics and Rural Insurgency in Yucatán, 1876–1915.* Stanford, CA: Stanford University Press, 1996.

Wenzlhuemer, Roland. *From Coffee to Tea Cultivation in Ceylon, 1880–1900: An Economic and Social History.* Leiden: Brill, 2008.

Wickizer, V. D., and M. K. Bennett. *The Rice Economy of Monsoon Asia.* Palo Alto, CA: Stanford University Food Research Institute, 1941.

Wilkins, Mira. *The Maturing of Multinational Enterprise: American Business Abroad from 1914 to 1970.* Cambridge, MA: Harvard University Press, 1974.

Wilkins, Mira, and Harm Schröter, eds. *The Free-Standing Company in the World Economy, 1830–1996.* Oxford: Oxford University Press, 1998.

Wright, Donald R. *The World and a Very Small Place in Africa.* Armonk, NY: M. E. Sharpe, 1997.

Yafa, Stephen. *Big Cotton: How a Humble Fiber Created Fortunes, Wrecked Civilizations, and Put America on the Map.* New York: Viking, 2005.

Yamamura, Kozo, ed. *The Economic Emergence of Modern Japan.* Cambridge: Cambridge University Press, 1997.

Yergin, Daniel. *The Prize: The Epic Quest for Oil, Money, and Power.* New York: Simon and Schuster, 1991.

# Acknowledgments

A synthesis like this would not have been possible if not for the superb existing scholarship on the history of specific commodities and on the period itself. As scholars specializing in Latin America, we especially benefited from the research of our colleagues working on Asia and Africa during this era. In particular, we thank Emily Rosenberg for her excellent editorial guidance; Kenneth Pomeranz, William Gervase Clarence-Smith, Jürgen Osterhammel, Matthew Klingle, Erika Rappaport, and Jennifer Scanlon for their very helpful comments; and Kathleen McDermott and Andrew Kinney at Harvard University Press for their editorial help and assistance in finding the right images. We also thank Natalia Topik for her help.

# Index